Perspectives
on
Hamlet

Perspectives

on

Hamlet

COLLECTED PAPERS OF THE BUCKNELL-
SUSQUEHANNA COLLOQUIUM ON *HAMLET*,
HELD AT BUCKNELL AND SUSQUEHANNA
UNIVERSITIES, APRIL 27 AND 28, 1973

Edited by

William G. Holzberger and Peter B. Waldeck

Lewisburg
Bucknell University Press
London: Associated University Presses

© 1975 by Associated University Presses, Inc.

Associated University Presses, Inc.
Cranbury, New Jersey 08512

Associated University Presses
108 New Bond Street
London W1Y OQX, England

Bucknell-Susquehanna Colloquium on Hamlet, 1973.
Perspectives on Hamlet.

Includes bibliographical references.
1. Shakespeare, William, 1564–1616. Hamlet.
I. Holzberger, William G., ed. II. Waldeck, Peter
Bruce, ed. III. Title.
PR2807.B78   1973   822.3'3   74–4844
ISBN 0–8387–1573–7

PRINTED IN THE UNITED STATES OF AMERICA

Contents

Preface

The papers constituting this volume were given at a Colloquium on *Hamlet* sponsored jointly by Bucknell and Susquehanna Universities and held on April 27 and 28, 1973, at Lewisburg and Selinsgrove, Pennsylvania.

The fundamental purpose of the Colloquium was to foster communication and cooperation among scholars of the two universities, and, through the selection of a topic of universal interest and appeal, to bring faculty and students together with outstanding scholars from other institutions. The selection of *Hamlet* assured a topic familiar to all, yet one capable of generating a wide variety of critical approaches. Thus, the papers of this volume are included not as representative samples of *Hamlet* criticism, but rather as fresh critical perspectives on the work.

While several of the authors represented are Shakespeare specialists, other more general critical points of view are also included. The result is a collection of nine essays that fall roughly into three categories: Literary Critical Studies (Hapgood, Eastman, and Rinkus); Psychological Analyses (Payne, Orbison, and Waldeck); and a third category roughly defined as Theatrical Considerations (Seltzer, Young, and Cairns). An Introduction, summarizing the origins and evolution of *Hamlet,* together with the principal lines of criticism, is also provided.

The success of the Hamlet Colloquium, and the excitement engendered by these papers, prove that *Hamlet* has by no means paled to extinction in the Age of Aquarius, but that the great play continues its influence into our own time, provoking fresh responses by new generations of audiences and critics.

We wish to acknowledge the contributions of the following persons whose special efforts and cooperation helped make the *Hamlet* Colloquium successful and this volume possible. We are grateful to Dr. Wendell I. Smith, Provost of Bucknell University, and to the members of the Division of Languages and Literatures at Susquehanna University, for providing financial and personal support; to Professors Harvey Powers and S. Ridgeway Kennedy, to Mr. Charles Pollock, and student members of the Bucknell University Players for their fine and entertaining performance of Charles Marowitz's collage version of *Hamlet;* to Professor Harry R. Garvin, Chairman of the English Department at Bucknell, and the members of the Harry Wolcott Robbins Lecture Committee, Professors Ralph Rees (Chairman), James F. Carens, and Louis Casimir, Jr., for permitting the Robbins Lecture, given by Professor Daniel Seltzer, to be included in the Colloquium. Finally, we wish to thank Professor George F. Folkers, Director of the German Program at Bucknell University, for his help in organizing the Colloquium; Professor Charles Rahter of the Susquehanna University Department of English for moderating the second day's meeting; student members of the Bucknell English Club for handling a variety of chores with efficiency and good humor; and also the faculty and students of Bucknell and Susquehanna Universities and of the several other colleges and universities whose attendance and participation made the *Hamlet* Colloquium a highlight of the academic year.

W. G. H.
P. B. W.

The Authors of the Papers
in This Volume

NANCY L. CAIRNS is Associate Professor of French at Susquehanna University. Her publications include an essay on the literary criticism of Émile Henriot, and a paper on the work of Maurice Scève presented at a meeting of the American Association of Teachers of French. She has also published original poems in English in various periodicals.

ARTHUR M. EASTMAN is Professor of English and Chairman of the Department of English at Carnegie-Mellon University. He was a Guggenheim Fellow in 1957–58, and is the author of numerous articles on Shakespeare and literature generally. He is co-editor of *Masterpieces of the Drama* (with A. W. Allison and A. J. Carr; New York: Macmillan, 1957; revised 1966, 1973), and *Shakespeare and His Critics* (with G. B. Harrison; Ann Arbor: University of Michigan Press, 1964); Coordinating Editor of *The Norton Anthology of Poetry* (New York: W. W. Norton, 1970); and General Editor of *The Norton Reader* (New York: W. W. Norton, 1964; revised 1969, 1973). Professor Eastman is author of *A Short History of Shakespearean Criticism* (New York: Random House, 1968. Reprinted by W. W. Norton and Co., 1974).

ROBERT D. HAPGOOD is Professor of English at The University of New Hampshire. A Shakespearean scholar, Professor Hapgood has published many studies of Shakespeare's plays in leading journals, and has also written a number of theater reviews.

WILLIAM G. HOLZBERGER is Associate Professor of English at Bucknell University and a specialist in American literature and intellectual history; he has, however, a continuing interest in Shakespeare and in *Hamlet* particularly. He is the editor of *The Complete Poems of George Santayana: A Critical Edition* (Lewisburg, Pa.: Bucknell University Press, 1975), and co-editor (with the late Daniel Cory) of *The Complete Letters of George Santayana* (in preparation, to be published by The University of Illinois Press).

TUCKER ORBISON is Associate Professor of English at Bucknell University. His field of major interest is English Renaissance drama and his articles have appeared in various journals. He is the author of *The Tragic Vision of John Ford* (soon to be published by The University of Salzburg).

MICHAEL PAYNE is Associate Professor of English at Bucknell University. A specialist in Shakespeare and the English Renaissance, he has published several articles on Shakespeare in professional journals. He is co-editor of *Contemporary Essays on Style: Rhetoric, Linguistics, and Criticism* (with Glen A. Love; Glenview, Ill.: Scott Foresman, 1969), of a modernized text of Sir Philip Sidney's *New Arcadia* (with Arthur Amos, James Holleran, and William Jones; in preparation), and author of *Irony in Shakespeare's Roman Plays* (University of Salzburg, 1973).

JEROME J. RINKUS is Assistant Professor of Russian at Pomona College. His essay in this volume reflects his interest in the effects of Western literature on Russian writers.

DANIEL SELTZER has been Professor of English at Princeton University since 1970 and Chairman of the Faculty Committee on McCarter Theatre, Princeton's Center for Performing Arts. He was from 1965 to 1970 Associate Director of the Loeb Drama Center at Harvard. In 1964 he was awarded a Guggenheim Fellowship. Professor Seltzer's teaching and research have been focused on the literature and practice of the theater, with concentration in the drama of the English Renaissance and of the modern period. He has frequently acted in and directed plays, and has authored numerous essays and reviews. Currently, he is at work on two book-length studies, one of Shakespeare's tragedies and romances, the other of modes of modern drama.

PETER B. WALDECK is Associate Professor of German at Susquehanna University and Chairman of the Department of Modern Foreign Languages. He has published a monograph on Hermann Broch (Munich: Wilhelm Fink Verlag, 1968), as well as articles on Broch, Lessing, Kafka, and on the theory of the comic.

DAVID YOUNG is Professor of English at Oberlin College and the editor of *Field,* a magazine of contemporary poetry. A poet himself, he has published two volumes of poems: *Sweating Out the Winter* (Pittsburgh: University of Pittsburgh Press, 1969), and *Boxcars* (New York: Ecco Press, 1973, and has translated poems from German, Italian, and Chinese. He is the Editor of *Twentieth-Century Interpretations of Shakespeare's Henry IV,* Part II (Englewood Cliffs, N.J.: Prentice-Hall, 1968). Professor Young has written two highly regarded books on Shakespeare: *Something of Great Constancy: The Art of A Midsummer Night's Dream* (1966), and *The Heart's Forest: A Study of Shakespeare's Pastoral Plays* (1972), both published by The Yale University Press.

Introduction

WILLIAM G. HOLZBERGER

Shakespeare is the greatest dramatist who ever lived, and his tragedy *Hamlet, Prince of Denmark,* is probably the greatest and certainly the most celebrated play of all time. More critical commentary has been written about *Hamlet* than any other play; indeed, it is the most discussed work of art in history. Not only has *Hamlet* fascinated literary critics for almost four hundred years, but it has inspired comment from great writers and thinkers in many fields. Philosophers Voltaire, Hegel, Emerson, and Santayana; poets Goethe, Coleridge, and T. S. Eliot; novelists Tolstoy, Turgenev, and James Joyce; psychologists Freud and Erikson—all have been stimulated to express opinions of the play. Whether they have, like Tolstoy and Eliot, pronounced *Hamlet* a failure, or, like Goethe and Santayana, celebrated it as a masterpiece, the fascination that the play has had for great intellects over the centuries is evident.

Hamlet is Shakespeare's most frequently performed play. From the first, it was the most popular of Shakespeare's works with actors and audiences, and later with critics and scholars. The title role has been interpreted by great actors of every age, from Burbage and Garrick to Gielgud and Olivier, and the text has been translated into a variety of foreign languages. Several films based on the play have been produced in England, America, Germany, Russia, and Japan. Grand operas inspired by *Hamlet* were composed by Domenico Scarlatti in 1715 and Ambroise Thomas in 1869, and Tchaikovsky based an overture-fantasia on the story in 1888.

Hamlet is the longest of Shakespeare's plays, containing more than thirty-eight-hundred lines, and the title role is his longest part, consisting of over fourteen-hundred lines. The work has almost invariably been cut in productions, even in Shakespeare's day, when performances customarily lasted between two and three hours. *Hamlet* contains seven soliloquies, and the role of Claudius offers a gifted actor perhaps as much opportunity for a tour de force as does that of the Prince himself.

Shakespeare and *Hamlet*

Shakespeare wrote *Hamlet* at the midpoint in his career. The drama was composed sometime between 1599 and 1602, at which time the poet was between thirty-five and thirty-eight years old, and it belongs to that period of seven or eight years during which Shakespeare's greatest tragic works were written: *Julius Caesar* (1601), *Othello* (1604), *King Lear* (1605), *Macbeth* (ca. 1606), and *Antony and Cleopatra* (1607). Shakespeare retired a few years later, probably in 1611, at the age of forty-seven, to the town of Stratford-on-Avon in Warwickshire, where he had, on about April 23, 1564, been born and spent his early life, and where, on April 23, 1616, at the comparatively early age of fifty-two, he died. Today, some three hundred and seventy-three years after its inception, *Hamlet* remains a great favorite, the very type of a literary classic.

Origins of the Story

For all the awesome magnitude of Shakespeare's creative power, the invention of plots and stories was not where his talent lay. Put more positively, a significant aspect of Shakespeare's genius was the capacity to perceive, in stories and plays already current, gripping plots and representative characters. These he adapted to his own uses, and, like Melville and other great plagiarizers, transformed and enhanced all that he borrowed.

The earliest written source of the Hamlet story is found in a Latin history of Denmark to 1186; entitled *Historia Danica,* and written by Saxo Grammaticus at the end of the twelfth century, it was first printed in 1514. Saxo draws upon oral tradition and lost Scandinavian sagas, and gives a highly if not purely fictional account of Hamlet (also called Amleth or Hamleth), son of Horvendill, a second-century B.C. king of Jutland, and his queen, Gerutha. The basic events of Shakespeare's *Hamlet* are found in Saxo, with certain differences. Horvendill is killed by his brother, Fengo, who then marries Gerutha. To save his life, Amleth feigns insanity. His mother, overcome by Amleth's reproaches, assists him in killing Fengo.

The story of Lucius Junius Brutus, a founder of the Roman Republic, in the sixth century B.C., who pretended madness while plotting to overthrow Tarquin, certainly contributes to Saxo's account of Amleth; however, several later legends have been suggested as being most contributory to Saxo's version. Basic to Saxo's account is a Scandinavian legend, the Icelandic saga of Amlothi (Amloði), the hero of a tale as old as *Beowulf*, Old English epic composed during the eighth century, whose manuscript in the British Museum dates from the latter part of the tenth century. No manuscript of the saga of Amlothi exists, if indeed it was ever written down, but Amlothi is first mentioned in writings by the tenth-century Icelandic poet Snaebjörn.[1]

Other origins of the Amleth legend found in the *Historia Danica* of Saxo Grammaticus have also been suggested. One of these attributes the original story to the Persian poet Firdausi, in his tale of Kei-Chosro and Afrasiab in a poem called *Shāh-Nāma;*[2] and another to Celtic history and legend, in the story of Amhlaide, recorded in the Irish annals for the year 917. A linguistic scholar has argued that Saxo's Amleth derives originally from Geatish tradition as developed in Jutland. The name Amloði is interpreted as meaning the "mad Onela" and is identified with the Swedish king Onela mentioned in *Beowulf*.[3]

1. An account of Snaebjörn's life and the few extant lines of his poem are given in Sir Israel Gollancz, *The Sources of Hamlet* (London: Humphrey Milford, Oxford University Press, 1926), pp. 1–14: "From the passages preserved it is evident that Snaebjörn was a sailor-poet, and the lost poem must have been descriptive of some voyage in the Arctic seas (p. 9)." "All that can be said at this point in the investigation is that the verse quoted [Snaebjörn's fragment] in the *Prose Edda* [a handbook of the Art of Poetry, composed by Snorri Sturlason about the year 1230] gives us a reference to some old legend concerning "Amloði," whose name is identical with that of the hero known to us as Hamlet" (p. 8).
   The Sources of Hamlet (pp. 94–163) also contains the complete text, in Latin and English on facing pages, of the story of Amlethus or Hamlet found at the end of Book III and the beginning of Book IV of Saxo Grammaticus's *Historia Danica*.
   2. Rudolph Zenker, *Boeve-Amlethus: Das altfranzösische Epos von Boeve de Hamtone und der Ursprung der Hamletsage. Literarhistorische Forschungen*, Heft 32 (Berlin and Leipzig: Schick and von Waldberg, 1905): "Die Hamletsage ist . . . eine Schwester der aus dem gleichen Quell entsprungenen persischen Sage von Kei Chosro und Afrasiab, welche in Firdosis gewaltigem Epos Schahname (d. i. Königsbuch) einen breiten Raum einnimmt, und auf deren Verwandtschaft mit der Hamletsage zuerst O. L. Jiriczek hingewiesen hat."
   3. Kemp Malone, *The Literary History of Hamlet: I. The Early Tradition. Anglistische Forschungen*, Heft 59 (Heidelberg: J. Hoops, 1923).

A later printed account of the Hamlet story reported in Saxo Grammaticus's Danish history is that which constitutes the fifth book of François de Belleforest's *Histoires Tragiques,* published about 1570. Belleforest's version is indebted to the writings of Matteo Bandello, the sixteenth-century author of tales, who, for fame as a storyteller in this period, is second only to his great predecessor and countryman, Giovanni Boccaccio. Bandello, through later intermediaries, became a principal source of plots for several Elizabethan playwrights, including Shakespeare. The story of Romeo and Juliet had been narrated by Bandello.

The fifth volume of Belleforest's work contains the essential features of the Hamlet story we find in Shakespeare's play. It is a story of adultery, fratricide, vengeance, and pretended madness; it includes the journey to England and an exchange of letters. The originals of Shakespeare's characters of Polonius, Rosencrantz and Guildenstern, Horatio, and Ophelia appear in Belleforest's history; in Shakespeare's play, however, they are thoroughly transformed by the poet's power of characterization.

A lost play, referred to as the *Ur-Hamlet* by analogy to the *Urfaust,* Goethe's early prototype of his dramatic masterpiece, stands between the version of the story in Belleforest and Shakespeare's drama. The missing link in the chain of development from primitive saga to Shakespeare's monumental tragedy was evidently based directly upon Belleforest's French text, since the fifth volume of his *Histoires Tragiques* was not translated into English until 1608, when it appeared in London as *The Hystorie of Hamblet,* whereas the *Ur-Hamlet* had appeared on the London stage in or before 1589, probably in 1588 or 1589.[4]

4. Gollancz's *The Sources of Hamlet* (pp. 164–311) contains the French text of the Hamlet story from Book V of Belleforest's *Histoires*

There is no evidence that the lost play, which provided the immediate source material for Shakespeare's tragedy, was ever printed. No manuscript of the work survives, and it was perhaps discarded upon the appearance of Shakespeare's masterful version. That such a play existed is evidenced by a derogatory reference made to it by Thomas Nashe in a preface he wrote to Robert Greene's prose romance *Menaphon* (1589). The authorship of the lost play is uncertain, although it has been attributed to Thomas Kyd (ca. 1557–1595) or one of his imitators.[5] Kyd was the author of one of the most successful plays of the period immediately preceding that dominated by Shakespeare. Called *The Spanish Tragedy*, and first published in 1594, this play is a story of vengeance, melodramatic and sensational in its effects. The missing play, or *Ur-Hamlet*, was probably, like Kyd's *Spanish Tragedy*, a revenge play in the Senecan mode. The tragedies of Seneca had a powerful influence on Elizabethan dramatists, and plays of revenge became very popular.

The missing *Ur-Hamlet* probably added a Ghost, a fencing scene (between Hamlet and Laertes), and a play within a play—all devices favored by Thomas Kyd. Although the piece was evidently never printed, it had appeared on the English stage during Shakespeare's apprenticeship as actor and playwright, and it is likely that Shakespeare acquired a copy of the "book" of the play, the copy from which performers worked.

Tragiques and the English translation of *The Hystorie of Hamlet* on facing pages.
    5. Gregor Sarrazin, "Der Ur-Hamlet," chap. 5, pp. 94–122, in *Thomas Kyd und Sein Kreis: Eine litterarhistorische Untersuchung* (Berlin: E. Felber, 1892).

Evolution of Shakespeare's Play

In an introduction to *Hamlet* for a complete works of Shakespeare published in 1908, George Santayana, with characteristic intuition, recognized that Shakespeare's *Hamlet* was a reworking of an earlier version of the play.[6] Santayana believed that the earlier version was also by Shakespeare. The personage of Hamlet, and also the episodes of the piece, he thought, show traces of expansion. Santayana points to certain passages in the play that give incoherence to Hamlet's character and incongruity to the dramatic events. Specific examples include Hamlet's words when he comes upon the praying Claudius. The reasons for sparing the King are, according to Santayana, "a remnant of bombast belonging to the old story, far more Christian and conventional in its motives than Shakespeare's is." [7] Similarly, the encounter with Laertes in Ophelia's grave is seen as a bit of bombast left over from a melodramatic predecessor. Also, the incongruous mixture of the comic with the highly serious—as in the scene following the encounter with the Ghost, where Hamlet says, "Ah, ha, boy! say'st thou so? Art thou there, truepenny? Come on; you hear this fellow in the cellarage," [8] and the other burlesque references to the Ghost in the underworld that we find in this scene—suggests to Santayana remnants of conventional farce carried over from the earlier state of the play. The present version of *Hamlet* may therefore be a re-working of an earlier version by Shakespeare himself, as Santayana believed, or

6. George Santayana, "Introduction to *Hamlet*," in *The Complete Works of William Shakespeare* (New York: Harper and Brothers, 1908); reprinted as "Hamlet" in *Obiter Scripta: Lectures, Essays and Reviews*, ed. Justus Buchler and Benjamin Schwartz (New York: Scribner's, 1936), pp. 41–67.
7. "Hamlet," in *Obiter Scripta*, p. 43.
8. *Hamlet*, 1.5.150–51.

perhaps the incongruous elements in the present version are direct carry-overs from the lost play, or *Ur-Hamlet*, attributed to one of Shakespeare's predecessors. It would not be remarkable for Shakespeare to have transplanted verbatim passages from the source into his own text. Enobarbus's description of Cleopatra in her barge in *Antony and Cleopatra*, taken almost word for word from Plutarch, is a famous example of Shakespeare's plagiarism.[9]

The version of *Hamlet* that we read and base productions upon today has been established through the labors of textual scholars. The first printing of the play is the First Quarto of 1603, called the "Bad" Quarto because of its obvious inaccuracies and incompleteness. The Second or "Good" Quarto, published in 1604, is the longest version; and the First Folio of 1623 is a rather abbreviated version of the "Good" Quarto of 1604, but adds material not found in either of the other texts. The present-day text of *Hamlet* is comprised of the Second or "Good" Quarto of 1604, with the addition of almost a hundred lines from the shorter First Folio of 1623. Modern stage productions and films of *Hamlet,* as observed earlier, are invariably abridgments of the complete text.

Patterns in Criticism

Historically, criticism of *Hamlet* has generally been character-oriented, with the personage of the Prince commanding central attention in analyses of the play; today criticism tends to subordinate character to action or theme.

9. *Anthony and Cleopatra,* 2.2.196–223. Plutarch, *The Lives of the Noble Grecians and Romans,* trans. John Dryden and revised by Arthur Hugh Clough (New York: The Modern Library, [1932]), "Antony," pp. 1118–19.

Current trends indicate antipathy toward psychologizing Shakespeare's characters, much less the poet himself.

Most famous and widely argued of critical questions on the play has been the cause of Hamlet's delay in fulfilling the Ghost's demand for vengeance, to which the Prince says he wishes to sweep "with wings as swift as meditation or the thoughts of love." [10] The so-called romantic view of Hamlet's delay is the most widespread and is associated with the interpretations of Goethe, Coleridge, A. C. Bradley, and Freud. According to this view, the reason why Hamlet continually postpones the vengeance to which he is sworn is that some personal incapacity prevents him from acting. This procrastination may result from neurosis, an essential irresolution, or a moral conscience that will not permit murder even in the cause of justice. Goethe effectively represents this latter view in his novel of *Wilhelm Meister*.[11] Wilhelm sees Hamlet as having been given a charge that he is constitutionally unfit to carry out. His noble and intensely moral nature sticks at the command to kill Claudius in cold blood. Only amid the chaotic passions of the final scene can Hamlet discharge the awful responsibility.

A counterpart to the "romantic" view is that which places the reasons for Hamlet's delay outside the character of the Prince. The situation in which the protagonist is placed and the characteristics of the revenge tragedy prevent Hamlet from quickly dispatching his obligation to kill Claudius. Had he done so there would be no play. According to this view, therefore, conditions of the plot and not idio-

10. *Hamlet*, 1.5.29–30.
11. Johann Wolfgang [von] Goethe, *Wilhelm Meisters Lehrjahre*, vol. 7 in *Gedenkausgabe der Werke, Briefe und Gespräche* (Zurich: Artemis-Verlag, 1949): 263–64; and *Wilhelm Meister's Apprenticeship and Travels*, trans. Thomas Carlyle (New York and Boston: H. M. Caldwell Co., [1882]), p. 223.

syncrasies of the character account for Hamlet's delay.[12]

Myriad other questions have been generated by the enormous body of criticism surrounding the play. Some of the most provocative are: Is Hamlet merely feigning madness or is he really mad? What is the essential quality of Hamlet's character? Is he cynical and cruel or idealistic and generous? Is he vacillating and indecisive, effete and excessively intellectual, or noble and heroic, sensitive and conscientiously reflective? Does Hamlet serve as a scapegoat or as a symbol of death? Is Hamlet a tragic figure in the classical sense? What is the true nature of Hamlet and Ophelia's relationship: do they love one another? Did Gertrude commit adultery with Claudius before King Hamlet's death? What is the best approach to the fullest understanding of *Hamlet* as a work of dramatic art: historical investigation; study of the imagery; analysis of structure, plot, and characterization; psychological analysis; symbolic interpretation; or some combination of these approaches? Finally, the evaluative question: is *Hamlet* a great dramatic masterpiece or a play that ultimately fails to be a complete work of art? [13]

Two twentieth-century views, combined in T. S. Eliot's famous essay on *Hamlet,* in which Eliot articulates his theory of the objective correlative, see the drama as an ultimate failure. The reasons given for this failure are Shakespeare's unsuccessful adaptation of the plot of the older melodramatic revenge play, or *Ur-Hamlet,* to his more realistic psychological interpretation, and that the poet's failure to achieve a complete coherence of theme and action was caused by his own psychological imbalance at the time

12. John Dover Wilson, *What Happens in Hamlet* (Cambridge: Cambridge University Press, 1951), 3rd ed. (1st ed. 1935), pp. 201–5.

13. A summary of "the main issues of *Hamlet* criticism" is found in Morris Weitz, *Hamlet and the Philosophy of Literary Criticism* (Cleveland and New York: The World Publishing Co., 1966), pp. 207–12.

of composition.[14] These negative criticisms of the play have been attacked as depending ultimately upon unknown source materials (the lost play or *Ur-Hamlet*) and objectively insupportable biographical and psychological speculations about Shakespeare himself.[15]

A comparatively recent interpretation of *Hamlet* sees the Prince as the instrument of Providence by which justice is achieved, reflecting the tendency of current criticism to subordinate character to considerations of action and theme.[16] The existence of this vast body of critical commentary on Shakespeare's *Hamlet* demonstrates the power of the piece to capture the interest and stimulate the imagination of readers and playgoers down through the centuries—precisely the quality that makes a work of literature immortal.

14. T. S. Eliot, "Hamlet and His Problems (1919)," in *Selected Essays* (New York: Harcourt, Brace and Co., 1950), pp. 121–26.

15. Eliseo Vivas, "The Objective Correlative of T. S. Eliot (1944)," in *Creation and Discovery: Essays in Criticism and Aesthetics* (New York: The Noonday Press, 1955), pp. 175–89.

16. See G. R. Elliott, *Scourge and Minister: A Study of Hamlet As Tragedy of Revengefulness and Justice* (Durham, N. C.: Duke University Press, 1951); Fredson Bowers, "Hamlet as Minister and Scourge," *PMLA* 70, no. 4, part 1 (September 1955): 740–49; and Eleanor Prosser, "Heaven's Scourge or Minister," in *Hamlet and Revenge* (Stanford, Calif.: Stanford University Press, 1967), pp. 172–204.

Perspectives
on
Hamlet

Hamlet
and Its Thematic Modes of Speech

ROBERT HAPGOOD

The most distinguished recent studies of *Hamlet's* dialogue
have focused on its most striking feature: its questioning
spirit. In *The Question of Hamlet* Harry Levin sees in Prince
Hamlet "the very personification of doubtfulness" amid "a
general atmosphere of uncertainty." [1] He seconds Maynard
Mack's observation that "Hamlet's world is pre-eminently in
the interrogative mood." [2] For Stephen Booth the same is
true of *Hamlet's* audience. He feels that as the play unfolds
we are kept in a quandary, again and again being forced
to realize that there are more things in heaven and earth
than are dreamt of in our philosophies. "*Hamlet*," he concludes, "is the tragedy of an audience that cannot make up
its mind." [3]

1. Harry Levin, *The Question of Hamlet* (New York: Oxford University Press, 1959).
2. Maynard Mack, "The World of Hamlet," *Yale Review* 41 (1952):
504.
3. Stephen Booth, "On the Value of *Hamlet*," in *Reinterpretations
of Elizabethan Drama*, Selected Papers from the English Institute, ed.
Norman Rabkin (New York: Columbia University Press, 1969), p. 152.

There is truth in this view of the play, but it is not the whole truth. In this study, I will try to balance what seems to me an overemphasis on *Hamlet* as a play of doubts and questions by stressing its certitudes.

Not that questions are unimportant in the play's dialogue. Almost all of the characters ask them. They range from the most matter of fact ("What hour now?") to the most speculative ("to be or not to be?"), from the most playful "What is he that builds stronger than the mason, the shipwright or the carpenter?") to the most urgent ("Is it the king?"). So striking are the questions, in fact, that they have made it possible to see a previously unrecognized feature of Shakespeare's dialogue: that in a given play his characters often share a proclivity not only for particular words and images but also for particular modes of speech. I call such modes of speech "thematic" because they recur and because they seem central to the play's meanings. Taking my cue from the recurring questions in *Hamlet*, I have elsewhere studied similar thematic modes of speech in the history plays from *Richard II* to *Henry V*, observing how often Richard and his enemies denounce one another, how often the characters in *I Henry IV* talk of the past, and so on. Interplaying with these dominant modes are contrasting "anti-modes." Of these the most interesting are used by Harry Monmouth: "in a world of retrospection [*I Henry IV*], his is the voice of the future; in a world of false report [*II Henry IV*], his speech is direct and true; in a world of dispute [*Henry V*], his call is to concord."[4] Looking back now to *Hamlet*, I find a similar interplay. By way of balancing the attention already given to its thematic questions, I want to emphasize its thematic modes of certainty. I propose to survey these modes

---

4. Robert Hapgood, "Shakespeare's Thematic Modes of Speech: *Richard II* to *Henry V*," *Shakespeare Survey* 20 (1967): 48.

and the "universe of discourse" that they help to create; then to focus on Prince Hamlet and his relation to this "universe," both in his speeches and in the inner processes of thought and feeling that underlie them; and finally to suggest how I as a "mute" in the audience participate silently in comparable processes.

I

Although the speeches expressing certainty are less striking than those expressing uncertainty, they are no less important. While the first scene begins with a question ("Who's there?"), it is followed by a command ("Nay, answer me. Stand and unfold yourself"). The "mood" of the play is imperative as well as interrogative.

Most of the characters seem notably sure of themselves and their world. Hamlet is an exception. Horatio and Claudius show some skepticism. But for the most part the residents of Elsinore talk confidently of their past, present, and future. So secure is their past that when they speak of it they sometimes lose their identities and become the voices of the events—so Horatio tells of King Hamlet's victory over old Fortinbras, Ophelia of Hamlet's silent visit, Gertrude of Ophelia's death. Present conduct is understood in terms of truisms and commonplace explanations of motives and purposes. The future seems readily predicted and managed. To Levin, the characters other than Hamlet "are even less sure of things than he is; Polonius obliges him by discerning three different animals in the same cloud; and Osric agrees that the weather is hot or cold, depending upon Hamlet's variable taste."[5] But surely Polonius and Osric are

5. Levin, p. 74.

here humoring their mad prince, or trying to ingratiate themselves with him. In general, those around Hamlet speak a language of certainty.

Everyone in Elsinore seems positive as to what others should or should not do and more than willing to tell them so, in detail. Even Ophelia ventures to warn Laertes against "the primrose path of dalliance." She herself, of course, receives admonishment from all sides—Laertes, Polonius, Hamlet. Sometimes the characters tell each other not only what to do but precisely how to do it. So Polonius instructs Reynaldo to check up on Laertes, so Hamlet instructs the players, so Claudius, more briefly, instructs his various accomplices.

At the center of the play's imperatives is the Ghost—the only major figure who never asks a question. (The others are the Player King and Queen and the Priest.) The ghost gives the key command ("Revenge") and the key prohibition, ("Taint not thy mind, nor let thy soul contrive/Against thy mother aught.") In addition, he explains, narrates, predicts, exhorts, denounces, philosophizes—all with ponderous certainty. Indeed, he is too vehement. In Prince Hamlet, as will be discussed, he evokes a paralyzingly excessive response. For us, he may well "protest too much" ("O, Horrible! O, horrible! most horrible!"). With due allowance for sepulchral rhetoric, King Hamlet seems not only assured but self-important ("What a falling off was there! From me . . .") and verbose.

Although Claudius often gives commands, he rarely does so when he can serve the same purpose by request or persuasion. Perhaps privately insecure in his usurped authority, he is publicly careful not to presume upon it. His directions are regularly accompanied by some explanation of his purposes. His speech is full of such expressions as "I pray you"

and "I entreat you," even to Rosencrantz and Guildenstern
—who feel constrained to point out that

> Both your majesties
> Might by the sovereign power you have of us
> Put your pleasures more into command
> Than to entreaty.

To Hamlet the king is particularly unctuous:

> we beseech you, bend you to remain
> Here, in the cheer and comfort of our eye,
> Our chiefest courtier, cousin, and our son.

Is "bend" accompanied by a gesture of bowing? Of course,
beneath Claudius's velvet glove is the image of "bending"
Hamlet to his will—as he in fact does here since Hamlet
does not contest the king's veto of his return to Wittenberg.

Like Hamlet, Claudius lives out the play's distinctive
overall pattern from untested certainty through a period of
questioning to new certainty and decisive action.[6] He of
course knows that Hamlet has good reason to be hostile
toward his father's murderer. But he at first seems sure that
Hamlet is ignorant and that he can be placated by blandly
talking him out of his "obstinate condolement" for his father
and ringingly pronouncing him "Our chiefest courtier,
cousin, and our son." In the face of Hamlet's "transformation," however, Claudius begins systematic inquiries, sum-
moning Rosencrantz and Guildenstern. Ostensibly, their
assignment is simply to search out the cause of Hamlet's
lunacy, but also, one suspects, Claudius hopes to find out

6. I am conscious here of the influence of Robert B. Heilman, "The
Lear World," in *English Institute Essays 1948*, ed. D. A. Robertson, Jr.
(New York: Columbia University Press, 1949), pp. 45–46, and of Willard
Farnham in his introduction to the Pelican *Hamlet* (Baltimore: Penguin,
1957), p. 23.

what Hamlet knows and intends. What a relief it would be for him if there were nothing more to Hamlet's distemper than lovesickness, as Polonius contends! Claudius tests that attractive explanation thoroughly before concluding that Hamlet is neither lovesick nor mad and should be sent to England. He is nevertheless willing to let his chief counsellor test the matter further by eavesdropping on Hamlet's interview with the queen. Above all, he is most concerned with determining whether or not Hamlet is a threat to himself and to his hold on his crown and his queen. Once *The Murther of Gonzago* confirms this threat, Claudius moves decisively, commanding England to kill Hamlet.

Except for Prince Hamlet, Polonius is the principal remaining authority-figure in the play. Many of his pronouncements unconsciously parody the various modes of certainty. As in a distorting mirror his overly artful presentation of the cause of Hamlet's lunacy reflects the stately rhetoric of the king's first speech from the throne, just as his pedantic comments on the First Player's speech anticipate Hamlet's instructions to the players. Not that Polonius is a complete fool. The precepts he gives Laertes may not be "few," but they are prudent advice for a young man setting off for Paris. They can be regarded as a prelude to the scene between the Ghost and Hamlet that follows, where another father seeks to dictate the conduct of his son. The theme then becomes farcical in the next scene, where Polonius attempts to instruct Reynaldo as to how to check up on Laertes. Here as elsewhere he gets so caught up in petty detail that he loses the necessary control of his language, verbally registering his slipping mastery of events.

Especially, Polonius unwittingly parodies the way Claudius and Hamlet reach the certainties upon which they act. Polonius goes through most of the same mental processes as they, but in the wrong order. On the basis of small evidence he leaps to the conclusion that Hamlet's intentions toward Ophelia are dishonorable and with characteristic overemphasis asserts his paternal authority, forbidding her "to give words or talk with the Lord Hamlet." On even less evidence he then makes the snap judgment that this break is the cause of Hamlet's lunacy, a theory that he devotes all his ingenuity to confirming. He loses his life in the effort.

For the most part, those who are commanded obey, and are often explicit about doing so. Thus Ophelia tells her father "I will obey," Gertrude tells her husband, "I shall obey you," Fortinbras "obeys" his uncle Norway, and Rosencrantz and Guildenstern positively abase themselves before their king:

> we both obey
> And here give up ourselves, in the full bent,
> To lay our service freely at your feet,
> To be commanded.

Aside from Hamlet, Laertes is the notable exception to the general obedience that characterizes the people of Elsinore. Claudius handles his rebellion masterfully. The soul of kingly aplomb, restrained yet firm, he allows Laertes to "demand" his fill before putting his obedience to the test:

> King.   Will you be rul'd by me?
> Laertes.   Ay, my lord.
>   So you will not o'errule me to a peace.
> King.   To thine own peace.

Not until the end is the King disobeyed:

> King.   Gertrude, do not drink.
> Queen.   I will my lord; I pray you pardon me.

The various kinds of speech that I have discussed—valid reports, confident plans, accurate predictions, vows, instructions, precepts, pieces of advice, admonitions—are of course very different from one another. I group them as "modes of certainty" because they assert or assume a sense of certitude about how things are and should be. In themselves, they might not seem noteworthy. But they take on importance when joined with the play's key commands (those ultimate modes of certainty, crystallizing assurance to the point of dictating action) and when contrasted with the ubiquitous questions.

It is interesting to observe how the modes of certainty and uncertainty interwork. It might seem puzzling that the same characters talk so positively yet ask so many questions. A close look at their questions, however, shows that they are mostly concerned with immediate, practical matters—"What is your cause of distemper?" "What have you done, my lord, with the dead body?" They are not primarily philosophical and speculative; only Hamlet and the First Gravedigger are much given to posing that sort of question. The "interrogative mood" of the play is not primarily musing but investigative, the natural reaction of ordinarily confident and strong-minded people to a court full of secrets.

On the other hand, the people of Elsinore are not truly so confident as they sound. Prince Hamlet apart, they talk a very conventional way of life, apparently secure in their truisms about human conduct and endlessly concerned with niceties of decorum. Yet, in their actions they run wild, into insanity, into raw exercises of will and power, into lawless passion. Nor is this disparity between word and deed merely hypocrisy. In the face of such tabloid scandals, it is no wonder that these society-page people feel the need to bolster verbally their hold on civilized codes. Except for the reticent Horatio, they all protest too much.

II

Hamlet puts his own touch on the modes of uncertainty and certainty, and on the rhythms in which the play moves from one to the other. He is the most searching of the play's questioners, especially as to whether the ghost is truly that of his father, both before and after he sees it with his own eyes. In his independence of mind, he is often inclined to "inquire too curiously," breaking out of the prevailing modes of certainty. About the past, he lacks the security and re-liability that the others show. In particular, he seems ob-sessed with maximizing his mother's guilt, repeatedly shrink-ing the time before her "o'erhasty" remarriage ("the funeral baked meats/Did coldly furnish forth the marriage tables") and even implicating her in the murder ("as bad, good mother,/As kill a king, and marry with his brother"). About the future, on the other hand, he is nothing short of pres-cient, divining his uncle's guilt ("O my prophetic soul"), the plot against his life in England, and the fatality of the fencing match.

About present conduct Hamlet is a generalizer. Where the other characters are tirelessly sententious, he character-istically extends particular instances to fresh universals, as he reflects upon his mother's frailty or the "dram of e'il" or Yorick's skull. He seems impatient with formulaic think-ing ("There are more things in heaven and earth, Horatio,/ Than are dreamt of in your philosophy") and suspicious of it. The immediate occasion of his outburst against Ophelia is her Polonius-like saw: "Rich gifts wax poor when givers prove unkind." Hamlet's response is: "Are you honest?"

Like the others, Hamlet believes he knows how life should be lived. No character is so generous in his praise, nor so harsh in his blame. He is a sermonizer. Fortunately, he knows it. He engagingly cuts short his fulsome tribute to Horatio with "something too much of this" and concludes his preacherly exhortation to his mother:

> Confess yourself to heaven;
> Repent what's past; avoid what is to come;
> And do not spread the compost on the weeds,
> To make them ranker. Forgive me this my virtue . . .

What chiefly redeems this trait is Hamlet's way of turning his searching questions and admonitions upon himself. He is not alone in this—Claudius, Gertrude, and Polonius all have such moments—but no other character comes close to such self-castigation as occurs in the soliloquies that begin "O what a rogue and peasant slave am I" and "How all occasions do inform against me."

In a compliant society Hamlet stands out by his intransigence. He does not take orders well, however graciously they may be phrased. To Claudius's overtures, he responds by telling his mother, "I shall in all my best obey you, Madam." When Rosencrantz and Guildenstern transmit the biddings of the king and queen, Hamlet replies at first with irony ("We shall obey, were she ten times our mother"), which turns to derision ("when demanded of a sponge, what replication should be made by the son of a king?"). Under the guise of his antic disposition, he by innuendo insults and commands the king. When Claudius demands, "Where is Polonius?" Hamlet replies: "In heaven. Send thither to see. If your messenger find him not there, seek him i' th' other place yourself."

Strictly speaking, Hamlet never fulfills a single one of the Ghost's injunctions. He taints his mind, he does not leave his mother to heaven, and his killing of Claudius is much more than an act of revenge. Why doesn't Hamlet obey these key commands? The reasons for his failure are complex and obscure. Without pretending to pluck out the heart of Hamlet's mystery, I would suggest that he is at once over-motivated and under-motivated. He vows to the ghost:

> thy commandment all alone shall live
> Within the book and volume of my brain,
> Unmix'd with baser matter . . .

But, in his zeal he defeats his father's purposes by trying too hard. The classic instance comes when he decides not to kill Claudius "at prayer" lest he send him to heaven not hell and his revenge be less than perfect. This decision is often regarded as a rationalization, disguising a deficient acceptance of his role as revenging son. To me, it seems excessively dedicated, literally honor bound. For zeal here postpones what ordinary duty would have achieved.

Yet Hamlet also feels a contrary pull, a reluctance to do his duty: "The time is out of joint: O cursed spite,/That ever I was born to set it right!" Partly this reluctance comes from a sense of inadequacy. Although he feels compelled to take the world on his shoulders, he knows that he is no Hercules. Largely, however, the problem is that the imperative is not his own.

Like most virtues in Shakespeare, a genuine sense of justice begins at home. Compare Hamlet's explicit motivations before his departure for England:

> . . . not for a king,
> Upon whose property and most dear life

A damn'd defeat was made.
                    (2.2.596–98)
                 How stand I then
That have a father kill'd, a mother stain'd . . .
                           (4.4.56–57)

with those after his return:

> Does it not, think'st thee, stand me now upon—
> He that hath kill'd my king and whored my mother,
> Popp'd in between the election and my hopes,
> Thrown out his angle for my proper life,
> And with such cozenage—is't not perfect conscience
> To quit him with this arm?
>   (5.2.64–69)

Before, Hamlet was fulfilling a role, chiefly on his father's behalf, retaliating for a wrong done "my" king and "my" mother. Further, he is no longer merely the son of the king but the crown prince, incensed at the successful rival who "popp'd in between the election and my hopes." Most of all, he is now fighting "for my proper life." Hamlet will not act until the wrong done him by Claudius is brought to its ultimates: he does not retaliate until he is physically attacked and Laertes and the queen confirm that it is the king's doing. The first time he kills the king, the act is the most instinctive kind of reflex to personal injury: "The point envenomed too?/Then, venom, to thy work." The second killing, as he forces the king to drink the potion, is accompanied by his final denunciation: "thou incestuous, murd'rous, damned Dane." Each word adds a further area of villainy on Claudius's part, against the family, society, God, and the state. What began as an imperative for familial revenge has become an act of physical retaliation and then one of cosmic justice.

In general in the last scene, Hamlet speaks with a new

assurance. He still asks questions, but they are now mostly incidental ("wilt thou hear how I did proceed?"). Even "These foils have all a length?" seems casual. His most significant questions now are rhetorical questions:

> ... is't not to be damn'd
> To let this canker of our nature come
> In further evil?
> ... since no man has aught of what he leaves, what is't
> to leave betimes?
> ... Is thy union here?

In further ways, he speaks with a new certainty. He becomes "the voice of the event" as he narrates his discovery of the king's "exact command" to England to strike off his head and the substitution of his own royally sealed command to put Rosencrantz and Guildenstern to sudden death. Instead of self-blame he now speaks in self-defense; it is now his madness, not himself, that he rebukes: "Was't Hamlet wrong'd Laertes? Never Hamlet." As he mocks Osric, he seems as sure as ever as to how others should act and speak. And he is never more prescient than toward the end, confessing to "such a kind of gain-giving, as would perhaps trouble a woman." At the very end, Hamlet speaks with the commanding assurance of a king, as he denounces the usurper and names his successor.

III

Recalling my own experiences as a spectator at *Hamlet*, I find that like the characters in the play I am trying to find my way past the mysteries and false certainties that abound in Elsinore to arrive—by an interplay of doubt and trust—at its home truths. Of course, such a quest for truth goes on to some degree in most plays. But in *Hamlet* it is especially pronounced and has a distinctive nature.

Like the characters, I am continually asking questions. Admittedly, there is not necessarily a direct relation between the question-asking of a character and my own. I question Othello's sagacity, for example, just because he does *not* ask the obvious and critical questions, even when other characters suggest that he should. Still, like most commentators, I do find that questions come to my mind during *Hamlet* and that they are the same sort of questions that most of the characters ask, investigative rather than brooding. I wonder: What *is* rotten in the state of Denmark? Is Hamlet really insane or isn't he? Does he love Ophelia or doesn't he? When it is all over I ponder profounder questions. And at certain points around the middle, at Shakespeare's explicit invitation, I question the ethics of suicide and murder. But for the most part experiencing *Hamlet* is much more like reading a mystery story than perusing an ethical treatise (although few critics seem to think so). Just as in a murder mystery, what seems suspect at first proves to be trustworthy and vice-versa.

Amid these questions, I find that I share the characters' imperatives toward certainty and follow their distinctive rhythm from untested certainty to doubt to new certainty. Sometimes I have the advantage over them and merely watch the pattern, as when Claudius tests out the cause of Hamlet's strange behavior. At other times, my own certainty is called into doubt. For instance, my initial confidence in the honesty of the ghost is shaken by Hamlet's doubt about it ("The spirit that I have seen/May be a devil") before being confirmed by Claudius's prayer.

The process of testing the honesty of the ghost also illustrates a more precise and distinctive rhythm of *Hamlet*.

In an article on the "dramaturgy of delay" in *Hamlet*,[7] I have pointed out how all of the leading characters in their actions and speech follow a pattern of arrest: a strong purpose is brought to a total standstill or deflected, before it reaches its final, unexpected fulfillment. The same rhythm can be seen in the spectator's patterns of understanding. By the end of Hamlet's soliloquy, I share his suspicion that the ghost may not be trustworthy and am almost as eager as he to test it out: the play's the thing. But does this happen? No, I am halted by Hamlet's soliloquy ("to be or not to be") and then diverted to the nunnery episode with Ophelia and then to Hamlet's theory of drama. My desire to see the mousetrap set is thus brought to a standstill and deflected. I am not at all so sure as Hamlet is that Claudius is guilty when he breaks up the play and calls for lights. My confirmation comes unexpectedly, and totally, when I hear him trying to pray.

Like Hamlet, I question Hamlet himself. Yet I doubt his judgment in a way that he never does. As I follow him in his search for the truth, I need constantly to correct his exaggerations, weigh his words. Hamlet's Polonius, for example, is not my Polonius. His is a mere fool and Hamlet treats him as such. Mine is a respected counsellor and solicitous father; a man wise enough to admit that he is a bit of a fool. It is easy to see that Hamlet glorifies those he loves and defames those he does not: his father is a Hyperion, Claudius is a satyr. When disappointed in a person, he can swing from one extreme to the other: Ophelia from "the celestial and my soul's idol" to a wanton, Rosencrantz and Guildenstern from "excellent good friends" to "adders fanged."

7. Robert Hapgood, *"Hamlet* Nearly Absurd," *Tulane Drama Review* 9 (1965): 132–45.

Yet I come to trust Hamlet as I come to trust his father's spirit. At first he seems aberrant and jaundiced, sick in an apparently healthy society. As the play goes on, however, I see that the world of Elsinore is in fact as bad as it seems to him, that he has a way of being basically right about people. When it matters most, Polonius is foolishly super-solicitous, Ophelia is dishonest. It is as though Hamlet can sense at the outset how they are going to be relevant to his tragedy and responds accordingly throughout. It is an aspect of his general prescience. In the same way his seem-ingly misplaced hope for his mother's better nature is vin-dicated at the end.

Hamlet thoroughly understands Claudius. His prophetic soul unerringly intuits his uncle's guilt and various plots. Although he gives Claudius credit for having a conscience and knows how to play upon it, Hamlet's Claudius is essenti-ally a smiling, damned villain. Through most of the play my Claudius is a much more sympathetic figure, a respon-sible ruler, a loving husband, and a self-tormented sinner. Before the play is over, though, he has become what Hamlet always took him to be. With Claudius as with the others, Hamlet's prophecies are self-fulfilling: he himself helps to drive these people to what they become. Yet his influence is never to pervert but only to catalyze qualities already there.

About himself, Hamlet shows all of the tendencies he shows in estimating others. At first he overrates himself: the true prince knows not seems and will sweep to his revenge with wings as swift as meditation. He then swings to the other extreme and exaggerates his own failings. As the play proceeds, however, and Hamlet not only continues to delay but lightheartedly does away with Polonius and Rosencrantz and Guildenstern, his self-denigration seems less excessive than prophetic. Nonetheless, he continues to have great expectations of himself. The context of his self-rebuke is characteristically not of denunciation (as toward Claudius) but exhortation (as toward his mother).

After his return to Denmark, Hamlet has entered a new phase. With his new assurance his zeal relaxes, he relinquishes his stewardship to "a special providence." Formerly he would have been intent on making the most of his interim before the arrival of the English ambassadors. Now, trusting in a divinity that shapes our ends rough-hew them how we will, he feels free, without self-rebuke, to joke and philosophize in a graveyard, bring Horatio up-to-date on his adventures, dally with a courtier.

This is Shakespeare's boldest twist on tradition. In Saxo Grammaticus and Belleforest, Amleth takes the initiative upon his return, not only killing his uncle but setting fire to the palace and destroying the courtiers. In *The Spanish Tragedy* Kyd's Hieronimo suffers paralyses of action and speech that anticipate Hamlet's, but at the end he takes charge, proposing, organizing, and presenting the catastrophic play-within-a-play. Titus Andronicus is even more impotent than Hieronimo; yet he is the "cook" of the fatal banquet.

Hamlet's change is subtler. Only at the very last minute does he act. Before that he passes through a new kind of inaction, a wise passiveness. We hear no more ringing vows and elaborate plans. It is Claudius who now tries too hard. Hamlet decides to "let be."

As a consequence, by the last scene, I as a member of the audience *have* "made up my mind." My readiness to trust Hamlet is complete. For the time I, like him, can relax my questioning of his judgments and acts, secure in his essential rightness, and can relax my own imperatives toward resolving the play's dilemmas. I too can "let be." And my trust is vindicated as Hamlet at long last does what I and he have been waiting for through most of the play—kills the king.

At this moment Hamlet's *Hamlet* and mine coincide. But the moment does not last. Hamlet dies believing that he has secured the preservation of his good name and the continuity of rule. I, however, cannot be so sure. Claudius is justly dead and damned, yet the loss of other human life is so general and indiscriminate as to approach the ludicrous. Horatio will survive to tell Hamlet's story, yet his summary version of the tragedy seems a sorry travesty of Hamlet's understanding of it and my own. Fortinbras promises stability to come; yet he is not a Dane but a Norwegian, and he seems something of a Claudius, with his booming peal of ordnance. When he says "with sorrow I embrace my fortune," can we help remembering how Claudius came to the throne with "an auspicious and a dropping eye"?

As so often at Shakespeare's finales, I have the feeling of circling back to the beginning, of "here we go again." The moment of confident certitude has passed. My doubts and questionings are not so anxious as they were in the first scene, but they have begun again.

I don't want, however, to end on this note. It has the smell of the sixties about it, characterized as that period was by a kind of inverted sentimentality. Instead of seeing the Shakespearean world through rose-colored glasses, this sentimentality saw it through dark-colored ones. Jan Kott's *Shakespeare Our Contemporary* and many of the productions it generated are illustrations. The Marowitz *Hamlet Collage* is another; it is truly closer to Pinter's *Birthday Party* than to Shakespeare's play. Part of what was so exciting about Peter Brook's production of *A Midsummer*

Night's Dream was that it found a way out of the sixties and into the seventies. Its mood was that rare thing, one of joy, the shared joy that comes from living one's way through to the other side of nightmare, of recognizing the mysteriousness and fearsomeness of the dark side of life, yet successfully coping with it—even embracing it.

In a much more somber way, the same spirit informs *Hamlet*. The note I want to end on is that although we as spectators, like the characters, find ourselves in a muddle, we do—thanks to Shakespeare—finally muddle through it. Whatever our forebodings at the very end, the overall sense of success is there. For me, this is founded on the feeling that I have encountered mysteries and horrors (especially the confrontation with death) that have shattered the minds and bodies of the characters in the world of the play on stage. Yet I have seen the experience through, lived through it, in fact feel more alive when it is over than when it started. It is no small thing to survive a Shakespearean tragedy!

Hamlet in the Light
of the Shakespearean Canon

ARTHUR M. EASTMAN

My concern here is to examine *Hamlet* in the context of
Shakespeare's other plays, to bring to it some of the illumi-
nation provided by parallels and contrasts. What I offer is
a series of notes, beginning with the play's first scene and
ending with its last scene but omitting many a scene along
the way. As you will see, the notes develop certain themes
that seem to me central to the play: God, sex, insanity. A
few notes focus on Shakespeare's dramaturgy, a few on the
play's inescapable ambiguity.

1.1.

Hamlet begins in murk. Midnight. The battlements of
Elsinore. The outer darkness cold; the inner, colder. Guards
sick at heart, nerves taut. Suddenly, harrowing with fear
and wonder, a ghost, stalking with martial gait yet, on the
cock's crowing, starting like a guilty thing—a ghost boding

some strange eruption to the state. The scene crests, troughs, crests, troughs. And in the troughs, when they can breathe and chat a moment, the watch contemplate the troubled state of the kingdom: the night not divided from the day nor the Sabbath from the week; the nation on a war footing, armaments mounting. Or they muse more largely on other troubled nations, other distracted times—when "A little ere the mightiest Julius fell,/The graves stood tenantless, and the sheeted dead/Did squeak and gibber in the Roman streets." [1]

A superb beginning to a troubled play, this scene carries its meanings quite adequately within its images, its rhythms, its actions. Yet other scenes from other plays—earlier, later —reinforce these meanings.

As *Julius Caesar* opens, rips and tears in the political fabric are evident. Caesar, issueless, superstitious, epileptic, deaf in one ear, filled with hubris, an easy prey to flattering manipulators—Caesar aims for the crown. The tribunes rally the populace against him while a clique of envious patricians eyes him warily. Cassius tempts Brutus. Then, even as Brutus rationalizes himself into the conspiracy and the assassination, it thunders and lightnings, the tempest drops fire, a common slave holds up his hand "which did flame and burn like twenty torches joined," men in fire walk up and down the streets, and "all . . . things change . . . To monstrous quality." As Horatio saw, the Roman experience paralleled Denmark's, and with comparable significance.

The same may be said of the beginning of *Macbeth*. "*Thunder and lightning. Enter* THREE WITCHES." "Fair is foul, and foul is fair." In the background, treason and civil war. Ahead, treason, "Lamentings hear i' the air, strange

1. All Shakespearean quotations are from G. B. Harrison, ed., *Shakespeare: The Complete Works* (New York: Harcourt, Brace, Jovanovich, 1952).

screams of death,/And prophesying with accents terrible/ Of dire combustion and confused events/New-hatched to the woeful time." Ahead regicide, usurpation, earthquake, Nature turned upon itself, the falcon slain by the mousing owl, Duncan's horses grown cannibal, Scotland drowning in its own blood.

The scenes from *Julius Caesar* and *Macbeth* reinforce the significance of *Hamlet's* opening. They underscore the theme of disease, of rottenness, within the kingdom. They suggest crimes already committed or under present contemplation. They foreshadow moral and political eruptions to come, and they witness insistently to the engagement of the powers of nature and the supernatural in the affairs of disordered states, divided families, guilty men.

1.1. (again)

In one of those pauses when emotions have quieted, Horatio undertakes to explain why Denmark prepares for war. Young Fortinbras, so the whisper goes, seeks to recover "by strong hand/And terms compulsory" the lands that his father, Fortinbras, staked on a duel with the elder Hamlet many years before. In that duel, says Horatio, "our valiant Hamlet—/For so this side of our known world esteemed him—/Did slay this Fortinbras."

This information explains the immediate political situation. It contrasts the king that was, a chivalric warrior, with the king that is, a political manipulator. It reinforces Hamlet's estimation of his father—"He was a man, take him for all in all./I shall not look upon his like again"—and the loathing Hamlet feels toward his uncle, the satyr, the "mildewed ear/Blasting his wholesome brother."

Horatio's information seems to fulfill its mission in the scene, or the act, of its deliverance. The same may be said of Hamlet's couplet at the end of Act I: "The time is out of joint. Oh cursed spite/That ever I was born to set it right!" Given that Hamlet has received from the Ghost the mandate of revenge and that revenge means ridding Denmark of its adulterate, incestuous, Machiavellian, regicidal, and usurping monarch; and given, too, that the Ghost's revelation has thrown Hamlet into distraction, into "wild and whirling words," we can understand the Prince's agonized conviction that the recovery of Denmark's health is his own unwanted, unwilled yet inescapable, personal mission. His lines, like Horatio's, seem, in doing their immediate business, to have done all their business.

And the same may be said of the information repetitively avouched by the Player King at the start of the Mousetrap —that he and his Queen have been married thirty years. The span of their conjugal happiness foreshadows by contrast the immediacy of the grief to come, the impending assassination, and the rupturing of the Queen's glib vow of eternal constancy. No other significance seems ascribable to the period of the marriage.

In the Graveyard, however, we learn that Hamlet was *born* on the very day that "our last King Hamlet o'ercame Fortinbras," and that Hamlet is *thirty years* old. And in the play's closing, Fortinbras himself appears to claim the throne. The beginning and the end of the play arc together, linked by the passages we have just been examining. The coincidences imply a larger pattern, a deeper significance than we have hitherto foreseen. What are we to understand?

Perhaps the underplot of *King Lear* can help us. In the opening we meet Gloucester, Kent, and Edmund. That Edmund is illegitimate, Gloucester immediately and gratuitously asserts: "Though this knave came somewhat saucily into the world before he was sent for, yet was his mother fair, there was good sport at his making, and the whoreson must be acknowledged." Subsequently Edmund betrays his brother, Edgar, then his father, who pays the price of his moral gullibility with his eyes. At the end, when Edgar defeats Edmund in a trial by combat, Edgar comments:

> The gods are just, and of our pleasant vices
> Make instruments to plague us.
> The dark and vicious place where thee he got
> Cost him his eyes.

To which Edmund replies, "Thou hast spoken right, 'tis true."

The pattern here is of a crime or sin that was committed long before the play's opening and that is finally punished in the course of the play—*as the consequence of the justice of the Heavens.*[2] The parallel is suggestive. Hamlet's father was a king, God's vicegerent on earth, his duty to govern his kingdom by God's will, to keep it healthy and whole. But this king, however honored by a debased chivalry, neglected God's will when he gambled a part of his kingdom on a duel. On the day of that gamble, when time went out of joint, his son was born, thirty years later to set time aright. And on that day thirty years later when Claudius and Hamlet meet their deaths, young Fortinbras appears, to receive Hamlet's dying voice and to claim a throne which, the Danish royal line now extinct, will revert to him. The sin, the punishment, and realization of divine

---

2. The same pattern may be seen in *Measure for Measure* where Duke Vincentio's failure to enforce the laws of Venice constitutes the original sin that is providentially punished and redeemed in the course of the play. Similarly, Prospero's ancient abdication of his gubernatorial responsibility sets in motion the punitive and redemptive chain of events that constitutes *The Tempest*.

justice would seem clear. This, I think, is the larger pattern, the deeper significance.

1.2.

In his first soliloquy Hamlet provides bitter personal definition for the pervasive malaise or rot that the opening scene has adumbrated. The world, he says, is "an unweeded garden,/That grows to seed, things rank and gross in nature /Possess it merely." If Claudius is the serpent in Hamlet's garden, Gertrude is its depraved Eve: with "most wicked speed" she has "posted . . . to incestuous sheets." This theme of lust or sexual dishonesty runs obsessively through the play. Laertes and Polonius harp on it. The Ghost speaks of lust's sating itself in a celestial bed and preying on garbage. Hamlet's school chums trade jokes with him about Fortune's privates. In her insanity Ophelia sings a song about seduction: "Young men will do 't, if they come to it,/By cock they are to blame." And Hamlet in the Nunnery Scene, at the Mousetrap, and again in his mother's closet spews out a kind of sexual vomit: "Nay, but to live/In the rank sweat of an enseamèd bed,/Stewed in corruption, honeying and making love/Over the nasty sty."

In earlier plays Shakespeare has dealt much with love, little with lust, though *Titus* and *Much Ado* are significant exceptions, and there have been snatches of callow or jaded sexuality in *Romeo and Juliet*. After *Hamlet* the theme is for a time ubiquitous—in *Troilus and Cressida*, *All's Well*, *Othello*, *Measure for Measure*, and *Lear*. Later it surfaces at length in *Antony and Cleopatra*, *Cymbeline*, and *The Winter's Tale*. Collectively these plays and the Dark Lady sonnets richly orchestrate their common theme, treating it in tones that run from cosmic moral indignation (King Lear) to phlegmatic acceptance (Pompey in *Measure for Measure*) to self-torturing if humorous complicity (the Dark Lady sonnets)—but they provide a commentary too rich to be analyzed here.

Two plays, however, offer special insights into Hamlet's attitude toward sexual dishonesty and his mother. One is *Othello*. Because we know that Iago has preyed on Othello's mind, turning it the seamy side out, and because we know that Desdemona is pure, we are more likely to recognize in Othello what is also in Hamlet—an imagination sexually diseased. Compulsively that imagination generates images of libidinous intimacies at which it stares in fascinated revulsion—as in the Brothel Scene, as in the Closet Scene. Compulsively it projects upon the world its own sexual cynicism —as when Othello cries, " 'Tis destiny unshunnable, like death./Even then this forkèd plague is fated to us/When we do quicken"; as when Hamlet berates Ophelia: "if thou wilt needs marry, marry a fool, for wise men know well enough what monsters you make of them." Though Ophelia is no Desdemona, neither is she a Gertrude. Even if she were, however, and thus conceivably deserving of Hamlet's barrage of sexual innuendoes during the Mousetrap, Hamlet's cynicism about all women is no less diseased than Othello's.

Othello can help us see that Hamlet's imagination is sick. He can also plunge us close to the heart of that sickness. Hamlet never defines it, never says explicitly that he feels implicated in his mother's bestiality, that inescapably he participates in her original sin; but in the Brothel Scene Othello says it for him. In that scene Othello contemplates his state as from a distance. He could have borne all kinds of affliction: "I should have found in some place of my soul/A drop of patience." He could have borne becoming "A fixèd figure for the time of scorn/To point his slow unmoving finger at!/Yet could I bear that too, well, very well." He continues: "But there where I have garnered up my heart,/Where either I must live or bear no life,/The fountain from the which my current runs/Or else dries up— To be discarded thence!/Or to keep it as a cistern for foul toads/To knot and gender in!" The lines about the fountain apply more directly to Gertrude and Hamlet than to Desdemona and Othello. Gertrude *is* almost literally the fountain from which Hamlet's current runs. He *is* discarded thence. It *has* become the cistern for foul toads to knot and gender in.

In his madness King Lear mirrors and magnifies Hamlet's sexual obsession, defining its ultimate meaning. Progressively Lear has denied the blood bonds that integrate families. He has called on the great force of generation to convey sterility into Goneril's womb. In the first of the storm scenes he has called on Nature to "Smite flat the thick rotundity o' the world" (the feminine principle) and spill all germens (the masculine principle) that make mankind. Never so explicitly or puritanically focusing on copulation as does Hamlet's imagination, Lear's in its settled madness pictures forth the radical reason for this will to annihilation:

> Behold yon simpering dame,
> Whose face between her forks [i.e., legs]
>   presages snow [i.e., cold chastity]
> That minces virtue and does shake the head
> To hear of pleasure's name.
> The fitchew, nor the soiled horse, goes to 't
> With a more riotous appetite.
> Down from the waist they are Centaurs,
> Though women all above.
> But to the girdle do the gods inherit,
> Beneath is all the fiends'.

> There's Hell, there's darkness, there's the
> sulphurous pit . . .

The vagina is the mouth of hell, the entry way of sin and death into this rotten world. That is what the mad Lear says. In the diseased state of his imagination, that is what Hamlet ultimately senses.

1.5.

With the Ghost's revelation there enters into the play a series of themes that Shakespeare explores early and late: fratricide, regicide, usurpation, revenge. I pass these by to touch on other matters. One is Hamlet's reaction to the Ghost's revelation—"O all you host of heaven! O earth! What else?/And shall I couple Hell? Oh, fie! Hold, hold my heart,/And you, my sinews grow not instant old/But bear me stiffly up." There follows the strange writing in his tables. As elsewhere, words, images, action adequately contain their own significance, but a passage in *Titus Andronicus* comments by parallel and by contrast on the state of Hamlet's tortured psyche.

There, by means of the staff that she holds in her tongueless mouth and guides with the stumps of her handless arms, Lavinia has finally revealed in the sands the rape perpetrated upon her and the names of the culprits. To this discovery Titus, like Hamlet, reacts with a cry to the Heavens: "Magni Dominator poli,/Tam lentus audis scelera? Tam lentus vides?" (Ruler of the great Heavens, do you so unconcernedly hear these crimes? So unconcernedly see them?—Harrison trans.). Marcus's comment, "Oh, calm thee," testifies that Titus, like Hamlet, is distracted. Titus, too, feels the need to make a written record of the monstrous revelation: "I will go get a leaf of brass,/And with a gad of steel will write these words/And lay it by." And Titus clarifies the distracted reasoning governing his conduct and Hamlet's: "The angry northern wind/Will blow these sands, like Sibyl's leaves, abroad,/And where's your lesson then?" Already reeling from its discovery of the world's monstrosity, then shocked yet more profoundly by fresh discovery of yet more heinous monstrosity, the mind fears for its own being. Memory, like the rational, moral standards that once seemed immutable, may dissolve and with it all knowledge of the horror, all capacity to take arms against it. Hence the obsessive effort to render objective and permament some evidence of the evil that has come into being, some redemptive imperative to guide the mind in the future.

Titus's words on brass, however, would simply have stated the facts—the fact of rape, the names of the culprits. Hamlet's words are different—not the fact of murder and adultery, but "A man may smile and smile and be a villain." The contrast exposes how oblique Hamlet's words are, how cunning, secretive, self-protective. Far more profoundly than Titus, Hamlet senses himself to be in a world where private intelligence has no privacy—unless it be covered, riddled, ironized. It's a Kafkaesque world: if actual, then cause for madness; if unreal, then the expression of madness; and if something of both, then hauntingly in-between.

1.5. (again)

Hamlet's response to the Ghost's revelation offers the first indication that his sanity threatens to succumb to the enormous pressures upon it. Before the scene is over he mentions, as a notion, that he may adopt an antic madness. In the months that follow he seems transformed, for "nor the exterior nor the inward man/Resembles that it was." Critics have been troubled how much of Hamlet's strange conduct in the rest of the play is to be construed as anticly mad—his rational will controlling his words and deeds—and how much is mad in fact—his suffering psyche issuing in words and deeds over which the prince exerts but little control.

Two of Shakespeare's plays define the parameters of the problem. In *Titus Andronicus* the aged warrior proceeds to send his nephew to the court with riddling accusations. (One thinks of the Mousetrap.) Although his brother, Marcus, considers Titus insane, we recognize his act as thoroughly if bizarrely rational, the oblique indictment of his enemies constituting a surrogate and self-protecting revenge. Then Titus summons his followers to seek Astrea, the goddess of justice. Some are to cast their nets into the sea to seek her there; others are to "dig with mattock and spade" down to Pluto's region to seek her there; and yet others are to shoot prayer-bearing arrows to Jove, Apollo, Mars, Pallas, and Saturn to beg her return to earth. Marcus again considers Titus insane, and this time we cannot but agree with him. Finally, Tamora and her guilty sons visit the lunatic, as they suppose him, pretending to be Revenge, Rape, and Murder. Titus invites them in with an aside that shows his sanity has returned: "I know them all, though they suppose me mad, /And will o'erreach them in their own devices."

King Lear provides the other contrast. In the first of the storm scenes, when the king addresses the winds, cataracts, and hurricanes, calling down destruction on man and bringing into being by the force of his imagination the Day of Judgment, though we recognize the profundity of his perturbation, we know that his mind lies still under the control of reason. When, later, he gathers to him Tom o' Bedlam as "robed man of justice" and the Fool as "his yokefellow of equity" to set up court and arraign Goneril, we know that his sanity has failed. And when, after restorative sleep and to the strains of harmonious music, he returns to consciousness in Cordelia's presence, then truly renounces his kingdom and the things of this world—content to find heaven, with Cordelia, even in a prison—we know his sanity has returned.

The state of the sanity of Titus or Lear is never in question. They are clearly now sane, now insane, now sane again. It may be that Hamlet should be seen in the same pattern, but one wonders. In those long stretches off-stage when he peaks like John-a-dreams unpregnant of his cause, when he is lapsed in time and passion, sunken into bestial oblivion—is he sane or not? In the hysteria with which he responds to the Ghost, Ophelia, the Mousetrap, and Gertrude in her closet, is he this side of the line or the other? Each spectator will decide for himself, but the contrasting clarity with which Shakespeare presents insanity in other plays forces us to see that the question profoundly exists, a fundamental response to the ambiguity, perplexity, mystery that are the mode of this play.

2.2.

Clearly anticly mad in this scene, Hamlet toys with Polonius, calling him a fishmonger, hinting at Ophelia's frailty, speaking words, words, words, and willing to walk out of the air—into his grave. "How pregnant sometimes his replies are!" murmurs Polonius. "A happiness that often

madness hits on, which reason and sanity could not so pros-
perously be delivered of." Immediately Rosencrantz and
Guildenstern enter and Hamlet is at them with interroga-
tions: "What have you deserved at the hands of Fortune,
that she sends you to prison hither?" "What make you at
Elsinore?" "Were you not sent for? Is it your own inclining?
Is it a free visitation?"

Perhaps this is as good a place as any to recognize that
Prince Hamlet combines two roles we customarily associate
with the comedies. One is that of the fool, who talks, it may
be, a good deal of nonsense, but talks, too, a riddling kind
of sense, assessing each character and situation with penetrating moral accuracy and challenging each alteration in
his environment with his wits at the ready—self-protective,
self-assertive, critical. Feste, in *Twelfth Night*, for example,
blathers a lot, but he also morally ticks off Olivia for her
sentimentality in grief, Malvolio for his egocentric sourness,
Sir Toby for his drunkenness, Maria for her husband-hunt-
ing, the Duke for his opalescent melancholy. And in each
new situation in which he finds himself—with Cesario,
with Sebastian—we see him fence, probe, judge. Feste is,
as Olivia says, "allowed." Hamlet plays the same game. He,
too, is allowed—by virtue of his rank, by virtue of his putative insanity. He too riddles and insults and penetrates as
he assesses those who surround him—King ("A little more
than kin and less than kind"), Queen ("A beast that wants
discourse of reason . . ."), Polonius ("These tedious old
fools"), Ophelia, Horatio, Rosencrantz, Guildenstern, the
players, Laertes, Osric. And with the same quick and defensive sensitivity as Feste's, Hamlet responds almost instantly
to changes in his environment. Scarcely has he met Horatio
than he demands to know of him why he's there. Similarly
he challenges Rosencrantz and Guildenstern. A false word or

two from Ophelia in the Nunnery Scene and he challenges her. A few words more and he demands to know where her father is. As Polonius discovers in the Closet Scene, Hamlet's protective wit is sharp.

Hamlet's second comic role, which he shares with Shylock, Jaques, and Malvolio, is what Northrop Frye calls the *idiotes*—that is, the private person who is idiosyncratic and resistant to the social and communal. Like the fool the idiotes is critical, but his tone shades toward the censorious —one thinks of Shylock's contempt for Christian liberality and license, of Jaques's rankling criticism of man in his speech on the Seven Ages, of Malvolio's censure of Olivia's dependents. Unlike the fool, though he of necessity participates in the community, the idiotes mentally refuses to belong. Shylock never becomes a Venetian Christian, Jaques a true follower of Duke Senior's court, Malvolio a fellow in the Illyrian fraternity. The idiotes sets himself apart from those he judges; he repudiates the frailties that bind men together. So Hamlet. From first to last he censures. From first to last he struggles to maintain his embattled, private identity. Though in the court of Denmark, he repudiates its frailty; and though he participates, no longer is he a citizen of this prison, the world.

Although fool and idiotes are akin, it is perhaps safe to say that the fool tends to engage us, the idiotes to repel us, for the one plays, the other is deadly earnest, the one acknowledges his kinship with humanity, the other denies it. In *Hamlet,* as in no other hero of Shakespeare's comedy or tragedy, the two roles uniquely meet. Perhaps this helps account for the fascinating if ambivalent hold he has upon our feelings—a point to which I shall return.

2.2. (again)

In the great soliloquy that terminates act 2, Hamlet first excoriates himself for not accomplishing his revenge ("Oh, what a rogue and peasant slave am I!"), then coolly reasons about his problem ("About, my brain!"). The speech images a divided mind in which passion, reason, and will are at destructive odds. In *Julius Caesar* Brutus has a soliloquy that seems almost a choral comment on Hamlet's peculiar case. He, too, has decided for just cause to kill the ruler, who in some ways is to him, as Claudius is to Hamlet, a surrogate and guilty father. From the time of his decision until the assassination itself, he lives in perturbation:

> Between the acting of a dreadful thing
> And the first motion [he says], all the
>   interim is
> Like a phantasma or a hideous dream.
> The Genius [i.e., the mind] and the mortal
>   instruments [i.e., the body]
> Are then in council, and the state of man,
> Like to a little kingdom, suffers then
> The nature of an insurrection.

So indeed it is with Hamlet before the acting of the dreadful thing to which he has sworn himself: inwardly he suffers an insurrection.

3.2.

Plays-within-plays in Shakespeare generally mirror the plays in which they are encapsulated. One thinks of "Pyramus and Thisbe" bombastically and parodically reflecting to the young lovers of *A Midsummer Night's Dream* a tale of true love that never did run smooth. One thinks of Hal and Falstaff trading roles as they take off the great scene, shortly to come, between the heartsore Henry IV and his scapegrace son; or of the hymeneal masque in *The Tempest,* symbolically projecting the future bliss of Ferdinand and Miranda. "The Murder of Gonzago" in *Hamlet* clearly fits the pattern.

Shakespeare's technique in certain of these encapsulated plays illuminates his dramaturgy in *Hamlet.* In *Love's Labor's Lost* and in *A Midsummer Night's Dream,* as in *Hamlet,* the focus repeatedly shifts from actors-as-actors to actors-as-spectators, the performance being interrupted or frozen, as it were. One function of the device, of course, is to characterize the spectators—to reveal the callow rudeness of Berowne and his colleagues as they ridicule their entertainers, or the benign amusement of the various lovers at the tragical farce served up by Bottom & Co., or the progressive malaise of Claudius and his court, the mounting hysteria of Hamlet, as the Mousetrap closes on its prey.

A second function is to weave the play-within-the-play into the fabric of the play as a whole. Set entirely off from the rest of the action, it would be, in effect, a set piece, stopping the play proper and usurping its claim on our attention. The comments of Berowne, Longaville, and Dumaine, of Theseus and Demetrius, of Hamlet, prevent this from occurring. They integrate the play-within-the-play with the play itself.

Certain of the plays-within-plays suffer a terminal truncation, as does "The Murder of Gonzago." In every instance one can see that the play-within-the-play has already done its job, already exhausted its own potential. One can see as well that having projected its conclusion—of six more Worthies no less absurdly ill-cast than the first three, of further hymeneal blessings echoing those already offered in *The Tempest's* wedding masque, or of Lucianus proceeding from the murder of Gonzago to the getting of the love of Gonzago's wife—the play-within-the-play by its abrupt truncation turns a heightened attention to the characters of the play proper—to the Lords of Navarre, to Prospero, to Hamlet and Claudius.

These things the encapsulated plays help us to see in *Hamlet* by parallel. By contrast, they offer or reinforce one further insight: that "The Murder of Gonzago" differs from its counterparts by its being no mere entertainment, however absurd or lofty. Shakespeare has made it Hamlet's device to catch the conscience of the King, the instrument of Claudius's discovery that Hamlet knows his guilt. Shakespeare has made it less commentary on character and plot than uniquely central to their revelation and development.

3.4.

Near the end of the Closet Scene, after Hamlet has purged himself of the disgust he feels for his mother, after the Ghost has crucially intervened, and after Gertrude has sighed, "O Hamlet, thou hast cleft my heart in twain," Hamlet advises his mother to refrain from sexual congress with Claudius. Initial abstinence will "lend a kind of easiness/To the next abstinence, the next more easy." And he concludes,

> when you are desirous to be blest,
> I'll blessing beg of you.

The language in context carries its own meaning, but a passage from *King Lear* reinforces that meaning. It comes after

Lear, his sanity recovered, finds himself, though captured and prison-bound, reunited with the daughter whom he had always truly loved but whom he had, in his tyrannous outrage, long since disowned. Lear has transcended his suffering, his insanity, his obsessive concern with his own kingship, with his daughters' ingratitude, with revenge. "Come," he cries,

> Come, let's away to prison.
> We two alone will sing like birds i' the cage.
> When thou dost ask me blessing, I'll kneel down
> And ask of thee forgiveness.

The lines are not identical to Hamlet's, but the formula is the same: a humbling of one member of a parent-child relationship to the other—out of forgiving, merciful love. Lear will no longer be father or authority only. He will be the inferior, the transgressor. And his asking of forgiveness, when he has hitherto been the severe dispenser of corrupted justice, expresses a tenderness, a vulnerable offering of the self in love, for which language finds few more exemplary instances.

Hamlet is not parent but child. He does not for a moment acknowledge a guilt that might beg forgiveness. But his language does express a deep desire for spiritual rapprochement, for reunion, after the agonized months of the disunion to which his first soliloquy testified and which his vituperation earlier in this scene has witnessed. The passage in *King Lear* helps us see that at this point Hamlet and his mother have finally found each other again. From this point, Hamlet is no longer so alone, so dis-eased.

4.6.

Of his interrupted voyage to England Hamlet writes
Horatio the following account:

> Ere we were two days old at sea, a pirate of very warlike
> appointment gave us chase. Finding ourselves too slow of sail,
> we put on a compelled valor, and in the grapple I boarded
> them. On the instant they got clear of our ship, so I alone
> became their prisoner. They have dealt with me like thieves
> of mercy; but they knew what they did—I am to do a good
> turn for them.

To the larger significance of this coincidence we shall come
shortly, but we may here recognize the episode as bizarrely
"romantic" in a play which, the ghost aside, has been remarkably realistic. A parallel from *Two Gentlemen of Ver-
ona* invites us to recognize the skill with which Shakespeare
has handled a potentially awkward matter.

In *Two Gentlemen* Valentine, like Hamlet, is cast out of
the kingdom, a price upon his head. Coming finally to a
forest (forests and deserts being earth's equivalent to the
trackless ocean), he is beset by "certain outlaws" (land's
equivalents to the ocean's pirates). These, too, are "thieves
of mercy." They find Valentine a fellow to their liking,
banishment making them all akin, Valentine's putative
crime no worse than theirs, his appearance handsome, and
his possessing "the tongues"—that is, knowledge of various
languages—a clear qualification for leadership.

In a trice they elect him their captain, deliver him homage, and put themselves and their treasure at his disposal.
Thus they place him, as the pirates place Hamlet, in a
position ultimately to resolve the plot. Later Valentine, like
Hamlet, intercedes for the outlaws and gains their pardon.

Though we recognize *Two Gentlemen* as a pleasantly

ridiculous play, the intrusion of this scene jars an audience
by its length (76 lines), by its fairytale absurdity, and by its
being presented rather than narrated—so that suspension of
disbelief is hard to come by. In *Hamlet,* by contrast, Shakespeare narrates his romantic coincidence; he retails it in the
language of reportorial objectivity, and he compresses it to
scarcely eight lines. Piqued the audience may be, but it does
not repudiate the play or throw up its hands in disbelief.
Rather, I think, it senses a special kind of strangeness quietly entering into the world of the play and, like the king and
Laertes, it eagerly awaits the outcome.

5.2.

At Ophelia's burial Hamlet leaps into the grave, grapples
with Laertes, strives to outrant him. His behavior is undoubtedly dictated by shocked indignation, which here and
elsewhere prompts him to sudden, violent action—the cursing of a deceitful Ophelia in the Nunnery Scene, the stabbing of Polonius through the treacherous arras; and most
readers and audiences, solidly supportive of the melancholy
prince, pay little heed to the moral dimensions of his conduct here.

A glance at Shakespeare's more obvious dramaturgy in
two earlier plays may invite reappraisal. In *Julius Caesar*
Shakespeare accents Caesar's repellent traits up to the
moment of the assassination—the superstition, the sus-
piciousness, the susceptibility to flattery and manipulation,
the hubris. In a sense Shakespeare may be said to be swaying
his audience to the conspiratorial side. He does much the
same thing in *Richard II*, initially underscoring Richard's
incapacity to command, his wanton extravagance and ruin-

ous taxation, his inveterate hostility to those of his own blood, his scorn for all but a handful of favorites among the nobility, his folly, and his egotism.

Then, with the death of one ruler, the overthrow of the other, Shakespeare sets himself to even the balance. He reveals Antony's love of Caesar; he reveals Caesar's benignity in the will that Antony reads; he exposes the conspirators clashing in petty and acrimonious dispute; he shows Caesar's partisans knitting together; and he presents Caesar's spirit on the final battlefield—still operant, grander than ever:

> O Julius Caesar [cries Brutus], thou art
>   mighty yet!
> Thy spirit walks abroad, and turns our swords
> In our proper entrails.

In *Richard* Shakespeare is less concerned to communicate a power that he has hitherto hidden than to arouse a compassion he has hitherto denied. First there is the hideous humiliation to which the deposed king is submitted, and the king's special kind of fortitude in facing up to his persecutors. Then York tells of Richard's trailing Bolingbroke as they enter London. To Bolingbroke the crowd has responded with idolatrous enthusiasm, but to Richard?

> As in a theater the eyes of men
> After a well-graced actor leaves the stage
> Are idly bent on him that enters next,
> Thinking his prattle to be tedious,
> Even so, or with much more contempt,
>   men's eyes
> Did scowl on gentle Richard. No man
>   cried "God save him!"
> No joyful tongue gave him his welcome home.
> But dust was thrown upon his sacred head,
> Which with such gentle sorrow he shook off,
> . . . .

That had not God, for some strong purpose
    steeled
The hearts of men, they must perforce
    have melted,
And barbarism itself have pitied him.

Thereafter we have the pathetic king in Pomfret, the ugly business of his assassination already afoot, Richard acknowledging his errors, responding warmly to the sympathy of the poor groom, suffering the knowledge that his steed, once fed from his own royal hand, has proudly entered Bolingbroke's service. Finally there is the heroism of his struggle against his assassins.

Shakespeare is a rhetorical no less than a realistic dramatist. He manipulates the feelings of his audience, and he is skilled enough so to alter emotional appeals, so to readjust moral frames, that he invites his spectators to change their minds.

Perhaps we should see him practicing the same magic, if more quietly, in *Hamlet*. At the start he sets Hamlet in opposition to the court, makes of him a pure idealist in a corrupted world, robs him of family solidarity and the companionship of society. He engages us then and long after in Hamlet's suffering. He bows his prince under the frightful burden of the Ghost's revelation and the mandate of revenge. He cripples him with a division of his mental powers. And always behind and around Hamlet he places the prying, probing, hostile figures of the King, Polonius, Rosencrantz, Guildenstern, and even, in her pathetic innocence, Ophelia.

But should we not see Shakespeare developing a counterappeal—as in *Richard II* and *Julius Caesar*? The obsessive sexuality, the verbal brutalization of Ophelia, the callowness over Polonius's body, the amoral relish Hamlet develops in his fencing with the King, the contemptuous carelessness about his murder of Rosencrantz and Guildenstern, the abysmal graveyard shallowness in the face of man's mortality—do not these matters invite to some modification of feeling? After the Closet Scene the suffering has markedly diminished. And here, morally outraged though he may be, we can see that Hamlet is intruding on private grief, trampling on the body of a woman whose insanity and death are directly of his making, grappling with the youth whose father he has slain. And if our moral ears are not totally stopped, when we hear Hamlet demand of Laertes, "Hear you, sir./What is the reason that you use me thus?" should not we experience some shift or distancing of our emotional allegiance?

5.2.

"There's a divinity that shapes our ends,/Rough-hew them how we will." So Hamlet tells Horatio; and a few moments later, commenting on his having had his father's signet wherewith to seal the forged commission to England, he observes, "even in that was Heaven ordinant." Years ago Bradley drew attention to these matters not as giving evidence about the world of the play but merely as expressing a change in Hamlet's attitude, the development of what Bradley called "fatalism" or "self-abandonment." [3] Bradley's reading need not be ours, however, if we have recognized that with the Ghost the supernatural entered the play, that behind the coincidence of Hamlet's being born on the day of the original duel there lies a shaping purpose other than

3. A. C. Bradley, *Shakespearean Tragedy,* 2d ed. (London: Macmillan, 1905), p. 116.

human, and that the singular accident by which Hamlet alone boards the pirate ship points to providential direction.

In our secular world we tend to resist such interpretation, but Shakespeare's other plays point the way. In *Measure for Measure* and *The Tempest* providential dukes manipulate human affairs to put time back into joint. In *Richard III* and *Macbeth*, before the battles that restore England and Scotland to health, God's intervention is invited by prayer or, in *Macbeth*, strongly intimated by the awed reverence paid to the succoring king, Edward the Confessor, who touches for the Evil—"A most miraculous work in this good King . . . He hath a heavenly gift of prophecy,/And sundry blessings hang about his throne/That speak him full of grace." On the eve of the climactic battles in *Richard III* and *Julius Caesar*, ghosts appear. A sudden visitation of the plague prevents news of Friar Laurence's machinations from reaching Romeo. In *Much Ado*, *Twelfth Night*, and *The Winter's Tale*, natural events turn tragedy into comedy, but the natural events have all of them the aura of the miraculous: Hero, Sebastian, Hermione suffer death and are resurrected. And at the close of *The Tempest*, the good Gonzalo speaks for the entire Shakespearean world when in profound emotion he prays,

> Look down, you gods
> And on this couple drop a blessed crown,
> For it is you that have chalked forth
> the way
> Which brought us hither.

5.2. (again)

After the fatal duel has been arranged, Hamlet confesses to Horatio a strange misgiving in his heart. Horatio urges him to cancel the duel. Hamlet demurs:

> There's special providence in the fall of a sparrow. If it be now, 'tis not to come; if it be not to come, it will be now; if it be not now, yet it will come. The readiness is all.

Years later Edgar in *King Lear* echoes Hamlet's final sentence. Having found his eyeless father desperately seeking release from this world's agony, Edgar has sought to educate Gloucester in patience. For a time, after the bold therapy at Dover, he seems to have succeeded: "Henceforth," vows Gloucester, "I'll bear/Affliction till it do cry out itself/ 'Enough, enough,' and die." But the defeat of France's army and the capture of Lear and Cordelia break Gloucester's resolution. He refuses to move. "A man may rot even here," he says. To which Edgar replies, "Men must endure/Their going hence, even as their coming hither./Ripeness is all."

Although there is a huge metaphorical difference between Hamlet's "readiness" and Edgar's "ripeness," let me focus on the parallels. Hamlet, no less than Gloucester, has been, in his suffering, impatient. Like Gloucester, from the moment of his first disillusionment he has yearned for death. Instead of abiding the burdens thrust upon him, he has impatiently sought to fashion events according to his own will: hence the Mousetrap, the Closet Scene—this latter despite the Ghost's specific injunction to

> Taint not thy mind, nor let thy soul contrive
> Against thy mother aught. Leave her to Heaven
> And to those thorns that in her bosom lodge
> To prick and sting her.

The great soliloquies beginning "Oh what a rogue and peasant slave am I" and "How all occasions do inform against me" testify to Hamlet's impatience, to his incapacity to make of himself simply an instrument for divine justice to achieve its end. Impatient, he has slain Polonius, driven Ophelia to madness and death, armed Claudius and Laertes against him.

Edgar's line, in context, invites us to see that Hamlet at this point has finally changed—aided, perhaps, by the recovered communion of the Closet Scene, perhaps by the salt air of the sea and the new awareness engendered on the pirates' ship. He is, finally, patient, ready to be instrument, not agent—of Claudius's death, of his own.

In this altered frame of spirit and mind, he accepts the duel, and Providence, itself infinitely patient, makes its move. The disparate figures converge—"Fortinbras from his pelting Polish wars, the English ambassador from the unintended executions of Rosencrantz and Guildenstern, Claudius expecting the end of his agony, Laertes expecting revenge and honor, Hamlet expecting momentary diversion —each seeking his own ends, each ironically fulfilling quite other ends, just so, as he moves in providential patterning. Laertes is unable to strike; Hamlet is unwilling to drink; Gertrude wishes to express her tenderness to the son she has regained; Claudius sits frozen as his best laid plans unravel. The duelists become incensed, each mortally hurting the other, Hamlet retaining just life enough to release himself from his mandate before achieving the felicity of death. In a sudden, mortally unplanned moment, the kingdom's rottenness has been purged, its throne firmly fitted by Fortinbras. It has happened providentially in Denmark.[4]

---

4. A. M. Eastman, *"Hamlet:* More Things," *The Discovery of English,* NCTE Distinguished Lectures, 1971 (Urbana, Ill.: National Council of Teachers of English, 1971), pp. 66–67.

Reflections on Turgenev's
"Hamlet and Don Quixote"

JEROME J. RINKUS

It is the purpose of this paper to examine critically Turgenev's essay "Hamlet and Don Quixote";[1] to relate Turgenev's ideas concerning Hamlet to major intellectual trends in Russian literature and literary criticism; and to compare Turgenev's ideas with important Western European critical interpretations of Hamlet.

Irving Ribner in his revised introduction of George Lyman Kittredge's edition of Shakespeare's *Hamlet* reviews the critical controversy that has arisen over the problem of the

1. Turgenev's essay was written between the years 1857–1859. It was delivered as a speech at a public gathering on January 10, 1860 in behalf of "The Society for Assistance to Needy Writers and Scholars." See Ivan Sergeevich Turgenev, "Gamlet i Don Kikhot," Sobranie sochinenij v desjati tomakh, 10 vols. (Moscow: Gos. izd-vo khudozh. iti-ry, 1962), 10: 250–63. For an English translation of Turgenev's essay see Ivan Turgenev "Hamlet and Don Quixote," translated by William A. Drake in M. J. Benardette and Angel Flores, eds., *The Anatomy of Don Quixote: A Symposium* (Port Washington, N.Y.: Kennikat Press, Inc., 1969), pp. 98–120. Henceforth all references to Turgenev's essay will be cited from the English translation and will be indicated in the body of the text according to page number.

74

interpretation of *Hamlet*. In Ribner's view, nineteenth-century romantic critics concentrated on the personality of the hero, "often removing him from his context in the play, and treating him as though he were a real person, the victim of some strange psychological disorder." [2]

Ribner's interpretation of the romantic view of Hamlet is similar to the view of Hamlet shared by Ivan Turgenev. Turgenev, like the romantics, viewed Hamlet not as a fictional figure but as a living human being who manifested psychological complexities common to all men. This predilection on Turgenev's part to relate fictional characters and problems to real life and immediate contemporary social and political questions was a general characteristic of nineteenth-century Russian literary criticism and was not necessarily confined to a romantic view of life.

Turgenev's view of Hamlet as a contemplative man so plagued by doubts that he loses his natural power of action has parallels with the romantic interpretation of Hamlet set forth by the English critics Coleridge and Hazlitt.[3] Likewise, Turgenev's view of Don Quixote resembled that of the English romantics who based their interpretation of Don Quixote on the premise that the comic actions of Don Quixote were unimportant in comparison to Don Quixote's nobility. Don Quixote was regarded as an idealist—as a tragic rather than a comic figure.[4] Turgenev's position concerning Don Quixote was essentially the romantic idealist position since Turgenev maintained that regardless of Don

2. Irving Ribner, "Introduction" in William Shakespeare, *The Tragedy of Hamlet, Prince of Denmark*, ed. George Lyman Kittredge, revised by Irving Ribner, 2d ed. (Waltham, Mass.: Ginn-Blaisdell, 1967), p. xiv.

3. William Shakespeare, *A New Variorum Edition of Shakespeare: Hamlet*, ed. Horace Howard Furness, 2 vols. (New York: Dover Publications, Inc., 1963), 2: 152–57.

4. Edwin B. Knowles, Jr. *Four Articles on Don Quixote in England* (New York: New York University Press, 1941), p. 111.

Quixote's comic mishaps "the ideal itself remains in its un-tarnished purity."[5]

Since the focus of this colloquium is on Hamlet, I will not dwell on the character of Don Quixote or "quixotism" but will refer to Don Quixote, as Turgenev did, in order to define and clarify important questions of universal significance posed by Hamlet. I would like to point out, however, that Turgenev may have underestimated the complexity of Don Quixote when he states that "Don Quixote . . . has less need of commentaries, thanks to the magnificent lucidity of the tale . . ." (p. 98), as evidenced by the diversity of critical literary opinion concerning Don Quixote, which is as varied as the opinion regarding Hamlet.[6]

I would like to proceed now with a summary and critical commentary on Turgenev's view of Hamlet in relation to Don Quixote.

In Turgenev's view Hamlet and Don Quixote represent two forces that propel the history of mankind—skepticism and enthusiasm. Hamlet is the incarnation of skepticism; Don Quixote is the embodiment of enthusiasm. The struggle between these two forces is the fundamental law of human life. Each of us bears within himself the resemblance to either Hamlet or Don Quixote. All human beings live according to their ideals, according to their conceptions of

5. Arthur Efron, *Don Quixote and the Dulcineated World* (Austin and London: University of Texas Press, 1971), p. 6. See also Ludmilla Buketoff Turkevich's chapter, "Turgenev," in *Cervantes in Russia* (Princeton: Princeton University Press, 1950), pp. 99–114 and Yakov Malkiel's critical commentary on Turkevich's work, "Cervantes in Nineteenth Century Russia," *Comparative Literature* 3, no. 4 (1951): 310–29.

6. For a survey of the range of readers' attitudes toward Don Quixote see John J. Allen, "Introduction" in *Don Quixote: Hero or Fool? A Study in Narrative Technique* (Gainesville: University of Florida Press, 1969), pp. 3–7. Other important collections include Lowry Nelson, Jr., ed., *Cervantes: A Collection of Critical Essays* (Englewood Cliffs, N.J.: Prentice Hall, Inc., 1969), and Angel Flores, ed. *Cervantes Across the Centuries*, a quadricentennial volume ed. Angel Flores and M. J. Benardette (New York: Dryden Press, 1948).

what is true, beautiful, and virtuous. Many, like Don Quixote, receive their ideal ready-made. "They pass through life, adjusting their habits and impulses to this ideal, sometimes receding from it under the stress of passion or circumstance, but never challenging it and never subjecting it to doubt." Others, like Hamlet, "constantly submit their ideal to introspective analysis" (p. 99). They are the skeptics and the doubters who constantly examine and reexamine their ideal.

Turgenev admitted the possibility that a skeptical attitude toward one's ideal as well as an enthusiastic acceptance of the ideal could be manifested in turn in the same person and that these two mental attitudes could even blend together. He did not deny the possibility of change or even contradiction in human nature.

Although Turgenev attempts to deal with both types objectively in his article, noting their strengths and weaknesses, nevertheless he basically establishes himself as an apologist for quixotism and a severe critic of Hamlet. In Turgenev's view Don Quixote is superior to Hamlet because he has "faith in something eternal, in something immutable, in truth—in short, in that truth which exists outside the individual . . ." (p. 100). He lives outside himself, entirely for others. He lives to exterminate evil and to frustrate the oppressors of the weak. He is a man capable of self-sacrifice. Hamlet, on the other hand, is the skeptic who is so preoccupied with introspective self-analysis that he is incapable of action and thus incapable of being of service to others. "What does the character of Hamlet represent? Pre-eminently, introspection and egoism, and therefore a complete absence of faith. Hamlet lives solely for himself; he is an egoist" (p. 102). Hamlet "berates himself exaggeratedly," he gazes into his own soul, recognizes his shortcomings, despises himself for them, "yet at the same time seems to derive a sustenance and pleasure from self-abasement. He has no faith in himself, yet is vainglorious; he does not know what he wants and what he seeks yet is devoted to life" (p. 103). Turgenev begins his analysis of the character of Hamlet with a passage from act 1, scene 2 of Shakespeare's play in which Hamlet expresses his disillusionment with the world upon the rapid remarriage of his mother, Gertrude, to his uncle, Claudius, after the recent death of his father, the King. Hamlet's disillusionment has led him to thoughts of suicide even before the appearance of his father's ghost, who reveals that he was murdered by his brother, Claudius, and now demands revenge. Hamlet reveals his world-weariness in the following soliloquy:

> O, that this too too solid flesh would melt,
> Thaw, and resolve itself into a dew!
> Or that the Everlasting had not fixed
> His canon 'gainst self-slaughter! O God! God!
> How weary, stale, flat, and unprofitable
> Seem to me all the uses of this world!
> Fie on't! Oh, fie! 'tis an unweeded garden,
> That grows to seed; things rank and gross in nature
> Possess it merely . . .

Although Hamlet is melancholy and disenchanted with the world, which he regards as "weary, stale, and flat," Turgenev maintains that Hamlet would not kill himself because he basically loves life. His dreams of discontinuing life through suicide are actually an assertion of his intense love of life. Such sentiments, in Turgenev's view, "are familiar in every youth of eighteen years—For blood needs burn and sap needs run . . ." (p. 103).[7]

7. It is unclear whether Turgenev has misinterpreted Hamlet's age or whether he simply wishes to stress that self-analysis and suicidal reflections are particularly acute in youth. Hamlet's conversation with the

Although discounting Hamlet's suicidal thoughts as basically the egotistical preoccupation of the young with themselves, Turgenev commiserates with Hamlet because Hamlet suffers. Hamlet's "sufferings are keener and more grievous than those of Don Quixote" because "Hamlet alone inflicts his wounds upon himself," through tormenting introspection (p. 103). Turgenev's analysis of Hamlet's character at this point strikes a modern note and is reminiscent of those characters of Dostoevsky who delight in self-laceration. Like Dostoevsky's Underground Man, Hamlet suffers because he is hyperconscious. His awareness and consciousness set him apart from ordinary men and are the source of his anguish. At the same time this anguish redeems him in our eyes and reconciles us to him. Hamlet is alienated and lonely. We can identify with his loneliness because, in the words of David Bevington: "Every human being is unique and believes that others can never fully understand or appreciate him. And every human being experiences some perverse delight in this proof of the world's callousness." [8] In Hamlet as in Dostoevsky's Underground Man we see a common human tendency to prefer estrangement.

Turgenev regards Hamlet as basically an idealist in spite of Hamlet's skepticism. Although Hamlet incarnates the spirit of negation, "his negation is not evil, since it is itself directed against evil." Hamlet's negation may cast a doubt upon the existence of virtue, but he does not doubt the

gravedigger in act 5, scene 1 of the play clearly establishes that Hamlet is thirty years old, since the gravedigger has been sexton for thirty years and assumed his post the day Hamlet was born. Harry Levin views Hamlet's malaise and suicidal thoughts as "the ennui of every sentient mind in mid-career pausing to ask whether life itself has a meaning or direction." Harry Levin, *The Question of Hamlet* (New York: Viking Press, 1959), p. 31.

8. David Bevington, "Introduction" in *Twentieth Century Interpretations of Hamlet*, a collection of critical essays ed. David Bevington (Englewood Cliffs, N.J.: Prentice Hall, Inc., 1968), p. 3.

existence of evil and "exhausts himself in a fierce struggle against it." When Hamlet attacks good "he does not oppose it in its true nature, but rather because he fancies it to be a counterfeit good, under whose mask are concealed his eternal foes, evil and illusion" (p. 111). Hamlet's skepticism "strives with relentless vigour against all that is not just and true and thus becomes the principal champion of that very truth in whose existence he cannot entirely believe" (p. 112).

In Turgenev's view, Hamlet's negation was the basis for his tragedy for "in negation, as in fire, there abides a destructive force. How shall it be possible to control this force within bounds; how to cause its activity to cease at the exact moment; how to designate what it is to demolish and what to spare, when those eternal opposites—good and evil, truth and illusion, beauty and ugliness—are so often cast and indissolubly bound together?" (p. 112). Turgenev raises in this section of his essay fundamental questions that tormented members of the nineteenth-century Russian intelligentsia in their desire to effect social and political change under an authoritarian and repressive tsarist regime. Should one seek evolutionary or revolutionary change? What would be the consequences of one's actions both before and afterward if one wished to effect social change? It should be remembered that Turgenev delivered his speech in 1860, when the majority of his countrymen were still held in bondage as serfs. There was widespread agitation for reforms and liberation as well as talk of revolution in intellectual circles. As a liberal and Westerner, Turgenev had already committed himself to the principle of emancipation by publishing his *Sportsman's Sketches* in 1852, in which he asserted the basic dignity of the peasantry as intelligent, imaginative, and humane human beings worthy of respect.

The work caused a sensation in Russian society upon its publication and has been frequently described as a "Russian *Uncle Tom's Cabin* without its blood and gunpowder." [9] It is well known that Turgenev's *Sketches* influenced the decision of the future emperor Alexander II to liberate the serfs.[10]

There is little doubt that Turgenev identified Hamlet's indecisiveness with his own uncertainty concerning the means one should employ to effect social change. It was a personal dilemma for Turgenev as well as for other members of the Russian intelligentsia. In his case I am inclined to agree with Richard Freeborn that Turgenev's dislike of violence and his love of peace were due in large part to the "epicurean slothfulness of his nature," but "it was also a love of peace which, in its abhorrence of violence, exalted the peaceful, civilizing virtues of European culture and enlightenment above all the fanaticism, political terrorism and police repression which had overtaken Russia." [11]

Turgenev felt the need for change and for action. In Hamlet he saw the tragedy of a man whose will was so paralyzed as a result of introspection that he was doomed to practical inaction. Turgenev's critique is at once a criticism of himself and of others around him, since he saw the number of ineffectual Hamlets increasing on the Russian scene. Turgenev's criticism was a common criticism of Russian intellectuals in the nineteenth century and may be a valid criticism of intellectuals of all countries in all ages. Significantly, the twentieth-century dissident Soviet historian

9. Dorothy Brewster, *East-West Passage: A Study in Literary Relationships* (London: George Allen and Unwin, Ltd., 1954), pp. 70–71. See also J. A. T. Lloyd, *Ivan Turgenev* (New York and London: Kennikat Press, 1972), p. 14.

10. Avrahm Yarmolinsky, *Turgenev: The Man, His Art and His Age* (New York: Collier Books, 1959), p. 128.

11. Richard Freeborn, *Turgenev: The Novelist's Novelist: A Study* (London: Oxford University Press, 1963), p. 135.

and playwright Andrei Amalrik in his analysis of the social composition of the New Democratic Movement, which has been emerging in the Soviet Union since the death of Stalin, has estimated that 45% of the membership of the movement is composed of academics.[12] The support of the movement by academic circles gives Amalrik little cause for optimism in the future of the movement since in his view scholars are the least capable of purposeful action:

> They [scholars] are very willing to "reflect" but extremely reluctant to act. It appears to me that scholarly work requires, in general, special exertion and total concentration. The privileged position of scholars in society militates against their taking risks, and the kind of thinking acquired through scholarly work has a more speculative than pragmatic character. Although at present workers represent a more conservative and passive group than scholars, I can easily imagine some years from now, large-scale strikes in factories, but I cannot visualize a strike in any scientific research institute.[13]

In view of the disorders on American campuses during the late 1960s as a result of widespread opposition to United States involvement in the war in Vietnam, it might appear that Amalrik's criticism of Soviet academic circles for their lack of purposeful action does not apply to the American scholarly community. Yet one can seriously question the effectiveness of the American scholarly community in awakening the conscience of the nation concerning the essential moral questions raised by the war and in influencing governmental opinion to bring the war to a rapid conclusion. Although there were massive strikes on college campuses throughout the United States during the Cambodian crises of 1970, one must bear in mind that the strikes

12. Andrei Amalrik, *Will the Soviet Union Survive Until 1984?*, preface by Henry Kamm, commentary by Sidney Monas (New York and Evanston, Ill.: Harper and Row, 1970), p. 15.
13. *Ibid.*, p. 16.

were initiated and led by students rather than by scholars. It might also be recalled that the civil rights movement in the South did not originate in the universities, which claim to be centers of moral awareness, but among preachers in the black churches of the South. The movement started in the churches and moved to the streets; the nation's intellectual academic community followed rather than led. It would appear that both Turgenev and Amalrik have discovered the Achilles' heel of the academic intellectual.

Turgenev's appraisal of Hamlet's lack of resolution is based on his reading of several lines from the most famous soliloquy of the play (act 3, scene 1) in which Hamlet raises the question "To be or not to be." [14] Turgenev cites the following lines to support his contention that Hamlet's will has been paralyzed:

> And thus the native hue of resolution
> Is sicklied o'er with the pale cast of thought. . . .

Now it may be true, as Levin has pointed out, that it has become commonplace in romantic criticism to state that the tragedy of Hamlet is that of a man who could not make up his mind, and that this point of view has been all but discredited by modern critics who point out that it is based more on the introspection of Goethe and Coleridge than on the actual behavior of Shakespeare's protagonist. [15] One is inclined to accept the revisionist view that Hamlet's prob-

14. For a lucid analysis of the alternative possibilities expressed by the proposition "To be or not to be," see Levin, *Question*, p. 69; also his diagram, fig. 1, p. 167.

15. *Ibid.*, p. 132. Levin also regards the misinterpretation of the play as a "tragedy of thought" as a result of the mistranslation of the German expression "Gedankenschauspiel" taken from A. W. Schlegel's lectures. In Levin's view "Schlegel wanted merely to underline the well-taken point that *Hamlet* was, above all, a drama of ideas, a dramatization of man's intellectual curiosity." P. 85.

lem is not one of inaction but of retarded action. Hamlet acts; he does not act swiftly enough. But this raises another more important question—the ethical question of the morality of revenge. Levin concedes that virtually all criticisms of *Hamlet* find "the code of revenge, the cult of blood for blood" a common stumbling block.[16] Turgenev does not dwell explicitly upon the ethical question of revenge in his essay and this may be considered an important moral oversight in his analysis. It has already been pointed out that he does raise the problem of man's inability to be certain that an action intended to do good may result in harm; but he does not raise the question of whether one has the right to take another's life or whether this particular problem torments Hamlet. Turgenev merely indicates that Hamlet perpetually vacillates concerning the "duty of vengeance" with which his father's ghost has charged him (pp. 104–5), apparently because it is in Hamlet's nature to procrastinate. Turgenev maintains that when Hamlet finally kills his stepfather he kills him "accidentally" ("sluchajno," p. 105). How are we to understand Turgenev's remark? I think we must conclude that for a brief moment Hamlet acts rashly without thinking and that this is totally out of character. When Hamlet forces his stepfather, Claudius, to drink the poison, it is a brief, spontaneous, unplanned act. At this point Turgenev comes remarkably close to the analysis of Levin, who maintains that although Hamlet "repines against his plight in general" he "never questions his duty of killing the King. On the other hand, he never deliberately acts upon it; and when he acts at the end, it is in *spontaneous retaliation* for several other deaths—including in a minute or two, his own." [17]

16. *Ibid.*, p. 35.
17. *Ibid.* Italics mine.

It would appear that Turgenev has not come to terms adequately with the important ethical question of the morality of vengeance raised by the play. Nor does Turgenev in his analysis of Don Quixote ever raise the question of whether the knight errant has the right in pursuing his ideal to take another's life. Turgenev consistently praises Don Quixote's enthusiasm over Hamlet's skepticism and seems prepared to justify enthusiastic action even when it might result in misfortune for the innocent as it does for the small boy whom Don Quixote rescues from a beating by his master only to have the master inflict upon the boy a punishment twice as severe immediately after the departure of his protector (p. 105).[18]

Turgenev saw much evil in the society of his day, as did Hamlet and Don Quixote. He longed to right the wrongs of his society but despaired when he saw the large number of Hamlets about him "thoughtful, discriminating, and often of profound comprehension but at the same time often useless and doomed to practical inaction inasmuch as they are paralyzed by their very gifts" (p. 112). And so Turgenev preferred to side with the Don Quixotes, whom he considered essentially useful to humanity because of their selfless devotion to an ideal but principally because of their ability to act. The Don Quixotes were "eccentric innovators" without whom "humanity should never have progressed, and the Hamlets should have nothing to reflect upon" (p. 118).

Although Turgenev lamented the decrease in Don Quixotes in Russian society and the increase in Hamlets, which boded ill for the future due to their eternal doubts and inability to believe in anything, he did not despair, be-

18. The incident between the small boy, Andrew, and his master, the farmer, appears in Part I, chap. 31 of Miguel de Cervantes Saavedra, *The Adventures of Don Quixote*, trans. J. M. Cohen (Baltimore, Md.: Penguin Books, 1958), pp. 273–76.

cause in his own words "by the wise dispensation of nature there are no Hamlets in the absolute sense, just as there are no absolute Don Quixotes" (p. 118). Turgenev attempts a synthesis between the dual principles of egotistical skepticism and selfless enthusiasm represented by Hamlet and Don Quixote. He formulates a fundamental natural law in which "all of life is nothing more than the eternal struggle and the eternal reconciliation of these two constantly separating and constantly merging forces": the centripetal or egoistic force represented by Hamlet and the centrifugal force of devotion and sacrifice represented by Don Quixote. "These two forces of inertia and action, conservatism and progress, are the fundamental motives of everything that exists" and provide us with "a key whereby we may comprehend the progress of the most powerful nations" (p. 113).

Although attracted to Don Quixote because of his enthusiasm, Turgenev realized that the quixotic element of man, although enabling man to act, would doom mankind to impractical action and consequently accomplish nothing. So in attempting to reconcile the principles of analysis and enthusiasm, inertia and action, Turgenev turned to another model from Shakespeare's play, Hamlet's friend, Horatio. In Turgenev's view one of the most valuable uses of the Hamlets of the world "consists in their capacity for moulding and advancing the cultural standards of such men as Horatio" (p. 119). Turgenev viewed Horatio as an "engaging type," "a typical follower," a "disciple in the best sense of the term." "Upright and stoical in character, warm in heart and somewhat limited in intellect, he is modest and aware of his shortcomings to a degree unusual in limited persons; he is, moreover, eager to learn, and for this reason he respects the wise Hamlet and gives him all the loyalty of his honest heart without demanding anything in return.

He feels himself subordinated to Hamlet, not as a prince, but as to a better man." Because of Horatio's receptive nature he is able to receive "the seeds of thought from Hamlet, nurture them in his heart and subsequently disseminate them to the rest of the world" (p. 118).

Other critics have been equally enthusiastic in their appraisal of Horatio, referring to him as "one of the very noblest and most beautiful of Shakespeare's male characters," praising his depth of feeling, his modesty, his unselfishness, and his "manly soul full alike of strength, tenderness and solidity." [19] Hamlet expresses his own admiration for Horatio in a speech in act 3, scene 2. Turgenev quotes Hamlet's words regarding Horatio because, in his opinion, they also reveal Hamlet's own "essential nobility of heart" and indicate that Hamlet's skepticism has not destroyed his "conception of the high dignity of man." Hamlet states:

> Since my dear soul was mistress of her choice,
> And could of men distinguish, her election
> Had sealed thee for herself: for thou hast been
> As one who, suffering all, has suffered nothing;
> A man that fortune's buffets and rewards
> Has ta'en with equal thanks; and blessed are those
> Whose blood and judgment are so well co-mingled,
> That they are not a pipe for Fortune's finger
> To sound whatever stop she please. Give me that man
> That is not passion's slave, and I will wear him
> In my heart's core, in my heart of hearts,
> As I do thee. . . .

Hamlet's admiration for Horatio as an integrated personality "whose blood and judgment are so well co-mingled" is an important psychological insight that helps us understand both Hamlet and Turgenev. Horatio has succeeded in integrating emotion and reason, head and heart. Hamlet and

19. See Hudson's remarks in *Variorum Hamlet,* 2: 179.

Turgenev, in contrast, were unable to achieve a similar synthesis. Turgenev, in analyzing the character of Hamlet, regarded Hamlet's personal tragedy as an inability to love. Hamlet can not love because, being an "egoist" and a "skeptic," his "very being is saturated with the corroding poison of introspection." Hamlet may be "sensual and even secretly voluptuous" but he does not love, he only pretends to love. His inclinations toward the innocent and pure Ophelia are either cynical or emphasize his "further preoccupation with himself" (p. 110).[20] Don Quixote, in contrast, is superior to Hamlet because he loves ideally and purely. "Don Quixote loves Dulcinea, an ideal woman created by his imagination, and he is prepared to die for her" (p. 109).

For Turgenev love ecstasy was man's highest goal. Love "transcended the boundaries of any rational understanding and penetrated into the realm of irrationality."[21] Turgenev did not believe that reality is totally encompassed by reason but rather believed with the German romantics that "the visible world, the spiritual world, and the transcendental world beyond both of them extending into infinity, all form an organic whole."[22]

Turgenev's views concerning the split between reason and emotion reflect the conflict between two schools of philosophical thought in the nineteenth century: the

20. Many critics have noted Hamlet's apparent inability to love. Some, like Boswell, maintain that because Hamlet is feigning madness he must assume a disguise in Ophelia's presence; he must restrain his expressions of affection. He appears rude and harsh toward Ophelia in order to conceal his tenderness. *Ibid.*, p. 197. A more convincing explanation has been advanced by Hartley Coleridge, the eldest son of Samuel T. Coleridge. Coleridge maintains that since Hamlet's task is to seek "revengeful Justice," he must extinguish in himself the last feeling of love for Ophelia. *Ibid.,* p. 199. Those seeking revenge can not love, for love does not harmonize with revenge.

21. Eva-Kagan-Kans, "Fate and Fantasy: A study of Turgenev's Fantastic Stories," *Slavic Review* 28, no. 4 (December 1969): 556.

22. *Ibid.*, p. 548.

rational, scientific philosophy and the transcendental, idealistic one. Turgenev's vacillation between these two philosophies represents the essence of his duality. He was both the rational man of science and the poet who was heir to the romantic tradition and who was himself seeking an escape. Turgenev's religious search has been described as a "conflict between two principles: a solemn acceptance by the mind of the scientific laws of nature and an uncontrollable revolt by the heart against these laws." [23] Like Don Quixote Turgenev felt the need for an ideal, a vision of beauty that would offer him redemption. His refusal to give up his ideal is apparent even in his masterpiece, *Fathers and Sons* (a title equally suitable for Shakespeare's *Hamlet*), in which Bazarov the rationalist, nihilist, and ultramaterialist, who ostensibly rejects everything, nevertheless discovers he has emotions and falls in love. Turgenev's belief in the power of love and in a transcendental life beyond the grave is revealed in the conclusion of the novel, in which he states:

Can it be that love, sacred, devoted love, is not all powerful? Oh, no! However passionate, sinning, and rebellious the heart hidden in the tomb, the flowers growing over it peep serenely at us with their innocent eyes; they tell us not of eternal peace alone, of that great peace of "indifferent" nature; they tell us, too, of eternal reconciliation and of life without end.[24]

Although by nature Turgenev himself was Hamlet-like in his questioning and personally identified with Hamlet's soul searching,[25] when confronted with a choice between

23. *Ibid.*, p. 546.
24. Ivan Turgenev, *Fathers and Sons; The Author on the Novel; Contemporary Criticism; Essays in Criticism*, ed. with a substantially new translation by Ralph E. Matlaw (New York: W. W. Norton & Company, 1966), p. 166.
25. Lloyd, *Ivan Turgenev*, p. 217. Cf. Avrahm Yarmolinsky's comments in *Turgenev*, p. 174.

Hamlet and Don Quixote he chose Don Quixote. Turgenev admired Don Quixote's willingness to serve the masses and lamented Hamlet's lack of service; he admired Don Quixote as a "poor man, almost a pauper, without means and without connections" (p. 105) and criticized Hamlet's aristocratic disdain for the masses, for Hamlet is an aristocrat by both "his fastidious instinct as well as his high birth" (p. 107). In Turgenev's view the Hamlets of the world can not be of service to the masses. "They offer them nothing. They cannot lead them anywhere, since they go nowhere themselves. How can they lead, when they are not certain even of the ground beneath their feet?" (p. 107).

Turgenev's acknowledgment of the necessity of service to the masses reflected his own acute awareness of the plight and suffering of the Russian masses of his day and the need for social and political change. As an aristocrat he undoubtedly questioned his privileged position in society, which was based on the misery and exploitation of the peasantry. Turgenev's admiration for Don Quixote's selfless devotion reflected his own idealism and strong democratic feelings. Significantly, in considering the inscription for his grave, Turgenev expressed this view: "My one desire for my tomb is that they shall engrave upon it what my book has accomplished for the emancipation of the serfs." [26] A man wants to be remembered by future generations for his good deeds. In concluding his essay "Hamlet and Don Quixote," Turgenev contrasts the deaths of Hamlet and Don Quixote as a means of reasserting Don Quixote's superiority to Hamlet. The death of Hamlet affects us deeply. "Hamlet's dying words are beautiful. He becomes humble and reticent; he bids Horatio live and gives his last utterance

26. J. A. T. Lloyd uses Turgenev's words as an epigraph to his study *Ivan Turgenev.*

to the favour of Fortinbras as his successor; *but his eyes do not search the way ahead.*[27] The rest is silence, says the dying skeptic; and after that, he becomes silent forever" (pp. 119–20).

"His eyes do not search the way ahead." Here I think is the key to understanding Turgenev's rejection of Hamlet and acceptance of Don Quixote. Hamlet does not provide us with a vision of the future. Don Quixote, on the other hand, embodies a future ideal. Don Quixote's death "overwhelms the reader with an unspeakably poignant emotion." When on his deathbed Don Quixote expresses the desire to be remembered as "Alonzo the Good" and the "full grandeur and significance of his personality becomes manifest to all." Turgenev states:

"Alonzo el Bueno!"
It is an evocative word; the mention of this epithet, for the first and last time, grips the reader. It is the only word that has still a meaning in the presence of death. All things will pass, all things vanish: the highest dignities, power, genius— all things will return to the dust and all earthly greatness scatter like mists; all save goodly deeds, which shall be more enduring than even the most splendid Beauty. All things shall pass, as the Apostle has written, and love alone shall remain . . . . (p. 120)

Now I am aware, as I am certain Turgenev was, of the vulnerability of becoming a spokesman for "quixotism" in an age that has become increasingly skeptical and cynical concerning human nature and the perfectibility of man. I am also aware that the idealist interpretation of Don Quixote is considered out of date. Modern criticism in evaluating Don Quixote considers him a "man who ruins himself and others by his romantic and generous illusions and by his over-confidence in the goodness of human

27. Italics mine.

nature." [28] This criticism reminds us that reality is superior to illusion, that one must remember that Don Quixote is mad, that his motives are not pure because, although he is "inspired by a passion for justice, he is also vain and egoistic." [29] But I do not think this criticism invalidates Turgenev's profound understanding of human nature as expressed in his essay. One must remember that Turgenev viewed Don Quixote's idealism, as he viewed Hamlet's skepticism, as inextricably merging elements of human nature. Idealism and skepticism exist side by side in every man. They may at times be out of balance, but their recognition and mutual interaction are essential for understanding man and his actions. Great masses of men will continue to assert their belief in idealism because the ideal is a source of inspiration. Like that representative of the masses Sancho Panza, they will follow and remain devoted to the Don Quixotes. Men have a capacity for abandoning themselves unselfishly to a cause (p. 108). Turgenev as an idealist assumed the unassailability of Don Quixote's cause. In spite of Don Quixote's comic mishaps, "the ideal itself remains in its untarnished purity" (p. 101). Thus at the end of his essay, when Turgenev contemplates Don Quixote's death, he notes that although Don Quixote has returned home apparently defeated, he, Turgenev, is able to maintain his own belief in the pure ideal that Don Quixote asserted. For Sancho is ready to continue Don Quixote's struggle. The ideal that Don Quixote expressed in his desire to be remembered as Alonzo the Good will live on in the memory of those he has left behind and will continue as a source of inspiration to others.

28. Gerald Brenan, "Cervantes" in *Cervantes: A Collection of Critical Essays*, ed. Lowry Nelson, Jr., Twentieth Century Views (Englewood Cliffs, N.J.: Prentice Hall, Inc., 1969), p. 17.
29. *Ibid.*, p. 30.

Now, it may seem incredible for an individual living in the twentieth century, with its wars and blood-letting, prisons and concentration camps, to continue to maintain a belief in the power of good and the eventual victory of good over evil. This enduring faith in the power of good, in man's unselfish devotion to an ideal, and in man's determination to preserve his essential dignity and freedom in the face of overwhelming odds is a nineteenth-century value preserved in Russian literature and transmitted as a humanistic legacy to the twentieth century. This humanistic tradition finds its most recent disciple in the contemporary Russian writer, Alexander Solzhenitsyn. In his Nobel Lecture Solzhenitsyn passed a severe judgment on the twentieth century for its materialism, its barbarism, and its cynical disregard for human life. His lecture is worth citing because it affirms the necessity for preserving those humanistic values which Turgenev cherished and which the world so desperately needs if mankind is to survive in "this cruel, dynamic, explosive world on the edge of ten destructions." [30]

Our twentieth century has turned out to be more cruel than those preceding it, and all that is terrible in it did not come to an end with the first half. The same old caveman feelings—greed, envy, violence, and mutual hate, which along the way assumed respectable pseudonyms like class struggle, racial struggle, mass struggle, labor-union struggle—are tearing our world to pieces. The caveman refusal to accept compromise has been turned into a theoretical principle and is considered to be a virtue of orthodoxy. It demands millions of victims in endless civil wars; it packs our hearts with the notion that there are no fixed universal human concepts called good and justice, that they are fluid, changing, and that therefore one must always do what will benefit one's party.[31]

30. Alexander Solzhenitsyn, *Nobel Lecture*, trans. from the Russian by F. D. Reeve (New York: Farrar, Straus and Giroux, 1972), p. 27.
31. *Ibid.*, p. 22.

Solzhenitsyn reaffirms the "universal human concepts called good and justice" and extolls the power of literature as the "living memory of a nation" to humanize and unify mankind by communicating the national experience of one nation to another and in so doing prevent the other nation from repeating the mistakes of the past.[32] It is a remarkable testament to the spirit of man that Solzhenitsyn, who has endured the sufferings and privations of the Stalinist prison camps, can still reaffirm his faith in the triumph of good. He is a source of inspiration for us all. His enduring belief in good is not unlike that of Svetlana Alliluyeva in the conclusion of her *Twenty Letters to a Friend*. As she concludes her memoirs of the cruel sufferings and deaths of so many of her countrymen, she still maintains her belief in eternal good. She urges:

> Don't ever forget what is good in life. Those of our people who have been through the war and the concentration camps (both German and Soviet), who have known prison both under the Czars and in Soviet times, these people who've seen every horror the twentieth century has unleased on mankind never forget the kindly faces of childhood. Each of them has small, sunny corners he can remember and draw strength from always, through all of life's sufferings. I can only pity anyone who has nothing of this kind to give him solace. Even those who are callous and cruel retain somewhere, hidden from others, such pockets of memory in the depths of their twisted souls.
>
> The Good always wins out. The Good triumphs over everything, though it frequently happens too late—not before the very best people have perished unjustly, senselessly, without rhyme or reason.[33]

As Svetlana concludes her letters she muses on the ver-

32. *Ibid.*, pp. 17–18.
33. Svetlana Alliluyeva, *Twenty Letters to a Friend*, trans. Priscilla Johnson McMillan, Discus Books (New York: Avon, 1967), pp. 241–42.

dict of history in passing judgment on that period of her country's history in which "millions were sacrificed senselessly, thousands of lives extinguished prematurely" [34] because a nation's leaders had not realized or had forgotten that one can not do good by doing evil, that the end does not justify the means because the means shape the end. She looks to a future generation who will read her letters and be led by that experience to live their lives differently. Her advice might be equally applicable to a future generation of Americans, who will have to pass judgment on their nation's Vietnam experience.

> We are all responsible for everything that happened. Let the judging be done by those who come later, by men and women who didn't know the times and the people we knew . . . . They will read through this page in their country's history with a feeling of pain, contrition and bewilderment, and they'll be led by this feeling to live their lives differently.
> But I hope they won't forget that what is Good never dies— that it lived on in the hearts of men even in the darkest times and was hidden where no one thought to look for it, that it never died out or disappeared completely.
> Everything on our tormented earth that is alive and breathes, that blossoms and bears fruit, lives only by virtue of and in the name of Truth and Good.[35]

Now it may seem that I have wandered from my topic, but I would remind my listeners that traditionally it has been the function of Russian literature and literary criticism to maintain the link between literature and life. Literature and especially literary criticism have served as vehicles carrying, and thus providing the means for examining, the pressing social, political, and moral questions of the day. And in a time of moral corruption and decay when indeed

34. *Ibid.*, p. 244.
35. *Ibid.*, pp. 244–45.

there is something "rotten in the state of Denmark," it would be remiss for any student of Russian literature or any true humanist for that matter not to comment on the truly important moral questions that beset us.

Turgenev was a humanist. He embodied in his personality and in his writings the essential values that the humanities in our educational system attempt to preserve. O. B. Hardison, Jr., the director of the Folger Shakespeare Library in Washington, has identified those values as "the spiritual values of freedom, dignity, and beauty, and the critical values of openness, toleration, and a measure of skepticism of all dogmas." [36] I think the fairness with which Turgenev tried to come to terms with the character of Hamlet and Don Quixote in his analysis testifies to his temperance, his compassion, and his understanding. In juxtaposing Hamlet and Don Quixote, Turgenev was searching for an understanding of what it means to be human. A rediscovery of the human spirit is perhaps the most important problem we face in modern technological society, in which men are subordinated to things and abstractions. A new positivism has developed based on the premise that "human beings are themselves things, that the human spirit is a ghost in a machine, a relic of the age of superstition, that the remedy for social problems—assuming there is a remedy—is to treat human beings like so many Pavlovian dogs, to be conditioned and programmed into docile acceptance of a do-it-yourself blueprint of the Good Life." [37]

Although in the words of Hardison "It's probably quixotic to oppose an idea as fragile and tentative as the idea of humanity to the enormous power of things and

36. O. B. Hardison, Jr., *Toward Freedom and Dignity: The Humanities and the Idea of Humanity* (Baltimore and London: The Johns Hopkins University Press, 1972), p. xxiv.
37. *Ibid.*, pp.xiv–xv.

abstractions," [38] such an opposition is our only hope unless we wish to survive without freedom, dignity, and beauty, in which case our society would become "a concentration camp for sullen, rebellious inmates, or a psychiatric ward for patients made docile by spiritual lobotomy." [39]

> In a culture corrupted by things and fragmented by abstractions and ideologies the social task of the humanities is to remind us that the life of humanity is the life of the spirit and that beyond all our differences we share a single community—what Croce called the aesthetic unity of the human race and what Schiller defined as the beauty by which man makes his way to freedom.[40]

Croce's call for the "aesthetic unity of the human race" parallels Solzhenitsyn's plea to reaffirm Dostoevsky's belief that "Beauty will save the World." [41] Solzhenitsyn bases his hope for the future on the premise that a keen sense of World Literature is developing due to the "instantaneous reciprocity . . . between writers of one country and the readers and writers of another." [42]

> I think that world literature has the power in these frightening times to help mankind see itself accurately despite what is advocated by partisans and by parties. It has the power to transmit the condensed experience of one region to another, so that different scales of values are combined, and so that one people accurately and concisely knows the true history of another with a power of recognition and acute awareness as if it had lived through that history itself—and could thus be spared repeating old mistakes. At the same time, perhaps we ourselves may succeed in developing our own World-Wide View, like any man, with the center of the eye seeing what is nearby but the periphery of vision taking in what is

38. *Ibid.*, p. xv.
39. *Ibid.*, p. xxi.
40. *Ibid.*, p. 157.
41. Solzhenitsyn, *Nobel Lecture*, p. 8.
42. *Ibid.*, p. 29.

happening in the rest of the world. We will make correlations and maintain world-wide standards.[43]

Although there has always existed a concept of world literature "as the link between the summits of national literature and as the aggregate of reciprocal literary influences," there has always been a time lag. "Readers and writers came to know foreign writers belatedly, sometimes centuries later, so that mutual influences were delayed and the network of national literary high points was visible not to contemporaries, but to later generations."[44] Due to modern communication systems this time lag no longer exists and thus we are presented with the opportunity of creating a new sense of the universality of our experiences.

Turgenev, like Solzhenitsyn, realized that a national literature reflects its own individual spirit but at the same time expresses values of universal significance for other nations. In *Hamlet* he saw "the spirit of the North: the spirit of reflection and introspection—a spirit that is oppressive, sombre, deprived of harmony and bright colours, and seldom rounded into elegant and minute forms; but strong, profound, versatile, independent, and dominant." In *Don Quixote* he saw the incarnation of the spirit of the South: "a spirit that is bright, happy, ingenuous and receptive, that does not probe deeply into life, nor endeavour to embrace and reflect all its phases" (p. 114). Turgenev viewed *Hamlet* and *Don Quixote* as both a reflection of the personalities of their creators, Shakespeare and Cervantes, and an incarnation of the national spirit of England and Spain. He tried to imagine how these two great and dissimilar poets who died the same year (1616) would have reacted had they read each other's works. He was especially intrigued by the

43. *Ibid.*, pp. 31–32.
44. *Ibid.*, pp. 28–29.

prospect that Shakespeare in his peaceful retirement at Stratford three years before his death may have read *Don Quixote,* since the novel had already been translated into English. "The picture is worthy of an artist-philosopher— Shakespeare reading Don Quixote!" (pp. 114–15). How would Shakespeare have reacted? What would he have said? I suspect that Turgenev, who was himself Hamlet-like and regarded Shakespeare as akin to Hamlet, may have imagined himself as Shakespeare reading *Don Quixote* as he wrote his essay and labored to achieve a synthetic understanding of human nature based on the characters Hamlet and Don Quixote. It is conceivable that Shakespeare would have responded to *Don Quixote* by asking the same question that Turgenev poses in his essay but never answers. That question is this:

> Must we necessarily be insane to believe in Truth? And is the intellect, when submitted to self-control, necessarily deprived of its capacities for action? (pp. 112–13)

But this is the subject of another essay; a question that each one of us should contemplate and act upon.

What's the Matter with Hamlet?

MICHAEL PAYNE

Pol. What do you read, my lord?
Ham. Words, words, words.
Pol. What is the matter, my lord?
Ham. Between who?
Pol. I mean, the matter that you read, my lord.
Ham. Slanders, sir.

What we ask and the way we ask it shape what we see
and the way we see it. Questions are treacherous in precisely this way: a question may lead us on a path of thought,
but it may also determine what path we take and thus may
limit or obscure what there is to be thought about. To ask
a question is to take a step that may help to simplify and
to manage experience. It is paralyzing and terrifying to be
troubled and yet not to know what question to ask that
might relieve the trouble. But the question that alleviates
anxiety may produce relief precisely because the question
itself denies the anxiety rather than enabling us to get at
the heart of it. Such questions put us further from genuine
relief and further from thought. Bernardo and Francisco
ask the same question of the shapes that appear to them

out of the darkness—"Who's there?"—but their anxiety is that the *who* may be a *what*, that the *thou* may be an *it*. Marcellus brings that anxiety to the surface of the opening scene of the play when he asks, "What, has this *thing* appear'd again to-night?" Bernardo and Francisco are mechanically locked into their role as sentries and so they ask the sentry's question. Marcellus is slightly more open, or so we think until we hear Horatio's question, which he puts directly to the Ghost:

> What art thou that usurp'st this time of night,
> Together with that fair and warlike form
> In which the majesty of buried Denmark
> Did sometimes march?

But even Horatio, who says he trusts only the "sensible and true avouch" of his own eyes, presupposes too much in his question. Far from being the usurper, the Ghost is the victim of usurpation. What these characters ask and the way they ask it shape what they see and the way they see it.

From Bernardo and Francisco to Marcellus to Horatio we move to questions that take us further into the play and further along a path of thought that the play leads us to pursue. In this sense, the opening scene instructs us in what questions to ask and how to ask them. Bernardo, Francisco, Marcellus, and Horatio all ask questions of identity; they ask who, or what, someone or something is. They all ask existential questions. "To be, or not to be: that is the question." But there are other questions that run directly counter to the play's existential questions. Claudius's first words to Hamlet are a question of this other sort: "But now, my cousin Hamlet, and my son,/ . . . How is it that the clouds still hang on you?" And here we have the first form of the question "What's the matter with Hamlet?" That this is the wrong question to ask is indicated by Hamlet's first words, which, as an aside, cut Claudius's question in half: "A little more than kin and less than kind." Here Hamlet's identity is asserted in the very midst of the kind of question that most threatens to obscure, to distort, and to deny his identity. Hamlet is not a collection of symptoms of one or more mental diseases, nor is he an intellectual problem to be solved. He is, however, surrounded by those who would, if they could, reduce him to a collection of symptoms or to a problem. "What's the matter with Hamlet?" everyone seems to ask. To Polonius, Hamlet is lovesick. To Gertrude, he is grief-stricken. To Rosencrantz and Guildenstern, he is the victim of his own frustrated ambitions. But as readers or audience, we come to see the limitations and the distortion not only of these reductive explanations of Hamlet's nature and behavior, but also of the questions that generate such explanations. "The serious problems in life," writes Jung, "are never fully solved. If ever they should appear to be so it is a sure sign that something has been lost. The meaning and purpose of a problem seem to lie not in its solution but in our working at it incessantly." The inadequacy of the questions about Hamlet that imply solutions to his problem is that despite the solutions offered, the problems remain. And we work at them incessantly.

"What's the matter with Hamlet?" is a tempting question to ask when we seek solutions or a cure. But when we ask it, we keep uneasy company with Claudius, Polonius, Gertrude, and Rosencrantz and Guildenstern. Yet the interpreters of the play who have asked this very question are, at first glance, a nobler lot: they include Goethe, Freud, and T. S. Eliot. Here is Goethe in *Wilhelm Meister*, recalling Hamlet to us:

Figure to yourselves this youth, this son of princes; conceive him vividly, bring his state before your eyes, and then observe him when he learns that his father's spirit walks; stand by him in the terrors of the night, when the venerable ghost itself appears before him. A horrid shudder passes over him; he speaks to the mysterious form; he sees it beckon him; he follows it, and hears. The fearful accusation of his uncle rings in his ears; the summons to revenge, and the piercing oft-repeated prayer, Remember me! . . . To me it is clear that Shakespeare meant, in the present case, to represent the effects of a great action laid upon a soul unfit for the perform-ance of it. . . . A lovely, pure, noble and most moral nature, without the strength of nerve which forms a hero sinks be-neath a burden which it cannot bear and must not cast away.[1]

Goethe so deftly, so affectionately condemns Hamlet by holding up the heroic model—just as Hamlet negatively compares himself to Hercules—and finds his specimen lack-ing "strength of nerve." But also like Hamlet, Goethe longs for another place in history, a quieter time before mental anguish, before consciousness, when a strong paternal pres-ence gave order to experience. But the greatest cruelty of the present moment—for Hamlet and Goethe—is that no escape from the present torment is possible. Here is Goethe again,

Impossibilities have been required of him; not in themselves impossibilities, but such for him. He winds, and turns, and torments himself; he advances and recoils; is ever put in mind, ever puts himself in mind; at last does all but lose his purpose from his thoughts; yet still without recovering his peace of mind. (p. 213)

Hamlet's problem is that he is disturbed, and his being disturbed disturbs Goethe. If Goethe could advise the Prince, his advice would be practical, wholesome common sense:

1. Quoted in F. E. Halliday, *Shakespeare and His Critics* (New York: Schocken Books, 1963), p. 213.

to thine own self be true,
And it must follow, as the night the day,
Thou canst not then be false to any man.

That Goethe's explanation is a rejection of Shakespeare's problematic vision is clear from the career of Goethe's hero. Goethe's Wilhelm leaves the theater and is promised a happy marriage; for Hamlet and for Shakespeare there is no escape from the theater of the world.

If Goethe shares the superficial wholesomeness of Polonius, Freud shares Claudius's desire to wrap Hamlet in an analytical web. Here is Freud:

> The plot of the drama . . . shows us that Hamlet is by no means . . . incapable of action. . . . What is it, then that inhibits him in accomplishing the task which his father's ghost has laid upon him? Here the explanation offers itself that it is the peculiar nature of this task. Hamlet is able to do anything but take vengeance upon the man who did away with his father and has taken his father's place with his mother—the man who shows him in realization the repressed desires of his own childhood. The loathing which should have driven him to revenge is thus replaced by self-reproach, by conscientious scruples, which tell him that he himself is no better than the murderer whom he is required to punish. I have here translated into consciousness what had to remain unconscious in the mind of the hero; if anyone wishes to call Hamlet an hysterical subject I cannot but admit that this is the deduction to be drawn from my interpretation. The sexual aversion which Hamlet expresses in conversation with Ophelia is perfectly consistent with this deduction.[2]

Hamlet's problem is that he is hysterical, and his hysteria makes Freud hysterical. If Freud would advise the Prince, his advice would be clinical, detached, rational:

2. *The Interpretation of Dreams*, in *The Basic Writings of Sigmund Freud*, trans. A. A. Brill (New York: The Modern Library, 1938), pp. 309–10.

'Tis sweet and commendable in your nature, Hamlet,
To give these mourning duties to your father:
But, you must know, your father lost a father;
That father lost, lost his, and the survivor bound
In filial obligation for some term
To do obsequious sorrow: but to persevere
In obstinate condolement is a course
Of impious stubbornness; 'tis unmanly grief. . . .
Take it to heart? Fie! 'tis a fault to heaven,
A fault against the dead, a fault to nature,
To reason most absurd; whose common theme
Is death of fathers.

Freud hopes, as Claudius hopes, that Hamlet's problem may indeed be basically—and merely—sexual. Such a reductive explanation of his behavior would make Hamlet manageable, since Claudius controls Polonius, who in turn controls Ophelia. But again and again the text of the play flies in the face of the Oedipal explanation. Three young men all seek to right the wrong done to their fathers: Fortinbras, Hamlet, and Laertes. Two of them lack both mother and lover; Hamlet has access to both mother and lover, whom he rejects after having endeavored to preserve them in the memory of their innocence before Eden became the unweeded garden.

If Goethe and Polonius, Freud and Claudius speak to Hamlet in chorus, T. S. Eliot shares with Gertrude a desperate search for objectivity. Here is Eliot:

Hamlet (the man) is dominated by an emotion which is inexpressible, because it is in *excess* of the facts as they appear. And the supposed identity of Hamlet with his author is genuine to this point: that Hamlet's bafflement at the absence of objective equivalent to his feelings is a prolongation of the bafflement of his creator in the face of his artistic problem. Hamlet is up against the difficulty that his disgust is occasioned by his mother, but that his mother is not an adequate equivalent for it; his disgust envelops and exceeds her. It is

thus a feeling which he cannot understand; he cannot objectify it, and it therefore remains to poison life and obstruct
action.[3]

Hamlet's problem is that he cannot understand his problem,
nor can he objectify it, and his failure of understanding and
objectivity leads Eliot to repeat the failure to understand
and objectify. Eliot thus dismisses the play. But if he were
to advise the Prince, his advice would be controlled, understanding, straining toward objectivity:

> Good Hamlet, cast thy nighted colour off,
> And let thine eye look like a friend on Denmark.
> Do not for ever with thy vailed lids
> Seek for thy noble father in the dust:
> Thou know'st 'tis common; all that lives must die,
> Passing through nature to eternity. . . .
> Why seems it so particular with thee?

Gertrude, "etherized upon a table," "pinned and wriggling
on the wall," or walking through the play as though in a
drugged state, cannot admit the legitimacy of Hamlet's
feelings without admitting the illegitimacy of her own. She
has become an object, "the imperial jointress to this warlike
state," but always, beneath the surface of her tormented
objectivity, there are the shame, fear, guilt, and passion that
we see only once, in the scene in her closet.

Surely it is perverse to equate Goethe with Polonius,
Freud with Claudius, and Eliot with Gertrude, though
Shakespeare habitually anticipates his critics' simplistic re-
ductions of his vision. As early as *A Midsummer Night's
Dream*, Shakespeare counters the excesses of literal and
analytic interpretation in the comments of Theseus and
Bottom on what they see or fail to see in plays and dreams.

3. "Hamlet and His Problems," in *The Sacred Wood* (New York:
Barnes and Noble, 1960), p. 101.

Theseus's set speech on the lunatic, the lover, and the poet
begins with his refusal to believe in "antique fables" and
"fairy toys," which make up one dimension of the play.
Bottom, who occupies the other extreme of the play's world
from Theseus, warns us that "man is but an ass, if he go
about to expound this dream." But there remains within *A
Midsummer Night's Dream,* within *Hamlet,* and within the
criticism of the plays willful misinterpretation, deliberate
misprision, a refusal to understand, an unwillingness to give
in to the shaped vision of the work. We see clearly what
Hamlet's analysts within the play do to him. They project
onto him their own misprision: Polonius sees his own
lechery in Hamlet; Gertrude, her own guilt and grief; Rosencrantz and Guildenstern, their own ambition; Claudius, his
own Machiavellian destructiveness. But this same misprision
is found in the critics of the play and in ourselves: the
play is a mirror held up to our nature, in which we are
shown the feature of virtue, the image of scorn, and the
form and pressure of the age and body of the time. But
we willfully, deliberately misinterpret, misperceive the
vision we are offered. If Shakespeare had not anticipated in
advance the interpretations of such brilliant critics as
Goethe, Freud, and Eliot, we might convince ourselves that
we simply see different things when we look into that tragic
glass, that *Hamlet* is what you will or as you like it. But
there, in advance, the interpretations are anticipated and
even parodied in the speeches of those who would advise
the Prince. It appears that the only possible interpretations
are misinterpretations.

In his brilliant new book, *The Anxiety of Influence,*
Harold Bloom helps us understand our misunderstanding,
helps us see our misprision. The history of poetry, Bloom
argues, is the history of poetic misprision, of the deliberate

misreading of one poet by another. Goethe or Freud or
Eliot turns to Shakespeare and is struck by the value and
the authority of the vision of his predecessor. But the
anxiety of the later poet arises in the struggle with that
predecessor in an attempt to command a free space for a
new vision. Misprision is an attempt "to clear imaginative
space for ourselves";[4] it is a means of coming to terms with
the influence of an earlier generation of poetic authority.
But this same misprision that Bloom sees as central to the
history of poetry is also central to the internal history of
Hamlet and to the external history of *Hamlet* criticism.

Within the play three worlds overlap: the world of
Hamlet's father, the world of Claudius, and the world of
Hamlet himself. The world of Hamlet's father is shaped by
the Prince into the myth of Hyperion, the sun god. Hyperion's was a world of moral clarity when the faces of
virtue and scorn could be clearly seen and clearly identified.
It was also a world of rarefied passion, when desires both
satisfied and enlivened the appetite. But how do we know
such a world ever existed? We have simply Hamlet's first
soliloquy, which compares the world that is lost to the one
that is present; Hamlet looks from the age of the sun god to
the age of Claudius, the satyr. Yet, when the influence of the
fallen Hyperion would be exercised upon the world, when the
father would influence the son—"Avenge this foul and most
unnatural murder"—there arises the anxiety. Hamlet deliberately, willfully misunderstands. The two things he is forbidden by the Ghost to do, he does: he taints his mind and
contrives against his mother. What he is explicitly commanded to do, he tries to avoid. But just as Hamlet looks
upon the older Hamlet and refuses to see what is there, so all

4. Harold Bloom, *The Anxiety of Influence: A Theory of Poetry*
(New York: Oxford University Press, 1973), p. 5.

those who surround the Prince look on him and refuse to
see what is there. The anxiety of influence moves through
two revolutions: from Hamlet the father to Hamlet the
son; from Hamlet the son to the world that resists his rule
and influence. Rosencrantz and Guildenstern erroneously
think that Hamlet seeks the fulfillment of political ambition,
but what he rather struggles toward is his own poetic
authority. And this he attempts to achieve by doing what
Shakespeare did so often: he rewrites a play in order to
catch the conscience of the king, in order to capture the
minds of the new age. He would show the age and the body
of the time its form and pressure. But the new age suffers
the anxiety of influence from its would-be scourge and minister, just as the son suffers the anxiety of influence of the
father. Claudius is as desperate in his search for a free space
for his own imagination as is Hamlet. Here is Claudius:

> In the corrupted currents of this world
> Offence's gilded hand may shove by justice,
> And oft 'tis seen the wicked prize itself
> Buys out the law: but 'tis not so above;
> There is no shuffling, there the action lies
> In his true nature; and we ourselves compell'd,
> Even to the teeth and forehead of our faults,
> To give in evidence. What then? What rests?
> Try what repentance can: what can it not?
> Yet what can it when one can not repent?
> O wretched state! O bosom black as death!
> O limed soul, that struggling to be free,
> Art more engaged!

We might well ask, Why does Claudius delay in killing
Hamlet? What's the matter with Claudius? Yet Claudius's
range and power of vision are great indeed. It is Claudius
alone in the play who looks beyond the realm of human
influence to the realm of a creator whose "action lies/In his

true nature." But such oneness, such wholeness of being, is terribly intimidating to the divided, tortured being of Claudius. Now the man who would be king finds himself "struggling to be free."

Harold Bloom distinguishes six forms, or revisionary ratios, of the anxiety of influence in the history of poetry. The sixth ratio he calls "apophrades," or the return of the dead, a word he takes from the Athenian dismal or unlucky days upon which the dead returned to reinhabit the houses in which they had lived. *Hamlet,* the play, reenacts apophrades not only in its theme and subject but also in the demands it makes on its readers and audience. The struggle we have in thinking our way through the play is intensified by Shakespeare's multiplication of our anxiety on every level of the play's structure. Our thinking runs the full range of critical response: At one pole is our concern for the minute details of form and structure. These can be seen clearly enough. We can talk with each other about the disease and garden imagery, about Shakespeare's handling of the strategy of suspense in the early scenes, about paralleling and counterpointing of scenes; and when we talk of these things, we can reach considerable agreement and understanding about what we see as the play's parts. But at the other pole from the minute details of form and structure is our own desire to find a free imaginative space for our own minds within the play. Once we "get into" the play, we seek a means of coping with the anxiety produced by the play's influence upon our imaginations. Here is where we passionately misinterpret the play as we must misinterpret it. "There are no interpretations but only misinterpretations, and so all criticism is prose poetry." [5]

When Hamlet dies, his anxiety obviously ends: "The

5 *Ibid.*, p. 95.

rest is silence." But for us, the end of Hamlet's anxiety is but the beginning of our own. Like Horatio, we are witnesses who are left alive to repeat what we have seen; Hamlet restrains Horatio and us together:

> Absent thee from felicity awhile,
> And in this harsh world draw thy breath in pain,
> To tell my story.

For us there is no silence yet, no felicity. We draw our painful breaths and tell Hamlet's story, a story infused with our own anxiety. The final movement of the tragedy occurs when the players become silent and we repeat the story in our own thoughts. Then we are beyond the question, "What's the matter with Hamlet," for the matter, or substance, of the play has become our main concern—and a focal point for our continuing anxiety. We work at the problem incessantly.

Pol.   What do you read, my lord?
Ham. Words, words, words.
Pol.   What is the matter, my lord?
Ham. Between who?
Pol.   I mean, the matter that you read, my lord.
Ham. Slanders, sir.

"This Distracted Globe":
Self in *Hamlet*

TUCKER ORBISON

Each night I meet him. King with Crown. Each night we fight. Why must he kill me? No. I shall not die. I can be smaller than a pinhead, harder than a diamond. Suddenly, how gentle he is! One of his tricks. Off with his Crown! Strike. Bash in his skull. Face streams of blood. Tears? Perhaps. Too late! Off with his head! Pith the spine! Die now, O King!

So R. D. Laing begins his prose-poem "The Bird of Paradise" at the end of *The Politics of Experience*.[1] Elsewhere in that book Laing writes, "We have to begin by admitting and even accepting our violence, rather than blindly destroying ourselves with it" (p. 49). I have been wondering whether or not the unconscious impulse to destroy may not be a clue to one pattern in *Hamlet*, that most difficult of Shakespeare's plays. Could it be that each night

---

1. R. D. Laing, *The Politics of Experience* (New York: Random House, 1967), p. 123. At the outset of this paper, I would like to note that it has profited from the sharp criticisms and valuable suggestions of Professor Phil Withim.

of Hamlet's life after his mother's remarriage he experiences in one of his "bad dreams" the horrifyingly joyful struggle, mutilation, and final murder described by Laing? Hamlet's "prophetic soul" has revealed to him his hatred of Claudius even before the ghost's harrowing tale of poison and fratricide (I follow Kittredge in thinking that "prophetic soul" does not mean that Hamlet already suspected Claudius of the murder).[2] The visit of the ghost brings to his consciousness the antipathy implied in his first soliloquy's reference to the King as a "satyr" and validates the foreboding he feels after Horatio tells him he has seen the apparition:

> My father's spirit—in arms? All is not well. I
> doubt some foul play. Would the night were come!
> Till then sit still, my soul. Foul deeds will rise,
> Though all the earth o'erwhelm them, to men's eyes.
> (1.2.255–58)

Whether it is "a spirit of health or goblin damn'd" (1.4.40), it makes the night hideous and, as Hamlet says, speaking for himself and his friends, it horridly shakes "our disposition/With thoughts beyond the reaches of our souls" (55–56). It terrifies even Horatio the skeptic, and one can believe that in 1601 Shakespeare's audience stared at the apparition with "oppress'd and fear-surprised eyes" (1.2.203), as did Marcellus and Bernardo. It is just possible that the ghost is "a dram of e'il" come from the unconscious in an attempt to destroy Hamlet's "noble substance."

This play has been the despair of many who have tried to come to terms with it. There is always the possibility that like the ghost it may draw us into madness; and Maynard Mack has said that Hamlet is not only mad himself

---

2. The text I have used throughout is that of George Lyman Kittredge, revised by Irving Ribner (Waltham, Mass.: Blaisdel, 1967).

but a cause that madness is in the rest of us.[3] Some believe that the staging of a Shakespeare play can help with problems of interpretation. But listen to a review of one year of *Hamlet* productions in England in 1970:

> It has been just one damned villain after another lately; that's to say, just one smiling, damned villain, one remorseless, treacherous, lecherous, kindless villain. A well-known newspaper has actually appointed a provincial Hamlet correspondent, and, though I cannot claim to have seen all that character's recent manifestations, there certainly seem to have been enough to justify one. There was Courtenay, the prim swot just back from his Wittenburg tripos; Williamson, the dour, implacable puritan, stalking through the Danish fleshpots; McCowen, the vivid extrovert, as bold a fellow as ever sprinted across a battlement in search of a ghost; Howard, tattered and scrawny, and dreaming of a career with the players; Bates, sharp-witted and sly, the barrow boy of Elsinore; and others. Each gave a distinct interpretation.[4]

No, an effective production of the play will provide insight, but will not solve the problem of *Hamlet* for us.

Shall we then despair of coming to terms with the play? One may feel more sharply with this play than with any other that, like Hamlet, it resists the attempt to pluck out its mystery, but after all, is it not the nature of all literature to act the part of a sphinx? And if we were finally able to answer the riddle, who is to say that the experience might not in some way destroy us? We would probably do well to adopt Leo Kirschbaum's attitude when he concludes that "the play itself gives no clear answers. That, I think, is the ultimate answer for *Hamlet,* that it should raise ques-

3. Maynard Mack, "The World of *Hamlet," Tragic Themes in Western Literature,* ed. Cleanth Brooks (New Haven: Yale University Press), p. 33.

4. Benedict Nightingale, "Shakespeare Is as Shakespeare's Done," *Theatre 71,* ed. Sheridan Morley (London: Hutchinson, 1971), p. 154.

tions but never give forthright answers." [5] Naturally, this
does not prevent us from seeking for meanings—by indirec-
tions finding directions out. Some critics conclude that the
play's very mystery *is* its meaning. Harry Levin has emphasized the play's interrogative mood and doubting stance,
and Maynard Mack finds that "mysteriousness" is a central
quality of the play.[6] I have little hope of throwing much new
light into the dark places, but I would like to make a suggestion as to why the play continues to hold such interest
for a modern audience (in England the plethora of those
performances in 1970 imposed a burden on British producers
to institute a temporary moratorium on productions of
Hamlet). Robert Bridges's conclusion that in writing *Hamlet*
Shakespeare deliberately set out to mystify the audience
hardly suggests the full answer,[7] namely that the play
fascinates because it mystifies. It *does* mystify and because
of this it *does* fascinate, but the fascination does not reside
in that single cause alone. I would like to argue that the
play tells us something very important that we need to
know about ourselves and that the structure of the play
gives the audience the sense of renewal that results from a
psychic release. Shakespeare is as much as saying to his
audience:

> Come, come, and sit you down. You shall not budge!
> You go not till I set you up a glass
> Where you may see the inmost part of you.
> (3.4.18–20)

I began with the suggestion that the visitation of the

5. Leo Kirschbaum, *Character and Characterization in Shakespeare*
(Detroit: Wayne State University Press. 1962), p. 97.
6. Harry Levin, *The Question of Hamlet* (New York: Oxford University Press, 1959); Mack, in the work cited.
7. Robert Bridges, *The Influence of the Audience on Shakespeare's
Drama* (London: Oxford University Press, 1927), p. 25.

ghost is the inciting incident of the play and that in some sense it forebodes the possibility of the destruction of Hamlet's soul; more specifically, that it represents the unconscious impulse to violence in Hamlet's psyche. That Shakespeare is dramatizing a *psychomachia*—a war in the soul—is everywhere apparent in the text and in the action. Perhaps the most direct evidence of this concern is the reduplication in the play of characters who are self-divided and are described as such. Gertrude's moral obtuseness prevents her from discerning her guilt until the closet scene, when she says to Hamlet, "Thou turn'st mine eyes into my very soul" (3.4.89), and the ghost bids Hamlet to "step between her and her fighting soul!" (113). In the prayer scene the whole of Claudius's long speech, like many of Hamlet's, may be seen as a psychic civil war: "My stronger guilt defeats my strong intent" (3.3.40). Try as he will, he cannot liberate his imprisoned better part: "O limed soul, that, struggling to be free,/Art more engag'd!" (68–69). The clearest case, in which a soul disintegrates before our eyes, is that of Ophelia. Torn between her duty toward her father and her love for Hamlet, frustrated in her innermost being, she becomes, as the King describes it, "divided from herself and her fair judgment" (4.5.83). And Hamlet himself uses language that suggests his own internal struggle: to Horatio he explains why he could not sleep aboard the ship bound for England:

> Sir, in my heart there was a kind of fighting
> That would not let me sleep. Methought I lay
> Worse than the mutines in the bilboes.
> (5.2.4–6)

In short, Shakespeare's own language reveals, even if nothing else does, that he is clearly concerned with the workings of the soul divided against itself. But now to take the next step: is there any justification for our thinking that some of the characters in *Hamlet* are in some way representative of elements in a single psyche—that the ghost, for example, is an objectification of an unconscious impulse? Or in thinking thus, can we be accused, as the mad Ophelia's hearers are, of botching the words up to fit our own thoughts? What needs to be shown is that Shakespeare deliberately forces such a way of thinking upon us.

He does this by setting up a series of parallels, analogues, mirrors, and correspondences (all of which have at one time or another been pointed to). It is particularly interesting that in *Hamlet* Shakespeare does not rely merely on our ability to perceive the likenesses, but he indicates them in the language. First he establishes in the mind of the audience the idea that the appearance of the ghost is a disruption of the cosmic order: "What art thou that usurp'st this time of night?" (1.1.46) asks Horatio, who then moves quickly to the conclusion that "This bodes some strange eruption to our state" (69). The connection between the unnatural event in the macrocosm and the disaster in the body politic is immediately reenforced when Horatio reminds us that, shortly before the assassination of Julius Caesar,

> The graves stood tenantless, and the sheeted dead
> Did squeak and gibber in the Roman streets;
> As stars with trains of fire, and dews of blood,
> Disasters in the sun; and the moist star
> Upon whose influence Neptune's empire stands
> Was sick almost to doomsday with eclipse.
> And even the like precurse of fear'd events,
> As harbingers preceding still the fates
> And prologue to the omen coming on,
> Have heaven and earth together demonstrated
> Unto our climatures and countrymen.
> (1.1.116–25)

This speech of course foreshadows the "carnal, bloody, and unnatural acts" (5.2.367) of the play. Next, the analogue is drawn early in the play between the body politic and the body of man when Hamlet compares the effect of the national habit of drunkenness on the reputation of Denmark to the effect of the vicious mole of nature on the noble substance of the particular man. The parallel appears time and again, but nowhere so clearly and directly as in Guildenstern's reference to the many bodies "that live and feed" upon the king (3.3.10). If the King is sick, corrupt, and divided, the people will become, as they do, "muddied,/Thick and unwholesome in their thoughts" (4.5.81–82). In the world of this play, the state, with Claudius at the helm, cannot retain its "health" (1.3.21), Francisco is "sick at heart" (1.1.9), the Queen refers to her "sick soul" (4.5.19), Laertes feels a "sickness in [his] heart" (4.7.55), and near the end Hamlet refers forebodingly to the illness about his heart (5.2.198). Last, the division and sickness in the realms of cosmos and psyche are brought together when Hamlet says to the ghost:

> Remember thee?
> Ay, thou poor ghost, while memory holds a seat
> In this distracted globe.
> (1.5.95–97)

The great globe of the cosmos is disrupted by the apparition there on the battlement, the ghost has as well upset the balance of Hamlet's brain, and the audience watching the play might catch a third reference, that to the particular playhouse in which they were seated. The idea that all the world is a stage was a commonplace, and by collapsing these meanings in the word *globe*, Shakespeare is also suggesting that all this stage is a microcosm,[8] the characters

8. This triple reference has been pointed out by Levin, p. 18,

representing, among other things, the psychic elements in the globe of a man's mind.

This conception was, of course, nothing new either to the Elizabethan audience or to the playwrights, for their dramatic tradition stretched back to the morality plays and moral interludes, in which personification allegory was a standard technique. Jonsonian comedy always used moral types, and London would have been well prepared to see tragedies like *The Revenger's Tragedy*, which contains characters with names like Vindice and Lussurioso. Dover Wilson has shown how Shakespeare used some of the medieval abstractions in constructing the character of Falstaff, and Bernard Spivak has connected Iago with the old Vice of the Moralities.[9] Nor is my proposal that we look at *Hamlet* as a psychic world a particularly new one. Indeed, it goes back at least as far as Ernest Jones, who in a section of *Hamlet and Oedipus* advanced the idea that in the play the mechanism of myth formation called "decomposition" is in operation. This entails the disuniting of the various characteristics of an individual and their distribution among other characters, which have been created to accommodate them.[10] Thus, for example, the figure of the tyrannical father of ancient myth is split into a loved father and a hated tyrant, who in *Hamlet* are brothers. Kirsch and Aronson have recently developed the notion that the world of this play is dramatizing the soul of the hero,[11] and Maynard Mack himself has

though he does not follow out the implications of the stage-mind correspondence.

9. John Dover Wilson, *The Fortunes of Falstaff* (Cambridge: Cambridge University Press, 1964), and Bernard Spivak, *The Allegory of Evil* (New York: Columbia University Press, 1958).

10. Ernest Jones, *Hamlet and Oedipus* (Garden City, N.Y.: Doubleday, 1949), p. 149.

11. James Kirsch, *Shakespeare's Royal Self* (New York: Putnam's, 1966), pp. 3–183, takes the same Jungian approach that I do, but we come to exactly opposite conclusions: Kirsch thinks that Hamlet's soul is

pointed to an analogous aspect of Shakespearean dramatic construction when he describes Lear's Fool as serving "to some extent, as a screen on which Shakespeare flashes, as it were, readings from the psychic life of the protagonist, possibly even his subconscious life, which could not otherwise be conveyed in drama at all." [12] In various ways, however, these critics fall short of doing justice to the complexity of Shakespeare's vision, often by simply not pushing the argument far enough or, in my view, by coming to untenable conclusions. So the question now becomes, what meaning does Shakespeare give to the psychic struggle that we watch in the play?

As many have said, the central consciousness in the play is Hamlet's. It is this with which we identify, from his first speech ("A little more than kin, and less than kind") to the end of the play. This does not mean, however, that, as one critic holds, we approve all that he does, that because Hamlet approves of revenge, we do not condemn it. [13] Though we identify with him, we also stand outside his consciousness, free to criticize and evaluate. Indeed, it is crucial that we do so, for it is only the spectator who can see how the

dead at the end of the play, whereas I believe that Hamlet achieves a triumph over his unconscious impulses. Alex Aronson, *Psyche and Symbol in Shakespeare* (Bloomington, Ind.: Indiana University Press, 1972), also approaches Shakespeare from a Jungian perspective, but his discussion of Hamlet's motive (a brief one) rests on Freud's theory (see p. 235), whereas my theory rests on no necessary assumption of the Oedipus complex; in addition, while my discussion focuses on the shadow in *Hamlet*, Aronson restricts himself, with *Hamlet*, to an examination of the anima.

12. Maynard Mack, "The Jacobean Shakespeare: Some Observations on the Construction of the Tragedies," *Stratford-upon-Avon Studies: Jacobean Theatre,* ed. John Russell Brown and Bernard Harris (New York: St. Martin's, 1960), p. 24.

13. Robert Ornstein, "Historical Criticism and the Interpretation of Shakespeare," *Approaches to Shakespeare,* ed. Norman Rabkin (New York: McGraw-Hill, 1964), p. 176, says that "we accept the morality of blood revenge instantaneously and unquestioningly because Hamlet the idealist does." Ornstein assumes, wrongly in my view, that there is no distance between Hamlet and the audience.

split self that Shakespeare has created can be reintegrated; that is, it is only the external perspective that allows awareness of both conscious and unconscious elements of the self (I use "self" as Jung does to refer to the total psyche—not simply that part of the psyche which the ego-consciousness senses, but the whole psyche: conscious, personal unconscious, and collective unconscious). All this granted and even insisted upon, the fact remains, nevertheless, that Hamlet commands our instant sympathy.[14] His consciousness becomes ours; hence, it becomes important to discover what it is that troubles him at the outset.

Hamlet is suffering from two causes. First, with the death of his father, Hamlet's ego-ideal has been destroyed: "'A was a man, take him for all in all./I shall not look upon his like again" (1.2.187–88). There is no question that for Hamlet his father is an image of all he would like to become. Then too his mother, who used to possess the "fair forehead of an innocent love" (3.4.43), has made her "marriage vows/ As false as dicers' oaths" (44–45) by posting "With such dexterity to incestuous sheets" (1.2.157). The speed with which she has married the "mildewed ear" is not merely a falling away from virtue; it amounts to a betrayal of Hamlet's idealized father as well, and the double shock has thrown him into a state of disorientation and despair. When the corrupt reality of his mother's nature replaces the virtuous appearance, his youthful romanticism pushes him to the extreme of thinking that he himself, as well as all women, is sullied by her action. (I accept the reading "sullied," rather than "solid," though Kittredge prints the latter.)

14. The main weakness in Tony Richardson's *Hamlet* was that Nicol Williamson as Hamlet failed to establish the necessary sympathetic relationship with the audience.

What has happened to Hamlet is the virtual destruction of his personal myth. Mark Schorer has defined myth as "a large, controlling image that gives philosophical meaning to the facts of ordinary life; that is, which has organizing value for experience," and he goes on to say, "Myth is fundamental, the dramatic representation of our deepest instinctual life, of a primary awareness of man in the universe, capable of many configurations, upon which all particular opinions and attitudes depend." [15] Each of us carries with him his particular configuration of ideals, attitudes, and beliefs, and when the controlling image that is formed from these is weakened, he becomes, as Jung puts it, "like one uprooted, having no true link either with the past, or with the ancestral life which continues within him, or yet with contemporary human society." [16] Of course, the ideal represented by the father continues. Were it not for that, Hamlet would have been totally lost. As it is, Old Hamlet's death is psychologically disorienting to the ego of the son, and in this condition he reacts with excessive sensitivity to the destruction of the ideal of the virtuous woman in his mother. Tainted as he feels himself to be (the ghost's later adjuration, "Taint not thy mind" has a terrible irony), his moorings lost, the world seems an unweeded garden possessed by rank and gross things, a place not fit to live in. His ego is on the verge of dissolution.

At this point in Hamlet's life the ghost of his father appears. What, on the psychological level, does this signify? Some sentences from Jung's book *The Undiscovered Self* will be helpful here:

15. Mark Schorer, "The Necessity of Myth," *Myth and Mythmaking,* ed. Henry A. Murray (New York: Braziller, 1960), p. 354.

16. C. G. Jung, "Foreword to the Fourth Swiss Edition," *Symbols of Transformation,* trans. R. F. C. Hull, 2d ed. (Princeton, N.J.: Princeton University Press, 1956), p. xxiv.

When any natural human function gets lost, i.e., is denied conscious and intentional expression, a general disturbance results. . . . The activation of unconscious fantasies is a process that occurs when consciousness finds itself in a critical situation. Were that not so, the fantasies would be produced normally and would then be followed by the usual neurotic disturbances. In reality, fantasies of this kind belong to the world of childhood and give rise to disturbances only when prematurely strengthened by abnormal conditions in the conscious life. This is particularly likely to happen when unfavorable influences emanate from the parents, poisoning the atmosphere and producing conflicts which upset the psychic balance of the child. . . . These effects develop only when the individual comes up against a situation which he cannot overcome by conscious means. . . . When the fantasies reach a certain level of intensity, they begin to break through into consciousness and create a conflict situation that becomes perceptible to the patient himself, splitting him into two personalities with different characters.[17]

I do not mean to suggest, by quoting this section of Jung's thought, that Hamlet, a dramatic character, has a childhood that we can discuss. I *do* mean to say that Shakespeare created in his play a situation that he intuitively felt contained psychological truths. Thus, what is more natural than that when Hamlet undergoes his psychic disturbance, the "pales and forts of reason" are broken down "By the o'ergrowth of some complexion" (1.4.27–28), as he himself describes the process ("complexion" refers to temperament, which is governed by the four humors, among them, choler.) The frustration and rage he feels toward his mother have been largely repressed, but now break forth in the form of a fantasy commanding him to commit a violent act. The splitting that Jung refers to helps to explain the apparent inconsistencies in Hamlet's behavior: at times the melan-

17. C. G. Jung, *The Undiscovered Self*, trans. R. F. C. Hull (Boston: Little, Brown, 1957), pp. 65–68.

choly Dane; at others, capable of drinking "hot blood" (3.2.372). Claudius is right when he says, "There's something in his soul/O'er which his melancholy sits on brood" (3.1.164–65). That something is choler—the impulse to destroy.

The problem presented to his consciousness, which the audience sees but Hamlet does not, is a complex one. It involves, essentially, the difficulty of achieving self-knowledge. According to Jung, knowledge of self requires the recognition of "the dark aspects of the personality," or to use his term, the shadow side of the psyche.[18] The central characteristics of this element of the psyche are its autonomous, "possessive quality," its primitive nature, its inability to make moral judgments, its obstinate resistance to moral control, and its assumption of inferior qualities, which the ego projects onto the shadow character. All of these characteristics are unconscious and if in fact they form the nature of the ghost, Hamlet will of course be unable to recognize that they belong to his own self. "It is often tragic," writes Jung, "to see how blatantly a man bungles his own life and the lives of others yet remains totally incapable of seeing how much the whole tragedy originates in himself, and how he continually feeds it and keeps it going. Not *consciously*, of course—for consciously he is engaged in bewailing and cursing a faithless world ["O cursed spite"] that recedes further and further into the distance." [19] The central problem Hamlet faces, then, involves first recognizing the "moral problem" represented by his unconscious impulses, then understanding that they constitute a challenge to his "whole ego-personality," [20] and finally achieving the kind of self-

18. C. G. Jung, *Aion: Researches into the Phenomenology of the Self*, trans. R. F. C. Hull, 2d ed. (Princeton, N.J.: Princeton University Press, 1968), p. 8.
19. *Ibid.*, p. 10.
20. *Ibid.*, p. 8.

control that allows the self to be reintegrated. No small task, but this is only part of it.

The other side of the problem develops because the inferior, aggressive elements are objectified in the form of Hamlet's ego-ideal, so that when the ghost commands Hamlet to revenge his murder, Hamlet naturally accepts the injunction as the command of his conscience:

> And thy commandment all alone shall live
> Within the book and volume of my brain,
> Unmix'd with baser matter. Yes, by heaven!
> (1.4.102–4)

For him, this is no base impulse, but a high calling. To be sure, he later questions the honesty of the ghost, but once that question is settled by the mousetrap, he never once explicitly questions his duty. How, then, does Shakespeare assure the spectator that the ghost is evil? By always including the suggestion that Old Hamlet was a violent man —even cruel—and that therefore Hamlet's vision is not unclouded. Horatio says that "this side of our known world" Hamlet's father was esteemed "valiant" (1.1.84–85), but immediately before, he has described him this way:

> Such was the very armour he had on
> When he th' ambitious Norway combated.
> So frown'd he once when, in an angry parle,
> He smote the sledded Polacks on the ice.
> (1.1.60–63)

Kittredge glosses "parle" as "conference before battle." What are we to think of a king who breaks the peace in a fit of temper? And when Horatio, in order to elicit a response from the apparition, is listing reasons why ghosts walk the earth, he phrases the last in a rather uncomplimentary way:

> Or if thou hast uphoarded in thy life
> Extorted treasure in the womb of earth
> (For which, they say, you spirits oft walk in death),
> Speak of it!
>
> (1.1.136–39)

The ghost himself refers to the "foul crimes done in [his] days of nature" (1.5.12), and considerable ambiguity attends Hamlet's description of his father's portrait: the phrase "An eye like Mars, to threaten and command" (3.4.57) suggests an authority figure capable of the sort of tyranny that ostensibly only Claudius possesses. Then, too, what are we to think of a father who lays upon his son a burden of revenge that will eventually destroy his life? This kind of uncaring self-centeredness is underscored when to his assertion of Gertrude's infidelity he adds the following invidious comparison:

> O Hamlet, what a falling-off was there,
> From me, whose love was of that dignity
> That it went hand in hand even with the vow
> I made to her in marriage, and to decline
> Upon a wretch whose natural gifts were poor
> To those of mine!
>
> (1.5.47–52)

No, there are too many indications in the text of a tyrannical, violent, egocentric, Mars-like character for us to accept Hamlet's adulation without qualification.[21] Rather, Shakespeare is leading us to see that Hamlet is, in fact, a

---

21. At this point an objection may be brought: if the appearance of the ghost sets in motion a train of events that leads to the restoration of order and justice, how can the ghost be thought of as evil? First, the question may in fact be based upon a wrong premise. Has not the train of events already been set in motion by Claudius's fratricide? That the King is brought to book can be seen instead as the working out of a "special providence," for one can argue that the King's evil acts fall justly on the inventor's head and that the ghost's desire for revenge (his

victim of the idealizing tendency described by Jung as the childish desire to cling "to illusions that are contrary to reality." [22]

To sum up what I have said about Hamlet's problem: the disoriented state of mind resulting from the loss of the ego-ideal represented by his father and the destruction of the ideal of virtue represented by his mother open Hamlet to the hidden impulses of the unconscious. These appear to him as a voice that commands him to avenge his father's murder, in other words, to commit an act the nature of which violates all his conscious sensibilities but which he feels duty bound to carry out. His nearly impossible task is to see what it is that the ghost is asking him to do (to perform a violent act of revenge), to recognize this violence as part of his own nature, and somehow to bring that impulse into a newly reorganized self. Like a later young man who must take a river journey down the Mississippi instead of a voyage to England, he must come to understand that the ethic of one's culture may be enslaving and, if so, must be rejected if one is to be truly free.

Confronted with such a task, Hamlet must summon up tremendous resources of courage. His consciousness is in mortal danger, as Horatio tries to tell him when he is about to follow the ghost:

> What if it tempt you toward the flood, my lord,
> Or to the dreadful summit of the cliff

only motive) is used by God as one of the means to achieve a just conclusion. Alternatively, one may adduce the Jungian theory that the shadow (the ghost) must be faced and integrated into the conscious self before the individuation process is complete. Thus, the ghost appears because Hamlet's psychic situation calls it forth to be confronted. Either way, the ghost is a means to an end, rather than a prime mover.

22. C. G. Jung, *The Structure and Dynamics of the Psyche*, trans. R. F. C. Hull, 2d ed. (Princeton, N.J.: Princeton University Press, 1969), p. 392.

That beetles o'er his base into the sea,
And there assume some other, horrible form
Which might deprive your sovereignty of reason
And draw you into madness? Think of it.
The very place puts toys of desperation,
Without more motive, into every brain
That looks so many fathoms to the sea
And hears it roar beneath.

(1.4.69–78)

Hamlet thinks that his soul is safe : "And for my soul, what can it do to that,/Being a thing immortal as itself?" (66–67), but he forgets that the ghost appeared immediately after his discussion of the dram of e'il. If Jung is right that the audience unconsciously receives archetypal impressions through poetry, then surely they would sense that Hamlet is in imminent danger of losing control of his ego. This would mean submersion into the primitive realm of the unconscious, of which the sea is the primary archetype. As Jung has put it, "the problematical state, the inner division with oneself, arises when, side by side with the series of ego-contents, a second series of equal intensity comes into being. This second series, because of its energy value, has a functional significance equal to that of the ego-complex; we might call it another, second ego which can on occasion even wrest the leadership from the first." [23] I am arguing that this alter ego does from time to time usurp Hamlet's consciousness with wild and whirling words and with aggressive, cruel behavior, at least until his journey to England. Even after he returns, he is able to say to Laertes as they wrestle in the grave, "Yet have I in me something dangerous,/Which let thy wisdom fear" (5.1.249–50). Hamlet will finally triumph over the force that tries to return him to an unconscious, chthonic state, though Ophelia will

23. *Ibid.*, p. 391.

not be so fortunate. Her death by water signifies the ego's failure to maintain itself, or as Jung puts it, "Psychologically . . . . water means spirit that has become unconscious." [24] Hamlet's tragedy is that in finding his way through the labyrinth of his self, he achieves too late the kind of internal integration that will enable him to control the dangers in the outside world, the clearest and most present of which is, of course, Claudius.

Each night, in those "bad dreams" that arise from his unconscious, Hamlet meets Claudius—King with Crown. Ernest Jones's suggestion that Claudius may represent part of the split in the primordial father archetype is important. As noted above, Jones sees Old Hamlet as the loved and loving father and Claudius as the hateful tyrant, but I believe that the psychic situation is more complex than this. Both Old Hamlet and Claudius appear, or *wish* to appear, the tender father. Thus, for example, to Hamlet's "Farewell, dear mother" the King replies, "Thy loving father, Hamlet" (4.3.48–49). But the underlying reality is that the two are true brothers—evil usurpers. On the literary level, Claudius is of course Hamlet's great adversary in the real world, but as a surrogate father he is also, like the tyrannical father of myth, a psychic antagonist. These two functions coalesce in the notion that just as Claudius has stolen "the precious diadem" of Denmark "and put it in his pocket" (3.4.100–101), so also he is the "cutpurse" of Hamlet's psychic empire. Whereas Old Hamlet represents unconscious violence, Claudius is a projection of another side of Hamlet's shadow self, the part that embodies other evils of which he accuses himself: to Ophelia he says,

24. C. G. Jung, *The Archetypes of the Collective Unconscious*, trans. R. F. C. Hull, 2d ed. (Princeton, N.J.: Princeton University Press, 1968), pp. 18–19.

I am myself indifferent honest, but yet I could accuse me of such things that it were better my mother had not borne me. I am very proud, revengeful, ambitious; with more offences at my beck than I have thoughts to put them in, imagination to give them shape, or time to act them in. What should such fellows as I do, crawling between earth and heaven? We are arrant knaves all; believe none of us.

(3.1.122–29)

Hamlet objectifies his offenses in a "Remorseless, treacherous, lecherous, kindless villain" (2.2.566)—everything that he consciously hates. He can never achieve a psychic integrity unless he destroys the tyranny of this part of the self. But how difficult! for the way in which Hamlet does this is all important. The ghost will never return to usurp the consciousness with its primitive spirit of the *lex talionis* if Hamlet can abjure the ethic of the violent revenge, an eye for an eye. To bash in the King's skull and cut off his head is not the way, though the King shows that *he* is capable of such an act when he orders the English King to strike off Hamlet's head (5.2.24). Rather, Hamlet must allow providence, which governs the fall of a sparrow, to arrange the fall of the King, and to do it in such a way that Claudius will be hoist with his own petard—*that* would be justice.

As the action of the play develops, however, Hamlet's consciousness becomes ever more possessed by the impulse to violence. The spectator can easily understand how this could happen. Consider the successive blows upon Hamlet's sensibilities: the death of his father, the moral corruption of his mother, his hopes for the crown dashed, the rejection by his beloved Ophelia, the betrayal by his friends Rosencrantz and Guildenstern—all this aggravated by the sense of being surrounded by spies like Polonius and burdened by a prisonlike existence (Denmark without, the ghost within). Despair and frustration well up and cause what today would only be described as neurotic behavior. Ophelia is wrong in thinking that his noble mind is o'erthrown, but we should not be surprised to hear that he has appeared to Ophelia in her closet looking "As if he had been loosed out of hell/To speak of horrors" (2.1.83–84). Is it difficult to understand why, given these circumstances, he acts cruelly toward her when he discovers during the nunnery scene that she has not simply rejected him, but is betraying him as well? "Wise men know what monsters you make of them . . . . I have heard of your paintings too, well enough. . . . Go to! I'll no more on't! it hath made me mad" (3.1.139–46). Astute as ever, the King perceives more clearly than the others:

> Love? his affections do not that way tend;
> Nor what he spake, though it lack'd form a little,
> Was not like madness. There's something in his soul
> O'er which his melancholy sits on brood:
> And I do doubt the hatch and the disclose
> Will be some danger.
> (3.2.161–67)

The two scenes in which Hamlet's destructive aggressiveness reaches its apogee come immediately after his discovery during the play-within-the-play that the ghost's information is correct. He catches the king alone and defenseless at prayer. Now Hamlet wants *more* than an eye for an eye: he wants Claudius's soul in hell, though Old Hamlet's soul at least has the chance to cleanse itself in purgatory.[25] To kill the king now would be "hire and salary, not revenge!" (3.3.79). So "Up, sword, and know thou a more horrid hent" (88):

> When he is drunk asleep; or in his rage;
> Or in th' incestuous pleasure of his bed;

25. In *Hamlet and Revenge*, 2d ed. (Stanford: Stanford University Press, 1971), p. 192, n26, Eleanor Prosser makes this same point.

At game, a-swearing, or about some act
That has no relish of salvation in't—
Then trip him, that his heels may kick at heaven,
And his soul may be as damn'd and black
As Hell, whereto it goes.

(89–95)

The savageness of this speech shows how close Hamlet has come to complete possession by the shadow side of his psyche.

The closet scene, which immediately follows, simply continues this fearful mood. As mentioned above, in Hamlet's view his mother has betrayed his ideal of virtue and stained the whole of her sex. Though he is not at first conscious of it, the audience can sense from the beginning that his whole relation with Ophelia, even if she were not to reject and betray him, is poisoned.[26] In the closet scene he takes revenge. He rationalizes that he will be cruel to his mother only to be kind, but his lack of conscious control is revealed when he comes as close as he ever does to homicidal rage, so that the ghost has to intervene in order to redirect Hamlet's violence. From the ghost's perspective, Hamlet's original revenge motive has become diverted: his job is to kill the King rather than attack his mother. She must be left to heaven. These two scenes, then, form the turning point of the internal drama of the psyche. Henceforth, the ego-consciousness will establish its autonomy, though not without difficulty.

At this point it becomes important to see how Shake-

---

26. R. D. Laing, *The Divided Self: A Study of Sanity and Madness,* (Chicago: Quadrangle, 1960), p. 136, describes a parallel situation in the case of Peter, whose sexual relations with all women but one were promiscuous: "With the one girl whom he regarded as 'pure', he maintained a tenuous and platonic relationship for some years. But he was unable to translate his relationship with this girl into anything more than this."

speare uses three mirror-characters to draw the play to a conclusion: Fortinbras, Horatio, and Laertes. It is not until Hamlet is on his way to England that we actually glimpse Fortinbras, a presence (though unseen) from the beginning. Perhaps too much has been made of the idea that Fortinbras parallels Hamlet in that both wish to avenge their fathers; no speech of his anywhere in the play suggests revengeful feeling. He simply wishes from Denmark the surrender of lands lost by his father. But from the outset Shakespeare has made it clear that Fortinbras is a young prince desirous, like Hamlet, of regaining his inheritance. Like Hamlet he is "Of unimproved mettle hot and full" (1.1.96), as Horatio describes him, and when Hamlet himself calls him "a delicate and tender prince" (4.4.48), there is no question that Shakespeare is asking us to see in Fortinbras an alter ego for Hamlet. In Hamlet's eyes, the contrast between the two is very clear. He, who has a portentous and noble cause, fails, "to [his] shame," to carry out his duty to kill the King; the other, who has virtually no cause, finds a "quarrel in a straw/When honour's at the stake" (55–56). This Fortinbras—impetuous, decisive, direct—is an alternate personality in the psyche, which Hamlet can choose to integrate into his permanent adult self, and he appears to be trying to do just that when he concludes his Fortinbras soliloquy with the thought that he must learn to be as active as Fortinbras in the pursuit of honor, an effort which, because the ghost of revenge is still in him, means that henceforth his thoughts should "be bloody, or be nothing worth!" (66). The soliloquy reveals a transition to his final position of stoical acceptance. He is still thinking that revenge is his proper motive, but he is only thinking it. He does nothing, even though left alone. If he could later escape his captors to board a pirate ship, one would think that he might be able to find a way to use Fortinbras's army to over-throw Claudius, as Laertes later uses the Danish people. The idea of honorable action leads him on, but his heart is no longer in the revenge. It is the concept of honor that makes him at the end give his dying voice to Fortinbras, but he will not use honor as a rationalization for revenge.

How it is that Hamlet moves to the stoicism just re-ferred to has puzzled critics, but I believe that Horatio pro-vides one key. When Hamlet returns to Denmark, his tran-sition from bloody revenger to philosophical stoic is almost complete. There is the momentary lapse in emotional con-trol at the graveside, but it is important to note that his anger at Laertes does not spring from any motive of re-venge; rather, Laertes' exaggerated expression of love for Ophelia reminds Hamlet of the depth of his own feeling, and the confused frustration and anger at her betrayal is commuted into such a powerful outpouring of emotion that he has nothing but scorn for Laertes' avowals. Furthermore, editors' interpolated stage directions usually suggest that, though Hamlet leaps into the grave, it is Laertes who first launches the physical attack: "I prithee," says Hamlet, "take thy fingers from my throat," and he adds that he is not by nature "splenitive and rash" (5.1.236–37). Even including this incident, then, the keynote to Hamlet's behavior upon his return is announced in his statement to Horatio that "There's a divinity that shapes our ends,/Rough-hew them how we will—" (5.2.10–11). This "fellow-student" is of course another mirror for Hamlet, an alternate self that provides a possible model. Kirsch thinks that Hamlet becomes more and more like Claudius throughout the play,[27] but in my view Horatio's is the attitude that Hamlet gradually adopts. Horatio is the first in the play to voice the idea that provi-

27. Kirsch, p. 42.

dence rules human life when to Marcellus's "something is rotten in the state of Denmark," he responds, "Heaven will direct it" (1.4.90–91). Horatio is the only person in whom Hamlet confides the secret given by the ghost, and in an important speech, which Shakespeare significantly places just before Hamlet's crucial test of the King during the play-within-the-play, Hamlet says to Horatio:

> Since my dear soul was mistress of her choice
> And could of men distinguish, her election
> Hath seal'd thee for herself. For thou hast been
> As one, in suff'ring all, that suffers nothing;
> A man that Fortune's buffets and rewards
> Hast ta'en with equal thanks; and blest are those
> Whose blood and judgment are so well comeddled
> That they are not a pipe for Fortune's finger
> To sound what stop she please. Give me that man
> That is not passion's slave, and I will wear him
> In my heart's core, ay, in my heart of heart,
> As I do thee.
>
> (3.2.61–72)

The struggle to adopt this attitude Hamlet does not win until just before the end of the play. Only after the chastening experience of coming to an awareness of the problematic nature of death in the "To be, or not to be" soliloquy, of facing the prospect of imminent death at the hands of Claudius and his two sponges, Rosencrantz and Guildenstern, of the *danse macabre* with the gravedigger and Yorick's skull, and of the direct descent into the grave itself can Hamlet perceive the larger patterns at work and reconcile himself to giving up his revengeful feelings. There is nothing left of the urge to violence, in his final comprehensive vision:

> we defy augury; there's a special providence in the fall of a sparrow. If it be now, 'tis not to come; if it be not to come,

it will be now; if it be not now, yet it will come: the readiness is all. Since no man knows aught of what he leaves, what is't to leave betimes? Let be. (5.2.205–10)

I do not mean to say that Shakespeare is holding up Horatio as his ideal man. Horatio is the scholar—somewhat pedantic in his knowledge of Roman history, skeptical of ghosts but learned in their ways, fearful of taking chances, a bit timid and unimaginative; but at the same time he is a true friend and confidant, always loyal and sympathetic. Hamlet unconsciously takes what he requires from Horatio, and what he requires is the ability to control his passions so that he can deal effectively with the corruption in Elsinore.[28] The final test will be the duel with Laertes.

Laertes is the only one of the three whose situation Hamlet finds parallel to his: "by the image of my cause I see/The portraiture of his" (5.2.77–78). The audience knows of course that Laertes is as lustful, treacherous, and tyrannical as Claudius, is indeed merely an extension of him, but Hamlet does not see any of this. Because Hamlet is by nature as Claudius says he is, "Most generous, and free from all contriving" (4.7.135), he never suspects that Laertes will betray him, though he does feel "a kind of gaingiving" (5.2.201). All this being so, it is most important to look at Hamlet's speech to Laertes before the fencing match begins, for in this speech that has puzzled so many critics the audience can see Hamlet's new stoic attitude dramatized in a human situation:

> Give me your pardon, sir. I have done you wrong;
> But pardon't, as you are a gentleman.

28. For a contrary view see D. G. James, *The Dream of Learning* (Oxford: Clarendon Press, 1951), p. 63: James believes that the "fall of a sparrow" speech reveals "a defeated Hamlet who has given up the struggle."

This presence knows,
And you must needs have heard, how I am punish'd
With a sore distraction. What I have done
That might your nature, honour, and exception
Roughly awake, I here proclaim was madness.
Was't Hamlet wrong'd Laertes? Never Hamlet.
If Hamlet from himself be ta'en away,
And when he's not himself does wrong Laertes,
Then Hamlet does it not, Hamlet denies it.
Who does it, then? His madness. If't be so,
Hamlet is of the faction that is wrong'd;
His madness is poor Hamlet's enemy.
Sir, in this audience,
Let my disclaiming from a purpos'd evil
Free me so far in your most generous thoughts
That I have shot my arrow o'er the house
And hurt my brother.
                              (5.2.212–30)

Many critics see this speech as evidence that Hamlet either
is a liar (in that he never was mad but was only putting on
an antic disposition) or is unconsciously exculpating himself
from the murder of Polonius. If the view developed so far
has any validity, Hamlet need not be thought of as doing
either. The audience has seen how the ghost of violence
has possessed him, especially during the scene with his
mother when that wretched, rash fool of a Polonius in-
truded, coming "Between the pass and fell incensed points/
Of mighty opposites" (5.2.61–62). Hamlet says he was not
entirely himself, and we can agree, but we are not to think
of Hamlet as mad when he stabbed Polonius. I believe that
Hamlet is simply admitting his lack of full self-control when
he unknowingly killed Laertes' father, and in order to regain
Laertes' friendship, which he sincerely wants, he uses the
rumor of his madness that Laertes undoubtedly knows about
to try to explain to him that his actions did not develop
from a "purpos'd evil." Thus, though the audience has

understood the depth of Hamlet's revenge feelings during the prayer scene and the closet scene, they do not attribute the death of Polonius to these feelings. Moreover, early in the last scene while talking with Horatio, Hamlet explains that a sudden self-protective reaction has its very definite uses. Referring to the impulse that made him unseal the commission of Rosencrantz and Guildenstern on the way to England, he says,

> prais'd be rashness for it; let us know
> Our indiscretion sometimes serves us well
> When our deep plots do pall . . . .
>
> (5.2.7–9)

The quick, rash response that Laertes himself reveals in raising the army against Claudius may well fit into the providential plan and therefore *per se* is not an evil thing; indeed, in the case of the commission it has saved Hamlet's life. Thus, the audience is not to condemn Hamlet when he says that the deaths of Rosencrantz and Guildenstern are not near his conscience, and I believe likewise that the audience knows what Hamlet means when he says to Laertes that his madness was to blame for Polonius's death, that it resulted from, as it were, a misdirected arrow.

The other important point to make about the speech is that it reveals to the audience a consciousness much more fully and clearly integrated than that revealed in Hamlet's first soliloquy. Hamlet is no longer cursing his fate, but instead is concerned about the feelings of another. He admits his culpability in reasoned, calm, orderly discourse. Abraham Maslow can be of some help here in describing for us what he calls at least a partial explanation of what an integrated self is. At certain times a person is more fully integrated than at others, he says, when to an observer he appears "less split or dissociated, less fighting against himself, less split between an experiencing-self and an observing-self, . . . more able to fuse with the world." [29] Furthermore, says Maslow, "the greatest attainment of identity, autonomy, or selfhood is itself a transcending of itself, a going beyond and above selfhood. The person can then become relatively egoless" (p. 105). Hamlet had earlier seen an example of a person's ability to fuse with the world when Laertes, in an act of self-forgetting, joined Ophelia in the grave, an act then imitated by Hamlet. Reviewing now Hamlet's speech to Laertes, we can find little sense of the weight of his problems, the inhibition of his freedom, or the lacerating self-criticism. Rather than being constantly at odds with the world, he wants to achieve an understanding with at least one whom he admits injuring. And at the end he is even able to forgive Laertes for betraying him. The deaths of Claudius and Laertes, like those of Polonius, Rosencrantz, and Guildenstern, are the result of sudden, rash responses to immediate dangers, not premeditated revenges. The advance in self-control since the closet scene is marked, for the violence is acknowledged, restrained, and subordinated to the civilizing values of contrition, humility, and compassion—values that set one free.

One way of seeing this tragedy of *Hamlet*, then, is to understand the protagonist as a representation of consciousness, the ghost as a visitation from the unconscious, Claudius as a projection, and other characters as alter egos, from which Hamlet must draw the necessary qualities to preserve himself: from Fortinbras a renewed sense of honor and revitalized energy, from Horatio a stoic willingness to allow divinity to shape events beyond his control, and from

29. Abraham H. Maslow, *Toward a Psychology of Being*, 2d ed. (New York: Van Nostrand Reinhold, 1968), pp. 104–5.

Laertes the intuitive feeling that emotional responses, even though rash, have their own validity. This newly integrated self—much finer than that of any single alter ego—is Hamlet's great victory, and it gives the play its peculiar transcendence in the midst of tragic loss. It is a brilliant stroke in Kozintsev's film for Hamlet, just before death, to leave the castle, which at the beginning had closed its portcullis and drawbridge on his back. When Hamlet makes his way out into the open air and sunlight, the audience can sense the new freedom he has won, even in death.

It is not at all clear that Hamlet understands much of what has happened to him; it is rather for the audience to see that the central consciousness has within it the potential for good and evil, so clearly objectified in the other characters. Shakespeare shows how it is possible for each individual to reject an outmoded, primitive personal myth and to generate a new personal conscience and consciousness in order to confront new situations in the external world. In this sense he has created in *Hamlet* what might be called the myth of the civilized man, the man who is able to throw off the psychic chains that tie him to the past and to his inferior impulses. Shakespeare has externalized and dramatized our deepest fears and anxieties and formed them into a myth that we as spectators can then internalize and make our own.[30] C. S. Lewis put it well when he wrote, "we read Hamlet's speeches with interest chiefly because they describe so well a certain spiritual region through which most of us have passed." [31] It may be true, as Claudius says, that Hamlet has been put "from th' understanding of him-

30. See Jerome Bruner, "Myth and Identity," *Myth and Mythmaking*, pp. 276–87.
31. C. S. Lewis, "Hamlet: The Prince or the Poem?" *Selected Literary Essays*, ed. Walter Hooper (Cambridge: Cambridge University Press), p. 101.

self" (2.2.9), but one of the great values of this play for us is that in understanding Hamlet we may come to a clearer understanding of ourselves. Or as Hamlet himself puts it, "to know a man well were to know himself" (5.2.135).

If it is true, as R. D. Laing writes, that "as a whole, we are a generation of men so estranged from the inner world that many are arguing that it does not exist; and that even if it does exist, it does not matter," [32] then I conclude that Anthony Burgess is right: *Hamlet is* the play we can least do without,[33] for in it Shakespeare has made his most direct attempt to mirror the terror, pain, frustration, and glory of this distracted globe that we call the human self.

32. *The Politics of Experience*, p. 33.
33. Anthony Burgess, *Shakespeare* (Harmondsworth, Eng.: Penguin, 1972), p. 192.

Anxiety, Tragedy, and Hamlet's Delay

PETER B. WALDECK

> O villain, villain, smiling, damned villain!
> My tables—meet it is I set it down
> (*writing*) That one may smile, and smile, and be a villain.[1]
> (1.5.106–8)

If each *Hamlet* interpretation discovers its own Hamlet in the play, then let us cast our lot with this startled and distracted prince who has just confronted his father's ghost and is formulating his task of revenge in his notebook. In thus programming his problem while trying to erase everything else in his mind, Hamlet expresses his difficulty in indirect, but unambiguous terms, despite later confusion and rationalization. He mentions the word *smile* three times in as many lines to emphasize his outrage and confoundedness, but also as a means for Shakespeare to underline the specific nature of his problem, as I shall discuss below.

Having seized upon this "Hamlet-of-the-Tables," let us step back again in order to prepare and focus our run at the

1. All quotations from *Hamlet* are taken from G. B. Harrison, ed., *Shakespeare: The Complete Works* (New York: Harcourt, Brace and World, 1952).

142

work. I would like not simply to view the play as a problem of character motivation, but to relate the analysis of Hamlet's delay to an overall conception of the work as a tragedy. The present context permits only the summary of the argument for a hypothesis regarding the nature of tragic catharsis. Even the lengthiest arguments about the nature of tragedy would as a matter of principle not convince most students of literature that they should accept any specific definition for a genre so varied and controversial. Thus simply to deduce conclusions about *Hamlet* from such a definition would be a fruitless undertaking. I will aim rather at two interrelated goals. I would like to examine *Hamlet* as an example of tragedy—a unique and ingenious example —to demonstrate the mechanisms of catharsis in a hypothesis, without planting in the work, I hope, anything foreign to it. Conversely, I would like to use the hypothesis for tragedy also as a conceptual frame of reference that will allow us to view Hamlet's delay in a connection I believe can be established within the text alone, but that calls for some discussion of theory beforehand to clarify the language used. On the one hand, therefore, I would like to use *Hamlet* to illustrate a theory that in principle cannot expect to be established in any deductively rigorous way; and on the other hand I would like to interpret the central dramatic structure of *Hamlet* as a textual whole separate from but silhouetted against an explicitly stated conceptual backdrop. Partly as a result of this dual focus on tragedy *per se* and *Hamlet* I must ask the reader's indulgence in the first section for a radical departure from the realm of the purely literary. I hope that the need for this empirical foundation will become evident in the following discussion of tragedy and of *Hamlet*.

I Anxiety

This view of *Hamlet* is rooted in a broad biological definition of anxiety. A specific mechanism for the tragic can also be found in this preliterary realm. One of the central concepts of modern psychology, anxiety remains manifoldly defined. Cattell and Scheier tabulated over 300 definitions.[2] For existentialist Martin Heidegger, at one extreme, anxiety results from "Being-in-the-World-As-Such."[3] Certainly broad enough, the philosophical language of the existentialists is too isolated from the more concrete information of psychology to be of much help for our purposes. At the opposite extreme, but containing many useful insights, Freud's examinations of anxiety were based somewhat too narrowly on an essentially internal psychic system. As a result of his observations of sexually inhibited patients, Freud first viewed anxiety as repressed, converted libido.[4] Later he approached anxiety from the broader perspective of defense mechanisms (*Hemmung, Symptom und Angst,* 1926). Here, resisting the obvious analogies to animals and avoiding a general biological approach, he focused on *separation* as the central cause of anxiety in various stages of human development—separation from the womb, from the presence of a mother in infancy, from the penis (castration anxiety), "social anxiety of conscience as a derivative of castration anxiety," and finally "fear of death (or fear for life), which is a fear of the superego projected on the powers

2. Eugene E. Levitt, *The Psychology of Anxiety* (Indianapolis, New York, Kansas City: Bobbs-Merrill, 1967), p. 55.
3. Martin Heidegger, *Being and Time,* trans. John Macquarrie and Edward Robinson (New York and Evanston, Ill.: Harper and Row, 1962), pp. 230ff.
4. Sigmund Freud, *Inhibitions, Symptoms and Anxiety,* in *The Standard Edition of the Complete Psychological Works of Sigmund Freud,* trans. James Strachey (London: Imago Pub. Co., 1959) 20: 78.

of destiny." [5] Crucial to this view is the idea that anxiety appears not as a biological energy in its own right, as do sexual drives, but as a secondary process resulting from early experiences. In developing this argument Freud discussed among other things two especially important ideas : the function of anxiety as a *preparation for danger,* and its role as a counter-cathexis (*Gegenbesetzung*) to dangerous external or internal stimuli (p.121). But he appears to have felt that these points, with their broad biological and environmental implications, complicated and disrupted his internal model of the psyche, in which external events are treated as internal sensory impressions (p.138). Thus he left these concepts in the background, focusing instead on anxiety as a *signal of the ego* to warn the organism or psyche of danger (particularly threats posed by the id) (p.138). The signal concept implies, in empirical terms, a secondary and rather abstract mental process, a mere pilot light to activate a psychic mechanism still built on the single pillar of Freud's sexual model of the psyche.

A main thrust of contemporary Freudian or Neo-Freudian thinking has been to develop a view of the ego-functions (where anxiety plays a central role) as *autonomous* from libido. In discussing the historical development of ego psychology, David Rapaport examined among other things the question of the source of energy for this autonomous anxiety function. He still viewed anxiety, however, as id energy that has "come to be at the disposal of the ego," including "sublimations, neutralisations of aggressive energies," and "other neutralized energy," without specifying what this might be.[6] While proceeding from Freud's sexu-

5. *Ibid.,* p. 140.
6. David Rapaport, *The Collected Papers of David Rapaport,* ed. Merton M. Gill (New York and London : Basic Books, 1967), p. 603.

ally based psychic model and still using his terminology of the signal concept, Rapaport and others agreed that the ego at least *functions* autonomously. This development brings the revision of Freudian thought closer to the positions of physiologists and their counterparts in psychology on this issue. For the physiologically oriented psychologists, biological and environmental perspectives implicitly acknowledged in the social orientation of the Neo-Freudians suggest not only a functional autonomy of anxiety, but an independent fundamental energy given with life itself. Grinker and Robbins speak in biological terms of anxiety as a

> direct derivative of protoplasmic irritability and animal vigilance. . . . Irritability is the property of all protoplasm, but the capacity of the organism to project itself into the future is only acquired late in the phylogenetic series and hence is found only in the more highly evolved animals. Anxiety in the human being is a capacity which accompanies delayed action, self-awareness, and choice among several of appropriate future responses.[7]

Leo Rangell associates this view with Brunswick's division of the instincts into the

> (a) erotic or vital libidinal instincts, related to the parasympathetic nervous system; and (b) defensive-aggressive instincts, related to the sympathetic nervous system. Under the latter, anxiety and defense are considered as much instinctual as rage or aggression, both serving the same function, i.e., protective.[8]

Both these views and developments in Freudian psychology

7. Roy M. Grinker and F. P. Robbins, *Psychosomatic Case Book* (New York and Toronto: Blakiston, 1954), p. 49.
8. Leo Rangell, "On the Psychoanalytic Theory of Anxiety: A Statement of a Unitary Theory," *Journal American Psychoanalytic Association* 3 (1955): 406.

point to a concept of anxiety as a broad spectrum of defensive energy. At one end is the mere maintenance of metabolic processes involving the same physiological mechanisms (such as the heartbeat) that play a role in more intense states of anxiety. At the other end are states of extreme panic and trauma. Between these two extremes ranges a variety of levels of anxiety, such as the alertness to perform perfunctory tasks of self-preservation (for example: looking both ways before crossing the street, or, on a social level, remembering to introduce a guest at a party).

The self that is protected by all this is not only the physical organism, but the self-concept as defined according to a variety of social roles. Two levels of self may even conflict, as in, say, a patriot's preference to die rather than compromise his patriot-self. On all levels anxiety-related behavior falls into the two basic categories of action *vs.* restraint, from the alternating paralysis and violent, uncontrolled motor behavior of people in extreme panic to ordinary social behavior requiring the performance of certain actions and the restraint or inhibition of others. Behavior may be subdivided further into Cannon's "fight-flight" alternatives.[9] For purposes of literature it is important that this spectrum of anxiety be viewed as a unity. The reduction of anxiety on an intense problem level reduces anxiety on a lower level as well, or, as Joyce Cary's Gulley Jimson puts it: "There's nothing like a good smash for getting rid of small worries . . . ."[10] This definition of anxiety permits the inclusion of many specific contributions of psychology important to literature, such as guilt feelings as a form of anxiety. Equally as important, it recognizes the essential

9. Rollo May, *The Meaning of Anxiety* (New York: Ronald Press, 1950), p. 62
10. Joyce Cary, *The Horse's Mouth* (New York: Grosset and Dunlap, 1957), p. 124.

unity and interaction of different levels, suggesting how the literary presentation and treatment of traumatic events may vicariously reduce anxiety in the spectator or reader on a level less intense than has usually been recognized as anxiety. I define anxiety, then, as a broad spectrum of defensive energy in preparation for danger. It includes a wide range of states such as tension, stress, fear, terror, and panic, and underlies all psychological defense mechanisms.[11]

II   Anxiety and Tragic Catharsis

The particular mechanism of anxiety of greatest interest in the context of tragedy is the way in which it is "bound" in a defense mechanism. While very little in the way of empirical analysis of this exists, and only a general idea of it seems suggested in Freud's old term *anxiety binding,* one experiment with parachutists illustrates a kind of anxiety binding particularly important in the context of tragedy. Epstein and Fenz found that novice parachutists who experienced great anxiety hours before a jump felt much *less* anxiety at the moment of the jump, while those who failed to worry earlier were seized with panic when the crucial moment arrived. Epstein and Fenz spoke cautiously of some sort of "inhibition" of anxiety, and refrained from all theorizing, although obliquely suggesting that it was a matter of getting rid of an excessive, debilitating and nonfunctional arousal.[12] But seen together with the concept of anxiety binding, much more suggests itself here—despite

11. The preceding material on anxiety first appeared, with minor differences, in *Susquehanna Studies* 9, no. 2 (June 1972), and is reprinted here by permission.
12. W. D. Fenz and S. Epstein, "Gradients of Physiological Arousal in Parachutists as a Function of an Approaching Jump," *Psychosomatic Medicine* 29 (1967): 33–51.

the fact that we must leave the confines of Epstein's and Fenz's empirical method in reaching for our conclusions. The parachutists appear to have bound their anxiety in a very functional way to provide a counter-cathexis or *Reizschutz* against the traumatic experience of falling. Once bound somehow in this psychic defense, the anxiety was no longer experienced as the highly unpleasant energy it is in its mobilized or free-floating state. The peculiar nature of the danger involved in this example, and one crucially important to tragedy, is that the parachutists do not attempt to overcome or avoid the feared event, but make rather a *decision* to undergo the jump, for example early in the morning when they check the weather for the day. At the moment of this decision, as Epstein and Fenz noted, the anxiety is greatest, then lessening as the jump approaches. This particular form of anxiety binding suggests the analogy to the physical steeling oneself before a collision when it is apparent that the impact cannot be avoided. The difference is that in the case of the parachutists this preparation occurs on a more purely psychic and perceptual level. A catastrophe or other traumatic event that is recognized as unavoidable and necessary is the key, therefore, to establishing this process vicariously in the spectator at a tragedy. Similarly, from an inductive examination of various tragedies, Oscar Mandel concluded that the *necessity* of catastrophe is its indispensable core.[13] Catastrophe without preparation is not tragic. Hence the spectator prepares (binds anxiety) vicariously for Oedipus's traumatic recognition that he has murdered his father and married his mother, and prepares all the more intensely as Oedipus fails to do so in his denial of the mounting evidence. When the traumatic realization occurs,

13. *A Definition of Tragedy* (New York: New York University Press, 1961).

the spectator feels inwardly prepared, and his anxiety, on a low vicarious level, has already been removed from its free-floating or unbound state and committed to a single, well-defined danger. After the traumatic realization and self-blinding have taken place, this bound anxiety, as preparation for a danger already past, becomes superfluous. Anxiety energy that has suddenly become superfluous may be discharged in laughter if the danger has been mastered and overcome, but in tragedy an opposing situation obtains. The relief occurs in a context of loss. The reaction to loss is grief. The vicarious reaction to the grief of another is pity.

The concept of the catharsis of pity and fear dominates Aristotle's theory of tragedy. It requires only gentle maneuvering to interpret this in the present terms. The catharsis of fear would appear as the binding of anxiety in preparation for a catastrophe. This process in itself provides, as we have noted, a degree of relief, and does so in a way commensurate with the—for modern critics—troublesome roots of the word *catharsis* in the crassly physical, as for example Plato used the word. But the catharsis relief of anxiety binding is not enough; it leaves the audience so to speak with teeth still gritted for a catastrophe.

A second phase of catharsis is provided by pity. *Eleos*, usually translated as pity, is less problematic than fear or *phobos* as a source of catharsis, but possibly more ambiguous in terms of its Aristotelian meaning. Aristotle noted that we feel pity when we must fear that the same painful event could happen to ourselves.[14] This psychological insight has generated on the part of Wolfgang Schadewaldt a line of thinking that attempts to divorce pity from *eleos*. Schadewaldt claims that pity is an invention of Christianity.

14. *The Works of Aristotle Translated into English* (Oxford: Clarendon Press, 1957) 11: 1385b.

He sees in *eleos* something more elemental, more closely associated with fear than with pity.[15] Schadewaldt may have erred in taking Aristotle's analysis for a definition *per se* and in making a biologically universal human emotion overly dependent on cultural influences. In any case, he concludes by equating *eleos* with the German *Jammer*, or grief. And grief, as I see it, is the emotion that gives rise to pity in the observer. If the possible alternatives to pity as the translation of *eleos* lead no farther afield than this, then we are most likely still on Aristotelian soil when we speak of pity and fear in broad biological terms of anxiety. From this point of view, at any rate, fear and pity both imply a form of catharsis. Fear is associated with catharsis as preparation or anxiety binding, and pity with the release of anxiety in grief. Fear basically precedes catastrophe; pity follows.

III *Hamlet* as a Tragedy

Lest it seem that I am attempting to reduce tragedy to a simple biological formula, let me hasten to point out that great tragedians frequently find ingenious and unique ways to treat the catharsis of pity and fear. Tragedy does not thrive on monotony and predictability. It must create and develop necessity somewhere between freedom and fatalism; it must prepare, and yet it must not let this preparation become tedious. Georg Büchner's Danton vainly asserts a bitterly comic superiority over the inexorable grind of the Reign of Terror leading to his execution, while tones of grief clash with crassness and cynicism in a carefully

15. *Antike und Gegenwart: Uber die Tragödie* (Munich: Deutscher Taschenbuch Verlag, 1966).

orchestrated final act. Despite his own totally un-aristotelian theory of tragedy, Friedrich Schiller creates continuous audience preparation for catastrophe while his heroine Mary Stuart alternates between fear and hope, until at the end she experiences a kind of satori and transcends reality into the realm of the ideal. The audience meanwhile is left behind with a more conventional catharsis of pity and fear.

In *Hamlet* Shakespeare also creates an ingenious and unique structure of these basic cathartic processes. As we seek now to gain access to *Hamlet* from this point of view, the definition of pity as vicarious grief immediately suggests a related approach in the *Hamlet* literature. This is Lily B. Campbell's analysis of the play in terms of excessive grief. In a work first published in 1930 she argued convincingly not only that Hamlet's grief over the loss of his father dominates his behavior, but that Shakespeare treats in detail various forms of grief as expounded in contemporary psychological literature.[16] This theme is well established. But it does not in itself explain why Hamlet cannot kill the king. The above discussion of grief emphasized, however, that, since the danger is past and the loss already suffered, anxiety as a preparation for danger becomes superfluous and is reduced or discharged. The various deaths prior to the last scene are all experienced retrospectively and thus excite grief and pity rather than fear. Hamlet's father died before the play opens and when Hamlet was off at school. Hamlet's slaughter of Polonius comes totally unprepared, and can therefore be grieved over but not feared. Here Hamlet's own callous reaction to this unfortunate event shows perhaps that he is resisting grief as best he can, that he is in fact inwardly binding anxiety in preparation for killing the

16. "Hamlet: A Tragedy of Grief," in *Shakespeare's Tragic Heroes: Slaves of Passion* (New York: Barnes and Noble, 1959).

king, despite his grief. While Hamlet dispatches Rosencrantz and Guildenstern with premeditation, he does so only indirectly and from a distance, and their deaths play no emotional role in terms of grief. As a form of relaxation of tension, grief directly contradicts Hamlet's preparation for a difficult task, and must be conquered inwardly before he can discharge his duty. Hence his madness, feigned or real, his callous reaction to the death of Polonius, his unhesitating disposal of Rosencrantz and Guildenstern tell us that we are witnessing not weakness or lack of resolution, but a grim, paralyzing entanglement of inner conflict. Augmenting his inner struggle, external events only continue to work against Hamlet. He learns of Ophelia's pitiful end, characteristically, only after returning from his sea voyage, in a context emphasizing not only loss and grief but also his own heavy burden of guilt. This guilt, as a punishment for the one instance where he did in fact act rashly, can only double the paralysis of his arm. Ophelia's madness and death both renew the sense of guilt for the death of her father and combine it with her own loss to Hamlet. Hamlet must experience both pity for her loss of her father and grief for his own loss of her. Inwardly the grave scene is the climax of the play, where Hamlet's mounting readiness to kill Claudius is smothered under a hellish atmosphere of pity, grief, and guilt. Shakespeare may have been completely conscious of this effect. At the beginning the ghost in fact seems to recognize that pity can only contradict the action Hamlet must take:

> Pity me not, but lend thy serious hearing
> To what I shall unfold.
> (1.5.5–6)

Through the player king Shakespeare expresses the laming

effect of grief when he observes that "purpose is but the slave to memory" (3.2.198), assuming that we can equate "memory" with the grief of Hamlet's memory of his father. Laertes is Hamlet's opposite. Quick to act, he is also capable of grief, but he can get it out of his system:

> Too much of water hast thou, poor Ophelia,
> And therefore I forbid my tears. But yet
> It is our trick—Nature her custom holds,
> Let shame say what it will. When these are gone,
> The woman will be out.
>   (4.7.186–90)

Hamlet's grief, in contrast, is introverted, does not appear on the surface, and is not easily expunged:

> But I have within which passeth show,
> These but the trappings and the suits of woe.
>   (1.2.85–86)

Whatever Shakespeare's own conceptualization of grief may have been, it emerges in *Hamlet* unambiguously as in some way opposed to action.

At this point the analysis of the play differs from what one might expect from the hypothesis. To be sure, the emphasis on grief is not new in tragedy. Euripedes' *The Trojan Women* is based almost solely on grief as opposed to fear. In contrast, Hamlet's pervasive grief functions not as a final catharsis, but as a hindrance to his primary concern, revenge. And the preparation he makes for the latter is also unusual. The real danger facing him is not death, either his own or that of loved ones. It is the prospect of failing to perform his duty. Therefore he does not bind anxiety for the purpose of passively withstanding a traumatic event, but for the purpose of preparing for a difficult task. This task, furthermore, is not physically, but psychologically, inwardly difficult.

Peculiar to this tragedy is the fact that Hamlet prepares for an event that will ultimately be decided successfully. "The readiness is all" (5.2.233), he finally declares in the fifth act, when the crucial moment is approaching. His success, his mastery of the danger facing him, is in principle and broadly speaking comic. Tragic is primarily the enormous cost of this victory. It is also peculiar that the necessity of the various deaths appears to follow only vaguely and indirectly from the ominous effect of Hamlet's prolonged paralysis. In *Othello*, for example, the murder of Desdemona and Othello's subsequent self-execution follow directly from the development of the action. I do not wish to suggest that the partially incidental quality to the final bloodletting in *Hamlet* is a weakness in the play. On the contrary, an ironclad necessity of catastrophe tends to become fatalistic. A certain element of accident, if not overdone, heightens the tragic effect, precisely because it erases any tone of the mechanistic and fatalistic.

As a tragic structure, then, the following two characteristics emerge as dominant in *Hamlet* and with all their subtleties and nuances provide its peculiar set of emotional overtones: First, grief pervades the overt emotional atmosphere throughout the play, rather than being concentrated at the end. This atmosphere is varied, but not fundamentally challenged at moments of genuine, if sarcastic comedy in Hamlet's wit. It is, however, inwardly tensed and pressured throughout the play by Hamlet's cynicism and callousness as an expression of his conflict. Second, the anxiety binding or catharsis of fear does not focus upon the catastrophe, but upon a task carried out successfully. This success mingles almost strangely with the concomitant tragic destruction of Hamlet's world.

IV Hamlet's Delay

But this analysis is not complete. We still do not know what makes all this disaster necessary, that is, why Hamlet's simple task should require such preparation in the first place. Hamlet is in fact capable, despite his grief, of many acts, including homicide. His grief prevents him only from a particular killing especially difficult for him. At this point the argument intersects with any number of divergent delay theories. This proliferation is aided by the text, which is replete with Hamlet's own confusion as to the reason for his delay and rationalizations as to the moral imperative for the task. The religious level of the work, for example, cannot be ignored in any comprehensive analysis of the play, but too much evidence contradicts the notion that a conscious religious scruple hinders Hamlet's action. Also, the possibility that the ghost is an apparition of the devil serves Hamlet as only a lame excuse for inaction. Somewhat more consistent with the text is the view first suggested by Freud and enlarged upon by Ernest Jones, that Hamlet is prevented by an Oedipal inhibition from killing a father-figure, which the king might fairly be described as being, since he is both the brother of Hamlet's father and the husband of his mother.[17] The Oedipal view also accounts for Hamlet's inability to understand his delay, since the Oedipal inhibition is unconscious. Jones asserts with some justification that the only person Hamlet cannot kill is the king, that therefore some special attribute of the king is the problem. Nevertheless, two difficulties in Jones's argument seriously weaken this interpretation. The inhibiting attribute of the king need not in fact be unique to him, but unique only among those

17. Ernest Jones, *Hamlet and Oedipus*, Doubleday Anchor Book (Garden City, N.Y.: Doubleday, 1949).

Hamlet does ultimately try to kill. Some factor other than the familial relationship might be found. The Oedipal theory also becomes dubious when one considers how completely and unambiguously Hamlet dissociates Claudius from his father, and that his father himself has appeared concretely on the stage to demand revenge. Thus, were Hamlet in fact to show unusual appetite for the quick performance of his duty, the psychoanalysts would be far better justified in claiming an Oedipal desire. Hamlet could then be seen as quite fortunate in finding an opportunity to kill a father figure and remove the competition for his mother's affection, and do so in perfect harmony with the duty to his own father. Still, these points do not entirely refute the Oedipal theory. Jones thinks Shakespeare may himself have been unaware of anything Oedipal in his play. It could be that some spectators today find some such satisfaction here. Even if this should be the case, however, it cannot satisfy the critic, who is entitled to demand that an adequate interpretation of Hamlet's delay generate more textual justification than does the Oedipal theory.

I have pointed out above that Claudius's familial relationship as a father figure need not necessarily be the cause of Hamlet's problem; it remains to find another principle to distinguish between him and the others Hamlet kills. Qualms about regicide do not suffice, for Hamlet would then have had to explain to the ghost that killing a king is forbidden. One can imagine how *that* would go over with the elder Hamlet. Another possibility is suggested by the role a broad concept of anxiety plays in inhibitions. An inhibition is not simply a static wall of some sort, but an active defense that requires anxiety energy to maintain itself. Inhibitions are also not limited to the pathological, but include quite normal, useful perfunctory restraints as well, many of which arise from the needs of civilization. One of these is the inhibition of killing. This idea is simple and reasonable. Ernst Heuse pointed out in a little-noticed study in 1898 that it is difficult for a man of civilized temperament to kill when not motivated immediately by anger, self-defense, or—of all things—love of the fatherland.[18] He also noted that killing is made easier if, for example, the victim is standing behind a curtain. He saw Hamlet as a real person instead of a "Theaterprinz" who would have no difficulty running Claudius through. Unfortunately Heuse mentioned only the death of Polonius to support his theory, and otherwise buried his original idea in a Wilhelminian analysis of the moral fibre of the various characters in the play and a discussion of dueling techniques. So simply stated, this explanation only slightly reinterprets the old Goethean view of a delicate prince unequal to his task. But if we keep in mind our "Hamlet-of-the-Tables," it becomes evident that what specifically invokes Hamlet's inhibition against killing is the concrete social reality of his opponent, and particularly his friendly or smiling face.

A considerable part of the text can be interpreted from this point of view. As the first important evidence for what I shall call Hamlet's social inhibition to kill, Hamlet emphasizes the smiling Claudius while programming his task. It is particularly through the face that social presence and the cause of this inhibition manifests itself, and it is specifically the smiling, civilized exterior of Claudius that concerns Hamlet when he writes in his tables. Even before this key passage and any possible awareness of his special problem Hamlet refers to the

18. *Zur Lösung des Hamlet-Problems* (Elberfeld, Germany: A. Martini and Grüttefien, 1898).

> o'er growth of some complexion,
> Oft breaking down the pales and forts of reason,

or

> . . . some habit that too much o'erleavens
> The form of plausive manners, . . .

that

> Shall in the general censure take corruption
> From that particular fault.
>   (1.4.27–36)

This might be understood to mean that a civilized custom, such as the inhibition against killing, when operating even against reason—that is, conscious intent—becomes a fault. The ghost urges Hamlet to show his nature, or basic emotions, in seeking revenge, and Hamlet promises revenge

> . . . with wings swift
> As meditation or the thoughts of love
>   (1.5.29–30)

hardly the best symbols for such action. Also, in vowing that the ghost's command shall live unmixed with "baser matter," Hamlet betrays his inability to act, if we associate "baser matter" with "nature" (1.5.101–4).

Despite this inauspicious beginning, Hamlet gradually evolves an elaborate plan, making use of opportunities as they arise, to prepare himself for his task. When the players arrive he immediately asks for a speech describing the slaughter of Priam at Troy. In this speech Pyrrhus first fails to kill the Trojan king, then rekindles his will to carry out the deed. This presumably appeals to Hamlet as a reflection not only of his general task, but specifically as a portrayal of a man who finds killing difficult, then manages to finish his work nonetheless. But when Hamlet hears the impassioned player's speech, he is amazed that the player is able to whip himself into outward emotional frenzy, while he, with every reason for such passion, remains paralyzed. The contrast between the facile make-believe of the theater and Hamlet's reality only accentuates his intimidation by his real problem.

In the third act Hamlet's plan goes into action. Noting that conscience—and possibly the social conscience of his inhibition rather than conscious values—makes "cowards of us all" (3.1.83), he somewhat pessimistically organizes his players to trap the king. He cautions them, mindful of the unreality of exaggerated theatrical emotions, not to overdo their parts, for he requires a "mirror up to nature" to transfer his reality to the stage. In this context the much puzzled-over dumb show might be explained as providing an opportunity for Hamlet to witness a reenactment of the murder that is as far removed from an actual performance as the performance is from reality, so that the following performance will in comparison seem real. Whatever the reason for the dumb show by itself, the performance as a whole serves two additional functions. It allows Hamlet to witness the *crime,* creating a concrete visual experience to counteract or counterbalance the concrete visual reality of the king's face. Second, it allows him to witness the *guilt,* specifically in the face of the king. This is intended to remove any doubt of his guilt and at the same time to disrupt the paralyzing visage of "custom" in a friendly countenance. As it turns out, Hamlet's trap succeeds in dissolving Claudius's facial composure, but it fails to convey to him any illusion of the reality of the reenactment of the murder: "What, frighted with false fire!" (3.2.277) he calls out, when the king rises to leave. Instead of charging after him, he only calls for the recorders, betraying the failure of his plan. Like Pyrrhus, however, he manages to rekindle his resolve a few minutes later, and finds the king at prayer.

In addition to its religious significance, prayer is a particularly peaceful activity, one not well suited to help Hamlet in his task. Therefore he rationalizes that it would be better to wait for some moment without the "relish of salvation" in it, and lists some examples. When the king is "drunk asleep" his conscious social presence is momentarily extinguished; when he is "in his rage" he is violent and can be goaded into enabling Hamlet to act in self-defense, or, as Hamlet later says in connection with the pirates' attack, with "compelled valor" (4.6.17); when he is in the "incestuous pleasure of his bed" he is acting privately, not socially, and Hamlet's rage at the marriage will come into play as well to help him show some "nature"; and finally, when the king is "gaming" or "swearing," his friendly and civilized exterior is also momentarily nullified (3.3.89–95).

Hamlet therefore proceeds to his mother's room, where, noticing that someone is listening, he stabs Polonius through the arras, hoping it is the king. It is significant that the arras makes the face and entire person of the victim invisible, in this way bypassing Hamlet's inhibition. Thus in the fourth act Hamlet marvels at the ability of Fortinbras to make war over an "invisible event" (4.5.50), thereby perhaps underscoring the importance of visual presence in relation to his own problem. Invisibility also contributes to his quick and easy removal of Rosencrantz and Guildenstern through the mail.

When it becomes clear to Hamlet that he must move before the king succeeds in destroying him, the need for action intensifies. And still, he succeeds only with the help of fortuitous circumstances. Drawn into the duel with Laertes, he does not realize until *after* he has mortally wounded his opponent that he is himself using a poisoned tip. At this moment, sword in hand, Laertes and his mother dying, he finally manages to run the king through without avoiding his social presence. It is significant that Claudius makes no attempt to defend himself. Hamlet must act without any such help in overcoming his inhibition. And yet even here Hamlet only wounds him, trusting expressly to the poison to do the real work.

At least Hamlet finally succeeds in avenging his father's murder, face-to-face with his opponent and with complete awareness of his action, the only time he could manage to kill in such a manner. He has done so at tragic cost. More specifically, he has swum against and conquered an emotional current of grief flowing in the wrong direction. Pity (or grief) and fear (or anxiety binding) tend to contradict one another, if not kept in the proper sequence. Shakespeare has turned these processes upside down and pitted his hero against them. In Hamlet, Shakespeare has created not Weak and Melancholy Man, not Religious, Oedipal, or Marxist Man, but Civilized Man. In the long theatrical tradition of stage violence, and particularly the English Senecan tradition, one easily forgets that the premeditated slaughter of a human being is a difficult task under normal social conditions. Laertes does not know this, because Laertes is a "Theaterprinz." Hamlet possesses an additional dimension of civilized human reality.

The Shape of *Hamlet* in the Theater[1]

DANIEL SELTZER

My title might suggest many approaches to the play and requires me to begin with an attempt at definition. I am not using the word *shape* as a metaphor, and my primary concern is not now with any traditionally understood sense of those stock-in-trade words of literary jargon, *form* and *structure*. I am concerned literally with the kind of shape of which one might speak as though he were referring to a pictorial image or a special kind of architecture, and which performance in the theater uniquely creates. So it may be worth saying again, although by now it is a principle to which those of us who are academics at least pay lip service, that the activity and experience of performance are not in themselves primarily "literary" experiences, although of

1. This paper, when delivered, was interspersed with dramatic readings from the play to help support interpretive comments regarding the variations of theatrical intensity, pitch of voice, speed of delivery, and so on. Such quotation, for the most part, has been eliminated for the printed version of the essay, since the quotations were almost invariably from the most famous speeches in the title role, and little would be gained from their simple reproduction on these pages. Sentences introducing these lines, then, have been slightly revised, with act-scene-line references incorporated in the text. These are from the edition by G. L. Kittredge (Boston and New York: Ginn and Co., 1936).

course in the plays of Shakespeare, in performance or in the study, the literary component is a more important element than is the case in other drama. Although dealing specifically with *Hamlet,* what I have to say about the shape of performance applies more or less generally to other plays from all periods of dramatic composition. Some conclusions of this paper may apply specifically, however, not only to *Hamlet* but to the other major tragedies and romances of Shakespeare as well.

Hamlet's famous advice to the Players who visit Elsinore (3.2.1–50) has become a text useful in many ways. We derive from it, for example, corroboration that the Elizabethans, whatever their styles of stage acting, believed their best examples of the art to be, as indeed all ages have considered good acting to be, intensely realistic. The advice to the Players tells us also something of what Hamlet is feeling at the moment about the values of moderation, of eschewing excessive action or empty demonstration of emotion—and these issues naturally relate to larger aspects of his personal problems of action. I would like to call attention to some useful phrases in one part of this speech, for they seem to me to suggest the need for a specialized critical vocabulary when one wants to discuss the *experiencing* of drama in performance. In emphasizing the great need to imitate nature as exactly as possible, which is, Hamlet says, the whole "purpose of playing . . . both at the first and now," he elaborates by remarking that good acting "[shows] . . . the very age and body of the time his form and pressure." This phrase suggests an effort on Hamlet's part to invent— perhaps, indeed, with only moderate success—a nomenclature that says what acting does in terms more pictorial and temporal than critical or specifically verbal.

Hamlet sees the arts of imitation, appropriate to a time

of human life, as mirroring a shape—a "form"—and in fact reflecting reality as one might speak of shaping, of molding ("pressure"). A play performed takes a shape, considered retrospectively, and is simultaneously a *process* of shaping: the way life is imitated involves creation of new life. The old image of the mirror reflecting nature (which was not in any case invented by Hamlet) is perhaps more confusing than helpful, for, as the great art historian Ernst Gombrich has pointed out,[2] art itself does not mirror nature: artists do; and the artist who is an actor does his job not in some once-removed realm of activity, but literally by conjuring up in himself and, therefore, in the beholders, not simply something that is "like" life, but a new reality itself. The acted life span of a play in the theater has very little to do with the pagination of a text, and it is that re-created life that has an architectonic of its own which literary critics do not often, if ever, take into account—for indeed that which describes its forms and its pressures must be a vocabulary that has little to do with literary criticism.

Before saying more about the shaping of drama in performance, and particularly the shape of *Hamlet,* it is of course necessary to acknowledge that the first tool of reference has to be the text of the play—which is all we have of Shakespeare's living creation—and it would be irresponsible not to observe (if only to get the point out of the way) that a number of different texts of *Hamlet* exist. If one is to talk about the shape of a play, he had better decide which text becomes its foundation, and establishes the coordinates of its temporal life span on stage. *Hamlet* comes down to us in three different but apparently related texts: first, the Quarto of 1603, known as the "bad" quarto, which

2. One of the fundamental arguments running throughout *Art and Illusion* (New York: Pantheon Books, 1960).

is probably a version abridged for acting purposes, but badly reported and inaccurately printed; the so-called good quarto of 1604–5, which is of course a vastly enlarged text, sometimes assumed to have been printed from Shakespeare's draft; and the Folio text of 1623, which may be based on the prompt-book used by the actors, and which contains additional lines and whole stretches of dialogue. General consensus now is that the Folio represents an authorized acting version of the play, but that the second Quarto represents, more or less, the full text as Shakespeare wanted it to appear, though in the Folio are cuts that may be efforts to shorten—again, for performance—a very long play. Modern editions almost always present a conflation of the second Quarto and the Folio, and although such a text is probably longer than anything Shakespeare could have seen performed, it is the best standard we have for assessing the movement of action as he conceived it—and even a slightly shortened version of it would contain still the thrust of activity in the fuller text. So my remarks about the play in performance refer to the version we all know and work with in our classes and researches, based mainly on the 1604–5 Quarto with additions from the Folio.

The shape of any play in performance is visual, aural, and temporal. It maintains the conditions of music and adds an image of action actually seen. Not only do words move through time, but so do human bodies, colors and textures, light or its absence, physical properties, and our perception of the space in which the activity of the play takes place. It is time, perhaps, to seek not only in the texts themselves, but in the phenomenology of drama, some new coordinates that may actually help us to understand Shakespeare better, to approach him in his own medium. The text will not stop being important, for it remains of course our primary source of data that can be analyzed, whatever our approach to such data may be. The world of the play itself should now be understood—and perhaps especially by teachers and students—as a world with its own realities, forms, and pressures; traditional scholarship hasn't the tools to define these, for they are dictated by theatrical artists' perceptions of the actualities of lifelike behavior.

A play may be said to exist in performance in terms of three bodies of sensory and understood data—forces felt and understood by actors and, to the extent that they have done so, by an audience—though each member of any audience will feel and understand them differently, and each performance will elicit differing degrees and kinds of perception. Everything that happens on stage during any performance (of any play) may be described, I think, as belonging to one of these bodies of data, which are built incrementally through stage time, much as sounds accumulate during a musical performance both at the present moment of their sounding and in the memory of the auditor. These three forceful components of performed plays are (first) *rhythmic,* having to do with the tempo and pace of physical and verbal activity in time; (second) *imagistic,* having to do both with what is seen—bodies, light or shadow, objects, and the like—or that which, when verbalized, conjures an aurally perceived structure, such as a continuity of words, or groups of peculiarly similar words; and (third) *intellectual,* having to do with patterns of ideas.

In more traditional terms, a critical discussion of what I have termed rhythm would concern a play's structure; but in terms of performance, the word refers to the deployment of events, seen and heard, across a period of time, so as to create, in this distribution, a shape of narrative. The traditional critical equivalent of the imagistic component would be of course our analytical procedures relating to poetics, to the uses of metaphor, to the idioms that individualize characters; but we do not often in more conventional criticism deal with that other aspect of a play's images in performance—that is, its purely visual forces, as these are set forth nonverbally. The intellectual content of a play relates to thematics, as these are conventionally understood—the "background of ideas" that form a context for a drama; but in performance these are presented not as demonstrating a preconceived idea that can be paraphrased afterwards; rather, they unfold as does the rhythmic component of a play, incrementally, as the thoughts of the characters force them to speak, or to move about physically, over the finite period of time during which their lives are exposed to us.

The nature of descriptive presentation forces me to speak of these elements of performance in sequence, as though they might occur on stage in some order of time or priority of importance, but during a performance they form a fabric of experience, both for performer and spectator, and often, of course, one component creates the experience of another, such as, for example, when the physical stage property of a crown elicits the cerebral data, now stock-in-trade for scholars, concerning Elizabethan notions of kingship and hierarchy. The sequence in which are presented, for example, the visual image caused by the presence in ensemble of different groupings of characters, will have much to do with the rhythmic content of a performed drama, since the very presence of these characters' bodies on stage together becomes, when set in conjunction or in juxtaposition with other combinations, an element of tempo of scenes.

The element of stage performance that is in question here, however, concerns the distribution of those phenomena of experience in *Hamlet,* as they create their performed pressure and form—their shape—in time. That element is primarily rhythmic, and requires that one assess the narrative of the play—quite simply, its story—in terms of the sequence of its presentation, together with that narrative's characteristics that in turn create variations of shape. It cannot be too much emphasized that this shape is deployed, like musical phenomena, in *time,* and that just as the varying tempi of a musical composition lay out its temporal boundaries, so the pacing of a drama establishes a format or pattern that may be discussed, for convenience, almost in pictorial terms. The coordinates that in drama establish such a rhythmic shape across a period of time, however, involve not only an assessment of substantive material that may move quickly or slowly, but an element that may be called intensity, this in turn deriving from the relative degrees of high- or low-pitched energies presented in the characters' stage lives themselves.

The shape of *Hamlet* in performance is a paradigm of Shakespearean tragedy in general; it may be analyzed in units of narrative action having little if anything to do with arbitrarily conceived textual "act" division, but denoted—again using convenient musical terminology—as movements or phrases of activity. These phrases suggest a movement from various levels of high energy, effecting a pulsation of rhythm that reaches its highest pitch near the end of the play, then subsides into an entirely new energy that carries forward a tranquillity hitherto unfelt in the action. It takes no ghost come from the grave to tell us, of course, that tragedy moves from chaos masked by apparent order, to an overt frenzy of action, returning finally to a genuine calm that accompanies the discoveries and achievements of the central character. But this description of the literary form of tragedy does not tell us much about experiencing drama, and indeed prevents us from discovering, for example, what seems to me in fact true—that Shakespeare's major accomplishments in the tragic mode, particularly *Hamlet, King Lear, Othello,* and *Antony and Cleopatra,* move in time with a rhythm suggestive not of the format of Elizabethan tragedies as that format is described· by Elizabethan or modern critics, but suggestive rather of that form of narrative most congenial to Shakespeare and many of his contemporaries, whether in writing for the stage or in narrative prose or poetry, namely, the pervasive form of romance. Indeed, the shape of Shakespeare's tragedies, as that shape pulses in stage performance, parallels most closely a comic mode in the purest sense—in the sense of Dante's *commedia,* moving from inner confusion and obfuscation to a long and introspectively oriented section during which lovers seek to repair their separation or a single hero seeks his own identity and proper function—a terrain of action, in fact, quite similar in nature to the long quests that occupy the central movements of late Medieval romances, moving finally to a phrase of activity in which (in comic terms) that which has been lost is found or (in tragic terms) an individual acknowledges how previous choices and decisions have led him to an inevitable ending place—a place where his own name becomes one with his action, and where self identification causes the tranquillity of acceptance and discovery. This sequence is a rhythmic pattern that informs the major tragedies, is much more obvious in *Antony,* and is the fundamental tempo purified in *Pericles, Cymbeline, Winter's Tale,* and *The Tempest.*

The rhythmic shape of the play *Hamlet* is much clearer to chart, interestingly enough, than that of any other major tragedy except *Macbeth,* in which, as in *Hamlet,* the tem-

poral architecture of the play is essentially that of the stage-
life of the title character. Once charted, however, it will be
seen that this shape resembles that of *Lear* and *Othello.* In
Hamlet, it is the Prince's energies, and his physical and
verbal expressions of them, that provide the form and pressure for the whole play; in hardly any other important play
in Western literature—even in that most archetypical
tragedy, *Oedipus the King*—is the title role so literally the
leading role : for it is Hamlet himself who forges the tempo
of our experiencing of *his* experience. This experience exists
in the time span of the play in terms of blocks of energy,
each expressed in dialogue or solo speech. These blocks of
verbalizations, we must remember, are more than a fabric
of words, even though it is the words that remain our
fundamental guide to all else. The substantive nature of
each event that prompts Hamlet to speak naturally influences *how* he is to speak, and I hope I need not discuss
the truth that of course different actors will make different
choices of detailed interpretation at each juncture in action.
But the range of choices is itself finite, and, in general terms,
ultimately describable.

As John Cage and Harold Pinter have reminded us,
silence is as important a factor in the determination of
rhythmic elements in performed art as sounds are; and, in
a consideration such as the one I am pursuing, one must add
that the physicalization of Hamlet's body is as important a
contributing element in the overall rhythm of the play as
are the articulations of his words. These blocks, or sections,
of speech which, taken in sequence, compose the shape of
Hamlet's stage life, are comparable to the blocks of sounds
that progress through a piece of "concrete" music. And, as in
such music, or even in a more traditional musical composition, the final effect of the shape of experience is incremen-

tal; for example, our full emotional and intellectual perception of the final rest that comes to the tragic hero is partly elicited by the tempo of the last measures of his activity, but is also partly due to our memorial—our remembered—experience of earlier activity, which is, by the time the end comes, gathered in our imaginations.

Our experience of Hamlet and his experience of himself —in performance these come to much the same phenomenon—exist in fifteen blocks of activity. Someone else might count them and describe them differently, but I think the differences would not be major ones. In counting these episodes, I omit only a few small sections of dialogue, most of the time merging in any case with more important junctures of action. These fifteen episodes include not only soliloquies and semi-solo speech and activity, but dialogues with other characters that are highly energized.

They are as follows: first, the soliloquy, "O that this too too sullied flesh" and the information about the Ghost that follows it directly; second, the scenes with the Ghost, including the oath of vengeance, surrounded on both sides with dialogue with Horatio and the others; third, the dialogue with Polonius while Hamlet reads his book and satirizes Polonius to his face; fourth, the dialogue with Rosencrantz and Guildenstern, concluding with the apostrophe to man as the "paragon of animals" as well as "the quintessence of dust"; fifth, the quick dialogue with the Players, which is followed by the soliloquy, "O, what a rogue and peasant slave am I!"; sixth, the "To be or not to be" soliloquy; seventh, the so-called Nunnery scene, with its savage verbal assaults upon Ophelia; eight, the "Advice" to the Players; ninth, the long set-speech of compliment to Horatio, on the subject of reason and moderation; tenth, the dialogue surrounding the actual performance of "The Murder of Gonzago," with Hamlet's responses to its conclusion; eleventh, the speech over the praying Claudius, in which Hamlet decides to put off his revenge until a more damning moment; twelfth, the scene between Hamlet and his mother; thirteenth, the episode in which Hamlet watches Fortinbras's armies and then speaks the soliloquy, "How all occasions do inform against me"; fourteenth, the long scene at Ophelia's grave, first with the Gravediggers and then the confrontation with Laertes; and, finally, the sequence of speeches to Horatio, describing his adventures at sea, then the short conversation with Osric, and the speech discussing the "special providence in the fall of a sparrow." These are the major units of Hamlet's life, with only short and mainly connective dialogues omitted. I think it fascinating that the stage life, which has elicited more imaginative response than any other fictional life in dramatic or nondramatic literature, is set forth for us in essentially only fifteen blocks of stage time, and that, although each is different from the others as well as various within itself, taken as an incremental sequence these blocks build a rhythmic shape that is also the mold of the whole drama.

Before describing this rhythm in more detail, with reference to specific speeches, let me dwell just a bit longer on the larger phrases of the play's action, for it is through them that a pattern emerges similar to that of the other tragedies, and very suggestive of the stage shape of the last romances. The phrases of the action begin and end with points of dramatic narrative, though not necessarily, or only accidentally, do they conform to textually marked act division. The first phrase, or movement, takes us through Hamlet's oath after seeing the Ghost; the second through the "Nunnery" scene and Claudius's determination that Hamlet must go to England; the third begins with the "Advice" to the

Players, goes through the play scene, and concludes with the "How all occasions" soliloquy; the fourth is an interlude in the role, for Hamlet is silent, off-stage, the action covering Ophelia's mad scene and Laertes' rebellion, Horatio's receipt of Hamlet's letter, Claudius's plot with Laertes, and Gertrude's description of Ophelia's drowning; the fifth movement begins in the graveyard and extends through the end of the action. The fifteen blocks of Hamlet's stage life are distributed across these phrases with remarkable balance: the first two are in the first phrase of action and the last two are in the fifth; and the two central movements—the second and third of the play—contain respectively five and six blocks of activity for Hamlet. Thus the first phrase becomes a kind of prologue, the last a coda, with the torso of the action containing in each of its major movements an approximately equal number of exposures, so to speak, of Hamlet's experience.

I have described the incremental rhythm of this life and this play as "pulsating" in performance. This is not simply a figurative adjective. Each block of activity, represented in the text by so many words but in performance by variations of movement and vocal pitch as well as by alternations of tempi, ebbs and flows higher in energy until a peak is reached when Hamlet watches Fortinbras's armies and proclaims for the last time his determination that his thoughts "be bloody, or be nothing worth." Following this his life is silent, as if anticipating that inevitable moment when all the "rest is silence," until his return to the graveyard. At this point a truly substantive alteration takes place, a difference in kind as well as in degree of projected energy, for from this juncture until the end Hamlet's verse is more flexible and supple than ever, his intellectual objectives gathered toward patience, and the pitch of physical activity

focused and aimed rather than loose and chaotically disorganized.[3]

Each of the fifteen exposures of stage life in *Hamlet* cannot be studied here in detail, but I would like to try to
suggest the way in which the ebb and flow of rhythm
effects the shape of the whole—literally causes our responses
and our experience of the hero's life. The two large areas
of activity in the first movement are syntactically, physically,
and visually disrupted, full of syncopated words and movement—first, the first soliloquy (1.2.129–59), full of incomplete
sentences and abrupt changes in the direction of thoughts,
and then the Ghost scenes and the oath (1.4.39—1.5), with
their expletives and flying language, a barrage of exclama-
tion and near hysteria. The first movement ends, as an actor
would say, high. The personality projected is intensely sub-

3. It may be of interest succinctly to compare the major phrases of
activity in *King Lear*. The whole play consists of twenty-three episodes of
action; of these only ten blocks of stage time and energy belong to the
title role, the rest filling out the contrapuntal texture provided by the
Gloucester story and a few scenes with the evil daughters and their
husbands, and their relationships to Edmund. Nevertheless, the rhythm
of the play, and specifically the beat of Lear's stage life within it, is
much the same as the pattern I have tried to reveal in *Hamlet*. The first
large phrase of *Lear* begins with the same great intensity, though at a
higher pitch of sound, as that of *Hamlet*. After the division of the kingdom,
the movement concludes on a crescendo of pitch and of inner and
physical intensity of action with Lear's great speech on human need, and
his expulsion to the heath, with original stage directions requiring rolls
of thunder. The second large movement is of course the sequence of
episodes on the heath, and ends with the mock trial in which Goneril
and Regan are arraigned by Lear, with Edgar, Kent, and the Fool as his
court. There follows, as in *Hamlet*, an interlude during which Lear is off-
stage and silent (and the actor is resting!), during which Gloucester is
blinded, and Lear's enemies prepare their armies and continue their
lustful disputes, ending with the scene in which Gloucester wishes to
commit suicide and is prevented by Edgar. The third large phrase of the
play begins in the middle of 4.6 with Lear's entrance and his heart-
rendingly astute, mad discourse with the blind Gloucester. Lear is on
stage again in this last movement only three times: the scene in which
he awakens to music and Cordelia's kindness; the short episode following
their capture by Edmund, during which Lear speaks of the permanence
their love will evoke in prison, triumphing alike over enemies and earthly
mutability; and of course the last time we see him, with Cordelia's body.

jective, the language more times than not chaotic, both in fluctuation of pitch and in actual syntax. The visual images alternate between the still figure of the man himself speaking the abruptly disjointed phrases of the first soliloquy to the quickly moving body and the flow of machine-gun emphases of the Ghost scenes.

The second movement offers five exposures of Hamlet—though perhaps there are six, if one includes the visual image not seen but vividly conjured up by Ophelia's description of him as he appeared in her chamber, acting in pantomime the typical melancholic lover; for Ophelia's memory causes Hamlet, silent but visually imagined, to rise in our own mind's eye.[4] The first three of the five blocks of activity in this movement constitute a flow of rising intensity from that still picture: first the sharply etched dialogue with Polonius (2.2.171–221), the prose sentences propelled in angry intention yet in perfectly balanced periods of sound, then, moments later and still in prose, the swelling crescendos of the little aria on man's worth, spoken as much to give vent to his own sense of ambiguity as to confuse Rosencrantz and Guildenstern (2.2.304–24), but culminating, and of course changing to verse, in the "Rogue and peasant slave" soliloquy (2.2.575–633), which itself contains three separate rising plateaus of intensity, climaxing not in chaotic grammar but in a febrile pitch of self-assault, this metamorphosing into a profound effort to think clearly. Almost immediately, however, the rhythm ebbs in vocal and visual intensity into the stillness, the innerly oriented probing of that most famous soliloquy of all, the "To be or not to be" (3.1.56–88), an introspective complement to the physicalized,

---

4. As indeed he literally did in Laurence Olivier's famous film version of the play, acting Ophelia's "stage directions" as we heard her voice speaking the lines.

outwardly oriented activity during the last twenty or thirty
minutes of stage time. Whatever our own variation of its
inflections may be, each of us remembers the way in which
this speech seems almost to make time stop, floating somehow unmoving and total in the air of the play. Immediately,
and in remarkable juxtaposition, is another outburst, as
previously withheld energy now finds a target and bursts
upon Ophelia (3.1.90–157).

Here at the conclusion of the second movement of the
play, the shape that is being established is one of high
energy alternating with low, emotional fury or intellectual
aggressiveness chained in—and then unleashed. Low beats
of vocal energy have been the first soliloquy and the third,
the peaks of swirling chaos surrounding them being the
oath after the Ghost, the "Rogue and peasant slave," and the
"Nunnery" episode. Intervening blocks of activity fall on
various points of the scale between these extremes, and
these areas of activity have been made real not only by
words but by the physical action required to express them :
the body still, the body in fast movement. Moreover, the
episodes themselves are syncopated; that is, they are not
evenly spaced. A long stretch of stage time separates, for
example, the oath after seeing the Ghost from the dialogue
with Polonius, whereas the "To be or not to be" soliloquy
comes directly before the "Nunnery" scene. On a purely
narrative level, Hamlet moves in various ways to impose
subjective response upon a habitually abstracted view of
life, and in doing so moves closer to a field of battle with
Claudius, even as he separates himself from familiar and
loved objects, activities, and people. Generally the pitch has
risen from the beginning of the play in spite of the interludes of relative quiet; and it has risen unevenly, its sequence
of exposed energies purposefully jarring.

The third movement, except for its warmly reasonable and calm address to Horatio, paying him the highest compliment Hamlet knows, is pitched even higher. It begins with the animated advice to the Players, the subject matter of which is careful choice and moderation of imitative activity—thus making it a logical companion-piece to the speech to Horatio that follows at once—and its energy level is slightly lower than that which concluded the beat at the end of the second movement, the "Nunnery" scene with Ophelia. But from this plateau the energy steadily rises, and now the tempo is not syncopated, the blocks of action separated unevenly from each other, but appear aurally and visually in regular tempo, one following the other: the bawdy chat with Ophelia before the play (3.2.116–30 and ff.), the hysterical reaction following it (3.2.282–306 and ff.), the furious intensity of the speech over the praying Claudius (3.3.73–98), and an apparent climax in the dialogue with Gertrude (most of 3.4, but especially 53–101, Hamlet's words topping each of the Queen's interjections). But the crescendo is not in fact over, for the exposed energy rises still further in the fourth major soliloquy, a peak of intensity absolutely vital to the total shape of the play, as Hamlet reacts to the march of Fortinbras's armies ("How all occasions do inform against me," 4.4.32–66).

This speech is the thirteenth of the major episodes in which the imagistic, rhythmic, and cerebral components of stage action combine to reveal to us Hamlet's experience of himself. All of these elements, taken together, though not always simultaneously, have effected a temporal architecture of energies that build from low to high, from the ebb and flow of confused syntax and perceptions to a steady stream of more feverishly pitched vocalizations and movements. The images of the play have kept Hamlet before us even when he is not physically on stage, and our sight of him has varied from immobility, his words seeming to hover in an absence of forward movement, to aggressively thrusting action, his words correspondingly energized.

Now, after this peak of energy, the charged, concentrated figure, his cerebral focus given over entirely to revenge, is gone from the stage for (more or less) forty minutes. Our aural memory holds, however, the high tempo of his last appearance. Now stage time is given over, in conventional patterns of plotting, to Claudius and Laertes— and the subject matter of revenge is itself transferred, as it were, from Hamlet to these two. Hamlet's own activity of vengeance, as we are to learn shortly, is sublimated in arranging the deaths of Rosencrantz and Guildenstern. His return to the world—to the stage and to our sight—is exactly equivalent in its placement in the measures of the drama, and in its qualities of visual and aural elements, to Lear's awakening in Cordelia's camp. Our own intellectual perception of the two heroes is somehow similar, too : though the feeling is difficult if not impossible to paraphrase, it will seem to us as though both have learned the same things over the earlier expanse of their stage lives, and that while they have been absent these things have altered their speech patterns, their habits of movement, and the very kinds of energy with which their personalities are communicated to us.

In the fourteenth block of his stage life, Hamlet's image (similar to Lear's, in the eighth and ninth blocks of his) is quieter, the rhythm of his words more often than not, now, the flexible, supple beats of very simple prose. Even when he leaps into the grave at Ophelia's funeral, his physical and verbal assault upon Laertes parodies the extremity of her brother's action and the rant of his words; Hamlet himself says so: "Nay, an thou'lt mouth,/I'll rant as well as thou" (5.2.306–7). Within a few minutes, his own summary of his actions, spoken to Horatio, contains a new quality of calmness (5.2.1–79). This calmness contrasts, indeed, even with the quiet moments in the role earlier, for it has none of the magically static characteristics of, say, the "To be or not to be." There is a new "stillness" now, found again, finally, in the speech through which our last memory of him is filtered (for, in the large view of the play, the duel is only a last cadence):

> Not a whit, we defy augury; there's a special providence in the fall of a sparrow. If it be now, 'tis not to come; if it be not to come, it will be now; if it be not now, yet it will come: the readiness is all. Since no man knows aught of what he leaves, what is't to leave betimes? Let be.
>
> (5.2.230–35)

The "stillness" of this speech is identical to that inner stillness which every successful actor must achieve as he steadies himself for the task of changing his identity. It is a feeling of inward peace without which even the best stage artist cannot accomplish the remarkable act of assuming new life—and perhaps without which no hero in tragedy can be prepared for a new sense of himself. There are equivalent moments toward the end of all the major tragedies and, of course, in the last romances; the substantive matter of the speech conveys tranquillity of a sort absent in any activity earlier in the play.

Naturally, our individual experiences of *Hamlet* will vary enormously, depending in large measure upon the emotional experience that is brought to the play, as well as upon that which the play exposes to the spectator. But although these variations will exist, the basic *pulse* of Shake-

spearean tragedy is, I believe, as I have tried to describe it
in *Hamlet*. Detailed discussion of *Macbeth, Othello,* and
King Lear would corroborate this pattern. Shakespeare's
experimentations in the plays written between those that
are called "the great tragedies" and the "last romances"
emphasize various components within the pattern, sometimes causing, indeed, stage experience that seems oddly
unbalanced (as in *Troilus and Cressida* or *Timon of Athens*),
or, more to the point, the presence of an emotional emphasis
upon a character or a series of events disproportionate to the
stage time used to distribute surrounding emphases. Surely
this is why those dramas we call the "problem plays" seem,
on stage or in the study, problematic.

Just as in terms of thematic criticism one might suggest
that the tranquillity of rediscovery, reunion, and the restoration of sexual or mercantile peace that exists at the conclusions of Shakespearean romance is parallel to the inner re-
discoveries and articulation of personal function that exist
at the conclusions of the tragedies, so it may be suggested
that the *theatrical* shape of the major tragedies is essentially
romantic in nature. The rhythm I have tried to describe in
Hamlet, and which I have suggested exists in many other
plays by Shakespeare, was of course first developed in forms
of literature—late Medieval and early Renaissance romances
—that were not in any case intended for the stage, and,
eventually, in theatrical terms, in some plays that were not
even by Shakespeare. The format of romance, first fully
developed in drama by Robert Greene, was distilled and
perfected by Shakespeare in the early years of his career,
and further developed during all the years he wrote for
the stage. The tempo and distribution of stage factors in
romance—setting forth physical and verbal images as well
as ideas—while essentially comedic in nature, come closer

to embodying the experience of Shakespearean tragedy than do other descriptive terms. While Shakespeare's development as a playwright was by no means orderly and is not describable in any pat nomenclature, his growth toward the compressed expression of the last plays on stage (and particularly, after the earlier elaborations of *Hamlet* and *Othello,* one thinks of the condensed structures of *Winter's Tale* and *The Tempest*) reminds one of Beethoven's progress from, say, the colossal elaborations of the Ninth Symphony and the *Missa Solemnis* to the economies of intensified but compressed expression of the last quartets.

Just as it used to be a cliché that Hamlet "delays," so now it is almost as great a critical commonplace to observe that, far from delaying, Hamlet is one of Shakespeare's most active characters. A study of the experienced shape of the play in the theater tells us in terms not so distant from those used by Sartre or R. D. Laing more exactly what the nature of the hero's action *is.* As this drama, and others like it, develop, what we see and hear is a furiously involved engagement of the self—or an effort so to engage—with all the outwardly perceived elements of life that in one way or another channel the individual's growing and authentic definition of *self*—not to put too fine a point on it, of *identity.* As Professors Lattimore and Else have pointed out, the most basic and ancient patterns of classical tragic plots are, perhaps more often than we make them out to be in our classrooms, quests and searches for a name joined with an action, frequently quite literally so. These searches and such a goal inform Shakespeare's greatest action as well. When personal identity is understood by the hero, a riddle is solved—not only intellectually but emotionally, as when some inner harassment has been removed, or translated into bearable terms.

This emotional end-point is the result of a theatrical rhythm, reinforced by visual and intellectual images, which moves from disorganized energies to a search for name and value. This search is usually fraught with danger. Stasis comes finally with a sense of discovery, or rediscovery, of an identifying function. The final movement is a recognition of and an acceptance of self, as the self's inner and outward experience has defined it, incrementally, during a certain time-span—whether this measured playing space be the several hours' traffic of a play or our own process through however many decades are allotted to us. I intend this comparison to be quite literal: great drama is not simply "like" life; it evokes life itself. The interim of which Hamlet speaks is his; but it is also mine:—ours.

The final effect of these great patterns, these shapes that performance articulates, is neither more nor less than a discovery of self, the self that is literally revealed and defined as the quality of what really is "in a name." Because we recognize the reality of these final discoveries, we contribute to them in some measure as Hamlet or Lear or Leontes do. Our closeness to these figures derives from the legitimate sensation of having participated in their creation, of having known their pulse of experience, and of recognizing in their final perceptions of self a potential understanding of our own, even though we lack their intelligence, or courage, and especially their guilt and suffering.

Hamlet, Son of *Hamlet*

DAVID YOUNG

In the background an army of Norwegians marches past, off to war with Poland over "a little patch of ground/That hath in it no profit but the name." In the foreground the tragic hero broods on the way this event, like so many others, seems to detect his inadequacy. Personified "occasions" that ought to be indifferent to his dilemma "inform against" him as if they were spies and courtroom witnesses. A curious combination of self-pity and self-criticism is present in the notion. He goes on to muse on human capability and the necessity for its use, then to speculate on his own failure in terms so inappropriate to the man as we have come to know him—"bestial oblivion," "craven scruple"—that it is difficult to take them seriously. "Examples," he then says, "gross as earth exhort me." We know that "gross" means mainly "large," but it already carried such additional connotations as "coarse," "indelicate," and even "obscene." That lends an interesting flavor to the lines that follow:

> Witness this army of such mass and charge
> Led by a delicate and tender prince,
> Whose spirit with divine ambition puff'd
> Makes mouths at the invisible event
> Exposing what is mortal and unsure
> To all that fortune, death and danger dare,
> Even for an eggshell.
>   (4.4.47–53) [1]

Hugh Kenner once cited these lines in a poetry textbook as an illustration of the way poetry can rapidly shift its tone and texture. Let's begin a scrutiny of them with his help:

> We start with an expansive gesture, its substance enforced by the prolonged sound and large abstractness of the words *mass* and *charge*. . . . What happens next? The army is re-placed by a single figure, and the sound becomes quick and delicate; you cannot make that line sound impressive no mat-ter how hard you try. What happens next? The prince is enlarged like a bubble, a balloon or a puff of smoke. . . . Note the force of *divine* in keeping this image clear of the ludicrous. What happens next? A sudden superimposition of the cannon's mouth, the commander's shout, and a rude ges-ture. . . . But surprisingly, the line maintains its dignity. What happens next? Mortality and uncertainty are surrounded by thunderous enemies . . . [and] the passage suddenly closes on an image which combines potentiality, fragility, and ap-parent insignificance . . . a series of surprising shifts of direc-tion and focus, from "Witness this army" to "egg-shell." [2]

That Kenner can take the lines on their own terms and subject them to such sensitive tracing, is one kind of evi-dence of the pulsing energy and ample fertility of meaning that are perhaps the major features of the language of *Ham-let*. When we tuck the lines back into their dramatic con-

---

1. Quotations are from the Signet edition of the play, ed. Edward Hubler, in *The Complete Signet Shakespeare* (New York: Harcourt-Brace Jovanovich, 1972).
2. *The Art of Poetry* (New York: Holt, Rinehart & Winston, 1961), pp. 135–36.

text we find a number of other matters of interest coming to light. The tensions in the passage keep pointing to that figure in the foreground, and his complex history. If the example of Fortinbras and his army was gross as earth to begin with, it is considerably refined by the time our hero has wrapped it in his rawer breath, for we spy in him the delicate and tender prince much more than we do in Fortinbras; we have heard him comment on ambition earlier ("I could be bounded in a nutshell and count myself a king of infinite space, were it not that I have bad dreams"); and we know how many meanings the phrase "invisible event" can gather to itself in this world. As for Fortune, to take one member of that trio against whom the stakes are thrown for the eggshell, we have heard her cursed as a strumpet in the player's speech, and she has been variously attributed with a cap, a navel, private parts, a recorder, slings and arrows, and an influence that asserts itself through a star. My mental nickname for this passage has always been "the eggshell speech," partly because the image is so striking, but probably also because that is the one detail in it that really constitutes an addition to the play's vocabulary.

What mixed feelings these lines arouse in us! Hamlet tells us that he is the negative half of the example, Fortinbras the positive, but how can we accept that? Even if we dodge the question of the morality of a prince who marches his army off to die for ends that are largely personal, we are bound to be left uneasy about the relation of Fortinbras's "divine" ambition to the goal in sight, which is, variously, "an eggshell," "a patch of ground," "a straw," and "a fantasy and trick of fame." Hamlet seems to find him the more admirable for the pointlessness of his endeavor; he felt the same way about the player's weeping for Hecuba. But we may feel, like Horatio, that in both cases he is considering too curiously. Our wonder and interest, at any rate, are not in question. We would rather listen to Hamlet all day than watch the Norwegian troops go off to battle; we know a hawk from a handsaw.

One more point about this moment before I turn to its application to my thesis: it is often cut from productions, when directors are trying to deal with the length and complexity of the play. Indeed, the soliloquy itself is omitted from the First Folio text; we have it only because we have the Second Quarto. Another instancing of the richness of *Hamlet.*

II

I have chosen this single example as a means of posing once more the perennial, unanswerable question that seems to lurk around so many discussions of *Hamlet:* what gives this play its astonishing expressive power, how can we account for its enormously vibrant way with language? For that is surely one of our keenest senses of its uniqueness. When Alfred Harbage says, "Throughout its great and turbulent length, there is not a shoddy line," [3] we know that his statement cannot be taken literally at the same time that we recognize, instantly, that he has found one means of expressing what it is that makes us care so much for this three hundred and seventy-year-old tragedy about murder, intrigue, and revenge in medieval Denmark.

Both Kenner and Harbage emphasize language, and insofar as they do so, we must recognize that one answer to our question lies in the affirmation that Shakespeare was a

3. *William Shakespeare: A Reader's Guide* (New York: Noonday, 1963), p. 340.

great poet, and that when he wrote *Hamlet* he was at the
height of his powers. We can admit the truth of that even
as we object that as a complete answer it begs the question;
we are talking not of a poem but of a play. To that objection
one might respond somewhat as follows: that Shakespeare's
poetic genius was, as C. S. Lewis has said, best expressed in
what he calls a "nibbling" style, the continually shifting and
glancing engagement of imagination and reality that Kenner
very ably shows the exemplary passage above to be; that
such a style was well suited to dramatic poetry; that in
Hamlet and his dilemma Shakespeare found a character and
a dramatic situation perfectly fitted to such a style, the
result being a play that called most fully and effectively
on the poet's own temperament and inclinations.[4]

Such an explanation is very persuasive, but I am not
completely satisfied with it because I think it slides too
easily over the issue of the peculiar conditions in which
great drama must come to being. To assign epic to Milton
(because his style is *not* a "nibbling" one) and drama to
Shakespeare, is to fix the gaze too much on varieties of
poetic expression and too little on the phenomenon of
drama, all the life and being and meaning of theatrical
performance. It is with this in mind that I am going to ask
you to consider once more *Hamlet's* relation to its source or
sources; I do this not from curiosity about Shakespeare's

4. "Where Milton marches steadily forward, Shakespeare behaves
rather like a swallow. He darts at the subject and glances away; and
then he is back again before your eyes can follow him. It is as if he
kept on having tries at it, and being dissatisfied. He darts image after
image at you and still seems to think that he has not done enough. . . .
He wants to see the object from a dozen different angles; if the undig-
nified word is pardonable, he *nibbles*, like a man trying a tough biscuit
now from this side and now from that." C. S. Lewis, *Rehabilitations and
Other Essays* (London: Oxford University Press, 1939), p. 162. Lewis does
not apply this to *Hamlet;* a student of mine, David Lebeaux, developed
the relation of the quote to the character of Hamlet, and it was through
him that the Lewis quote came to my attention.

artistic debts or even, in this case, his working habits as a dramatist, but out of an interest in what might be called the *ecology* (I know the word is overused these days) of the play, the interaction of dramatist, theater, audience, actors, and sociohistorical conditions that made the existence and importance of *Hamlet* possible. A counterweight, if you like, to the very legitimate claims made on behalf of Shakespeare's poetic genius.

Let me sketch out a few principles on which I think we can effectively proceed. First, that the *condition* of drama lies in the expectations of the audience. In speaking of the theater as an artistic medium we talk of actors, staging, costumes, and so on, but we often neglect the fact that the simultaneous response of a large and usually heterogeneous group of people is what the dramatist must work with. Whatever he hopes to accomplish must succeed through effective evocation and control of that response; such is the peculiar and vital condition of his art.

Out of that principle grows a second. If the dramatist must work with the expectations of his audience, then all drama will be a combination of the familiar and the surprising. A purely novel drama, in which nothing was familiar, *like* life or *like* other dramas, is impossible to imagine. However inventive the dramatist, his inventions must begin as variations on what his audience knows and/ or has some reason to expect in the theater. This is as true of Beckett and Ionesco as it is of Shakespeare and Molière.

If we next consider the kinds of familiarity a dramatist can call upon as matrix for his orginality—ritual and myth, known events (contemporary or historical), familiar character types, situation and conventions that have grown up with a particular theatrical tradition, and, indeed, other well-known plays—we can begin to see a third principle taking shape: as drama grows more sophisticated within a given line of development, its sources of familiarity grow more complex, since dramatists will inevitably draw upon earlier plays held in common by the audience, as well as upon known events and myths. Greek tragedy affords an obvious example of this process, as for instance in the three versions of the Electra story by Aeschylus, Sophocles, and Euripides, each play complicated (for better or for worse) by its audience's knowledge of the previous dramatizations of the same material.[5]

III

Suppose we ask of *Hamlet,* then, what were the expectations of its audience, and, in turn, what was familiar in it and what was novel and surprising? These questions can be answered in more detail than you might expect, and they may very well lead us to a better understanding of Shakespeare's achievement in the dramatic medium, and of what might be called the interpenetration of his abilities as a poet and as a playwright.

First, a piece of familiar knowledge: there was an older play about the Hamlet legend, not by Shakespeare, quite familiar to Elizabethan audiences. The *Ur-Hamlet,* as it is called, has not survived, but contemporary references allow us to characterize it fairly effectively. Here is Thomas Nashe, in 1589, in the preface to a pamphlet, making fun of English translators and imitators of Seneca, and of one in particular, almost certainly Thomas Kyd:

5. Lionel Abel, in his *Metatheatre,* uses this example in a discussion of *Hamlet,* but he does not, in my opinion, follow through on its implications.

yet English *Seneca* read by Candlelight yeelds many good
sentences, as *Blood is a begger,* and so forth; and if you
intreate him faire in a frostie morning, hee will affoord you
whol Hamlets, I should say handfuls of Tragicall speeches.
But O griefe! *Tempus edax rerum,* whats that will last al-
wayes? The Sea exhaled by droppes will in continuance bee
drie, and *Seneca,* let blood line by line and page by page, at
length must needes die to our Stage.[6]

The earlier play, then, was a Senecan tragedy of revenge,
bloody and bombastic, probably by Kyd, "the English
Seneca." In Kyd's surviving play, *The Spanish Tragedy,* we
have a good example of the type, and in Shakespeare's
early *Titus Andronicus,* a close imitation. Complex structures
of intrigue, exalted rhetoric, bloody incidents, obstacles that
frustrate the hero's revenge until the very end and that
result in his only partially feigned madness, and a spectacu-
lar device by which revenge is finally accomplished: in
The Spanish Tragedy a play-within-a-play, in *Titus* a Thy-
estian banquet. These are the characteristics of the type,
and we can see them surviving in *Hamlet.*

If, as we suspect, Thomas Kyd was the author of the
Ur-Hamlet, then we must add another factor to our sense
of the conditions that made Shakespeare's *Hamlet* possible.
For Kyd stands out among the playwrights of his time for
the degree to which his sensibility was attuned to the possibilities of theatricality as a metaphor for existence; his play
begins with an Induction that makes all that follows a sort
of command performance for the benefit of a ghost and the
personification of Revenge. Illusion and artifice are thus
stressed from the outset, and they are strengthened by
various kinds of role-playing and disguise until the play
reaches its climax as the revenging hero Hieronimo stages a

6. Geoffrey Bullough, *Narrative and Dramatic Sources of Shakespeare*
(New York: Columbia University Press, 1973), 7: 15.

court performance in which he is able to make an acted tragedy a true event and the supposedly feigned deaths of his enemies the reality he has sought throughout, discharging the tension of seeming and being that has persisted from the beginning. Since one of the things we value most about Shakespeare's *Hamlet* is its exploration of the interdependence of seeming and being, its use of its own medium —actors, plays, histrionic behavior, a theater in which the bait of falsehood takes the carp of truth—to take us ever closer to an understanding of the nature of illusion and reality, we must acknowledge that Shakespeare's transformations from Kyd are not simply a great artist turning negligible junk to gold, but rather a kind of homage from one artist to another, or, to return to my risky ecological metaphor, a marvellous recycling of illusion that seemed to have lost its power to catch the carp of truth or the conscience of the king or the attention of a more sophisticated audience.

IV

The most memorable part of the old *Hamlet* seems to have been the ghost, a typical Senecan device for introducing the information and the impulse to revenge. In a pamphlet written in 1596, an evil spirit is described as looking "as pale as the Visard of the ghost which cried so miserably at the Theator, like an oister wife, Hamlet, revenge." Even greater familiarity is implied in a comedy (1602) where a character facetiously exclaims, "my name's Hamlet revenge," which suggests that the ghost's cry had become a kind of slang term.[7]

7. Both references quoted from *The Reader's Encyclopedia of Shake-Speare*, ed. Campbell and Quinn (New York: Thomas Y. Crowell, 1966), pp. 925–26.

We know then that the earlier play, beyond its general Senecan emphasis on gore, madness, and revenge, had a demanding ghost that was a theatrical favorite. Let us see if that knowledge will help explain an especially strange moment in Shakespeare's play. You will recall how the issues of appearance and reality, truth and illusion, are continually called to our attention as the first act builds toward the climactic interview between dead father and living son. The injunction is issued, the ghost disappears, and the hero, shaken and half-hysterical, finds himself once more in the company of his friends. There now follows one of the oddest scenes in all of Shakespeare. As Hamlet asks Horatio and Marcellus to swear silence, he also begins to make fun of the ghost, who is speaking from beneath the stage :

Ghost cries under the stage
GHOST
  Swear.
HAMLET
  Ha, ha, boy, say'st thou so? Art thou there truepenny?
  Come on. You hear this fellow in the cellarage.
  Consent to swear.
HORATIO
                Propose the oath, my lord.
HAMLET
  Never to speak of this that you have seen.
  Swear by my sword.
GHOST (*Beneath*)
                Swear.
HAMLET
  Hic et ubique? Then we'll shift our ground;
  Come hither, gentlemen,
  And lay your hands again upon my sword.
  Swear by my sword
  Never to speak of this that you have heard.
GHOST (*Beneath*)
  Swear by his sword.

HAMLET
Well said, old mole! Canst work i' th' earth so fast?
A worthy pioner! Once more remove, good friends.
HORATIO
O day and night, but this is wondrous strange!
(1.5.149–64)

Indeed it is. We may try to explain it away by saying that Hamlet is trying his antic disposition on, that he is suffering from whatever sort of shock may be said to afflict people whose fathers rise from the dead to reveal murder and order revenge. But none of those factors seems to me a sufficient explanation. Consider what is happening in terms of actual performance. The ghost is offering up gruesome sound effects from beneath the stage, as he undoubtedly did in the old play. Probably that reiterated cry "Hamlet revenge" kept floating up from underneath during the *Ur-Hamlet*. Its occurrence in this version is too much to take seriously, so Shakespeare daringly breaks the tension by letting his hero mock it; if the audience does not remember the old play, he certainly jogs their memories and strengthens their sense of the general staginess of the ghost with words like "truepenny," and "pioner" and "mole" and "cellarage" (true not for the castle battlement, but true enough for the stage of the Globe, where there was an underneath area, available through a trapdoor and associated with cellars, graves, hell, and the appearance and disappearance of devils and spirits).

When we have said that Shakespeare seems to want here to deliberately evoke a histrionic and moldy old play, we have not yet understood why. We might suppose that he wants, invoking the theory about the collocation of familiar and surprising, to give the audience what they want and at the same time take them beyond the taste that made them want it. No doubt there is truth to that, but I think that there is another, even more interesting, way of accounting for it. I think he has found a way of connecting a series of relationships—past and present, father and son, old play and new play, simplicity and complexity, illusion and reality, death and life—that is the equivalent, theatrically, of the rich, expressive language we were examining earlier. The strain on the theatrical medium is, for a moment, enormous, but the effect of the gesture will spread meaning through the entire play. And Shakespeare allows us, meanwhile, to drop into more familiar recognitions; at the Ghost's last "Swear," Hamlet reacts not as a theater critic or an actor or a dramatist, but as a son: "Rest, rest, perturbed spirit." That response is something like a relief; we are back in the new play again, and the Ghost is not the old play, or Kyd, or an actor who played in the *Ur-Hamlet* eleven or twelve years ago, but, more reasonably, what we took it to be in the first place: Hamlet's father's spirit.

V

I have suggested that Hamlet's jocular savage response to the ghost beneath the stage means a number of things at once to the audience. What it means to Hamlet himself is well worth exploring too. In his response to the old mole in the cellarage we suddenly catch a glimpse of a man who is, perhaps rather painfully, aware of his situation as that of a figure in a crude and outdated story. Suddenly, and without warning, he has been cast as a sort of Laertes or Fortinbras, a man of action who must proceed straight to his task without questioning its rightness or its alternatives. But a sensitive and thoughtful man cannot act such a part without considerable discomfort. This theme—it surely deserves to be called such—will preoccupy us for much of the play, but to raise it by reminding the audience of the older play and by making the hero aware both of his own deficiencies and of the shortcomings of the situation in explicitly theatrical terms is really a master stroke.

One immediate effect, as I suggested earlier, is to bring a number of opposites together in an emphatic dialectic. It is ironic, really, that "To be or not to be" should be the most famous line in *Hamlet,* for its posing of opposites between which one is supposed to have to choose is far from characteristic of the play; "to be *and* not to be" would be more to the point, given the tendency for opposite states to exist simultaneously within characters, situations, and the meanings of spoken lines. We have just noted that Hamlet manages both to be enormously respectful and astonishingly disrespectful to his father's ghost; we have heard Horatio, following Marcellus's account of the legend that roosters crow nightlong during the Christmas season and thus ward off evil spirits, say "So have I heard and do in part believe it" (1.1.65); and Hamlet himself has talked, just before the appearance of the Ghost, of men who may be mainly good and noble yet accidentally carry "some vicious mole of nature in them" that is their undoing. (I do not *insist* on connecting this kind of mole with the old mole under the stage, but the conjunction of the two words is certainly interesting.)

One purpose these examples of dialectic may serve is to provide us with a means of relating some of the more incidental matters to the main action; in the next scene, for example, we see a father sending his servant to spy on his son for the boy's own good, explaining laboriously how truth and falsehood, direction and indirection, necessarily interact. I am more interested, however, for the moment, in exploring the dialectic as it can be perceived in the tragic hero: in the sense in which, for example, it can be said that Hamlet both does and does not accept his role. For Polonius has no sooner dispatched Reynaldo than Ophelia enters, breathlessly, to report Hamlet's peculiar visit to her "closet." It is our first encounter with the "antic disposition," which we cautiously assume he has put on to further the accomplishment of his revenge.

I say "cautiously" because I think that Shakespeare does some extremely complicated and subtle things with Hamlet's "lunacy." Once again, as with the ghost, he begins with a *given,* in this case a feature long associated with the story; here is Saxo Grammaticus:

> Amleth beheld all this, but feared lest too shrewd a behaviour might make his uncle suspect him. So he chose to feign dulness, and pretend an utter lack of wits. This cunning course not only concealed his intelligence but ensured his safety. Every day he remained in his mother's house utterly listless and unclean, flinging himself on the ground and bespattering his person with foul and filthy dirt. His discoloured face and visage smutched with slime denoted a foolish and grotesque madness. All he said was of a piece with these follies; all he did savoured of utter lethargy.[8]

Saxo's Amleth is suspected, and various tests intended to trick him into betraying his sanity are used without success; in his cunning he is often able to speak the truth in a way that seems ludicrous and unbelievable to his listeners, as when he chops up the body of the Polonius-figure and feeds it to the pigs, a fate grotesque enough that when he announces that the pigs have eaten the missing courtier, he is, as Saxo says, "flouted."

8. Bullough, p. 62.

Early on, then, the madness of Hamlet began to have an ambiguity about it, being both less sane and more sane than the norm. Just how fully this possibility was exploited in the *Ur-Hamlet* we do not know, although it seems reasonable to suspect that it was present in a far cruder fashion than in Shakespeare. The curious German play *Der bestrafte Brudermord* (Fratricide Punished), which may well have been derived from the earlier play, shows Hamlet mad mostly in terms of not recognizing people he knows and a bit of modest raving at Ophelia. This fools Polonius (here called, as in the First Quarto, Corambus!), but it does not fool the king. Moreover, there is no doubt that, as in Saxo's version, it is completely assumed.

It is difficult to know whether we ought to announce that Shakespeare has intensified something he found in his sources, or simply transcended them altogether, so striking a device does he make the lunacy for projecting the sense of duality, the tension between seeming and being, familiar and surprising, that we have found elsewhere. Consider: Hamlet's visit to Ophelia is taken for madness, and we in turn take it for crafty role-playing. But that it also perfectly expresses his feelings—he loved her, his new duty makes an end to that, he here takes his farewell—seems evident. When Ophelia says that he looked "As if he had been loosed out of hell/To speak of horrors," we know how close she comes, for we understand how this connects him with his father and binds new play to old. Given the actual circumstances, there is scarcely anything unreasonable about his behavior.

Consider too his next appearance, an interview with Polonius in which, once again, he is able to conceal his feelings and vent them at the same time. His "nonrecognition" convinces Polonius—"Yet he knew me not at first. A' said I was a fishmonger"—while it simultaneously strikes us as a more accurate "knowing" of the old meddler and peddler whose smell gives away his profession immediately. The effect in this case is comic, but the portrait of the hero who has replaced the traditional virtues of courage, stoic patience, and honor with the more fluid characteristics of guile, cunning, and a rapid wit, is being built up in a consistent manner.

Yet it is not simply a matter of our admiration for Hamlet's ability to play for two audiences at once, or to project both falsehood and truth with the same phrase or gesture. For the question of his self-control, as already raised in the platform scene, is not easily disposed of. This is why I would emphatically reject Dover Wilson's suggestion that Hamlet be given a silent entrance so that he can overhear the plotting of the "nunnery" scene; it resolves uncertainty where Shakespeare seems to have deliberately created it.[9] Watching the interview with Ophelia (and, later, the interview with Gertrude), we find that we are losing some of our assurance about Hamlet's acting. Is this a role, based on his suspicion that Claudius and Polonius are listening nearby, or is he really on the brink of madness? It is as though the duality, the ability to incorporate opposites, has begun to affect his behavior and our confidence in him. Such questions, as I have said, tended to be clarified in the sources; yet there is a marvelous sequence in Saxo, when Amleth is in England, where he seems to reveal magical powers that were not a part of our simpler sense of his cunning, and which lead Saxo to say:

O valiant Amleth, and worthy of immortal fame, who being shrewdly armed with a feint of folly, covered a wisdom too high for human wit under a marvelous disguise of silliness![10]

9. Dover Wilson's suggestion is advanced in his *What Happens in Hamlet* (Cambridge: Macmillan, 1935).
10. Bullough, p. 70.

We do not get a sense of "wisdom too high for human wit" if we pluck out the heart of the mystery with cut-and-dried explanations of Hamlet's madness and his every act and speech; he must incorporate heaven and hell in a fashion that sometimes makes them indistinguishable.

VI

Another way of understanding the extension and transformation that Shakespeare is accomplishing with his sources, in particular the old play, is to examine the theatrical metaphor on which so much of the action and imagery is based. There is no need, surely, to document all the instances of theatricality in the play, but it is a useful exercise, I think, when we have recognized Shakespeare's Hamlet as a man who is unhappy with the role for which fortune has cast him, to consider the extent to which he tries to abandon the role of actor for the more authoritative roles of director and playwright.

That is one way, at least, of looking at his seizing on the device of the play-within-a-play. Time does not permit me to examine the arrival of the players in detail, but let me ask you to consider once more the famous speech that precedes Rosencrantz's announcement of their approach:

> I have of late, but wherefore I know not, lost all my mirth, forgone all custom of exercises; and indeed, it goes so heavily with my disposition that this goodly frame, the earth, seems to me a sterile promontory; this most excellent canopy, the air, look you, this brave o'erhanging firmament, this majestical roof fretted with golden fire: why it appeareth nothing to me but a foul and pestilent congregation of vapors.
>
> (2.2.292–99)

Let me pause here to note that this is a good description of an Elizabethan theater—promontory stage, overhanging canopy decorated with gold and meant to symbolize the firmament—and that the "look you" may be a literal invitation to Rosencrantz, Guildenstern, and the audience to consider the building they are standing in. It is a still-life of the world as theater and theater as world, a foul fairness, a pestilent excellence. And it is capped with the similarly inclusive portrait of man as angel and quintessence of dust. Both portraits are still points in the turning world, both hold in balance the dialectical knowledge, embracing opposites, that so excites and unnerves Hamlet and his audience. When the arrival of the players is announced, however, Hamlet's style suddenly shifts from descriptions of passive comprehension of opposites to a welter of fulfilling theatrical activities:

> He that plays the king shall be welcome; his majesty shall have tribute of me; the adventurous knight shall use his foil and target; the lover shall not sigh gratis; the humorous man shall end his part in peace; the clown shall make those laugh whose lungs are tickle o' th' sere; and the lady shall say her mind freely, or the blank verse shall halt for it.

This catalogue of events is both a standard set of theatrical types and shabby plots, and a list that has wonderful parallels in the action of the play. But the encompassing gesture is one that foresees activity; Hamlet has seized the initiative. He will use true illusion against false reality, and he will begin from now on to sound more like a director—giving critiques of acting, assessing a speech from an old play, instructing the company before the performance—and like a playwright—plotting a far cleverer play than the one Polonius stages with Ophelia as bait—to give him "grounds more relative." Perhaps we cannot quite decide whether he is doing this to evade his more difficult task or to strengthen and justify it. But we sense that things have begun to move, and we delight, for awhile, in Hamlet's apparent success.

His staging of *The Mousetrap* is an assertion of his mastery over illusion, his ability to discriminate between seeming and being, and a reshaping of the action so that his impetus to revenge comes not from a ghost—a "seeming" outside his control and understanding—but from the power of feigning to expose a guilty creature. But the very success of the play-within-a-play, as Hamlet fails to notice in his elation, is illusory, for it returns the action to the beginning and it does not dispose of Claudius. Its worst effect is to give Hamlet an overconfidence in which he passes up the opportunity to kill Claudius in favor of a more dramatically appropriate occasion; but this is decidedly an error of judgment, since Claudius only *appears* to be praying. Hamlet's error of overconfidence is confirmed in the next scene when he stabs through the arras, thinking he has the king in the appropriate placement for revenge, and kills Polonius. The immediate effect is a kind of hysteria in which he suffers, alone, the reappearance of the ghost, a signal that he has not succeeded in rewriting his part at all; the more far-reaching effect is to reestablish his destiny as doomed tragic hero. When he returns from England he will have accepted his role, as written, relapsing from directing to acting, and his comments on the larger forces that represent destiny will have shifted from the images of strumpet Fortune to a "heaven" that is "ordinant" and a "divinity that shapes our ends,/Rough-hew them how we will." Those comments may or may not announce metaphysical truths, but they effectively define Hamlet's new attitude toward the play and his part: the authoring of events is out of his hands—only readiness will serve him effectively. The fatalism carries him

into the last play within this play, the real-mock duel staged
by the king and Laertes. That Hamlet can still be deceived
—he says of Laertes, having earlier upstaged him and criticized his acting in the graveyard, "by the image of my
cause I see/The portraiture of his"—makes no difference
in this changed context.

VII

I turn away from the theatrical metaphor reluctantly, so
rich is it and so fruitful to our attempts to understand this
play. But it has been discussed elsewhere, and is available
to any careful reader.[11] I want to take a moment to point
out one further aspect of *Hamlet* that derives, I think, from
what I have called its theatrical ecology, its complicated
relation to an earlier dramatic version (less visible, alas, than
the Ghost). That is its special ability to create involvement
and detachment, to move with celerity from one to the
other, to intertwine them astonishingly. Again, the sudden
reversal of attitude toward the ghost exemplifies what I am
talking about, as do the line-to-line shifts in the poetry that
Kenner called our attention to. But this quality is surely
most of all associated with the hero, who turns emotional
corners on two wheels, as it were, and whose breathless
passengers the audience in a good production must inevitably come to be. I suppose this ebb and flow of engagement
and detachment, to use the pair of terms Maynard Mack
employs,[12] is what we refer to in a fairly confused way when

11. Other discussions include Abel's, Anne Righter's, in her *Shakespeare and the Idea of the Play* (London: Chatto and Windus, 1962),
and Charles R. Forker, "Shakespeare's Theatrical Symbolism and Its
Function in *Hamlet,*" *Shakespeare Quarterly* 14 (1963): 215–29.
12. "Engagement and Detachment in Shakespeare's Plays," in *Essays*

we say that Hamlet is dangerously given over to contemplation (i.e., helplessly detaching himself when he ought to be engaged), or that he cannot make up his mind. There must be countless ways to illustrate the way this quality informs the play, but I shall restrict myself to a very brief comparison of two scenes: the interview with the ghost, and the scene in the graveyard.

There are a number of interesting parallels between these two scenes. Both involve, for example, the area below the stage, in the first instance the source of the Ghost's injunctions to swear secrecy, in the second the grave where the sexton-clown, visually not much more than a head sticking up from a grave and bandying jokes with the hero (shades of Beckett!), produces the skull of Yorick, the king's jester, a death's-head who grins and silently provokes some marvelous twists and turns in our hero's imagination. Associating the skull and the ghost makes us consider Yorick as a kind of alternate father to Hamlet. This one, a fellow of infinite jest and excellent fancy, has borne Hamlet on his back a thousand times and kissed him as often. But if he sounds like a sort of spiritual parent, we must consider him a kind of counterpart as well. Yorick was "a whoreson mad fellow . . . a mad rogue," and the jester's part in this play has been taken by the prince, who found madness and foolishness more congenial and useful than heroism. For an instant, a whole set of opposites join in a flash of insight— Hamlet's image closing with that of his father in a different way from what it did when he found his father's signet in his purse and, writing a letter of state, played for the first time the role of king—and then Hamlet tosses the image of

on *Shakespeare and Elizabethan Drama in Honor of Hardin Craig* (Columbia, Mo.: University of Missouri Press, 1963), pp. 275–96.

Alexander, a smelly old piece of bone, to one side and the play goes on.

I think the difference in our feeling about the two scenes in which Hamlet confronts these manifestations of the undiscovered country from whose bourn no traveler returns is measured by the difference in his feeling. Both he and we seem to have come a long way from that platform where the figure of the father harrowed us with fear and wonder, and where the jesting and mocking urge created a terrible tension, to this place, quiet except for the steady sound of the shovel and the singing of the old sexton, where we can be grave and witty at once, as father and son, life and death, seeming and being, meet and are at ease. The distance is of course the whole action of *Hamlet,* but it is also the accommodation of the old play and the new. I can't *prove,* obviously, that there was no graveyard scene in the old play, but it is surely clear why I feel I have every right to suspect it. For the ghost scene, surely, is the kind of scene that Shakespeare had to work with as he began, while the graveyard scene, just as surely, seems to be what he was working toward. The tendency that forced Hamlet at first toward opposites, violently, painfully, to be *or* not to be, involvement *or* detachment, has moved, with a success that takes one's breath away, to a detachment that is involvement ("the readiness is all"), a man looking thoughtfully into the eyes of a skull. Just how it all came about is not easy to understand, but it had something to do with making an old play new, reconciling a man to his fate, killing a king that a kingdom might survive.

We can return to my opening example, "gross as earth":

> Witness this army of such mass and charge
> Led by a delicate and tender prince,

Whose spirit with divine ambition puff'd
Makes mouths at the invisible event
Exposing what is mortal and unsure
To all that fortune, death and danger dare,
Even for an eggshell.

(4.4.47–53)

A swarm of words transforming a simple and silly event to something of great interest and beauty by darting around it from all directions. It is Hamlet's way. It was Shakespeare's. And if we do not have the advantage of his audience in knowing the old play and witnessing the transformations directly, we have something like the equivalent in the way that *Hamlet* has come to bear such an enormous cultural weight for us that it begins to bore us with what we think is our familiarity and its triteness until we pick it up again or have the good luck to see a strong performance, and are suddenly confronted again with its fierce energies and its apparently endless power to quicken and create where we thought there was mostly dust and death.

Hamlet, Gide, and Barrault*

NANCY LEE CAIRNS

Comprehension of the challenges and enormous pitfalls that awaited the French actor-director Jean-Louis Barrault, who had the temerity to undertake Shakespeare's *Hamlet,* is impossible for one unfamiliar with the history in France of the "monstrous farce," as the play was christened by Voltaire two centuries ago.[1] In the "Forward" to her inclusive study, *Hamlet in France,* Helen Phelps Bailey has stated the problem succinctly.

> Of all Shakespeare's dramatic works none, of course, presents so many problems as his *Hamlet,* none would seem less

* The translations of all French texts are mine, unless otherwise indicated, and are purposefully literal rather than literary, because I feel this best serves the interest of clarity. For the texts dating from the eighteenth century, I have used Randle Cotgrave, *A Dictionarie of the French and English Tongues* (London, 1611. Reprinted by George Olms Verlag, Hildesheim and New York, 1970). And for the others, *Harrap's Shorter French and English Dictionary,* rev. ed. (1967), and *Le Petit Robert* (1970).

1. In "Lettre XVIII" of his Lettres Philosophiques (1734), Voltaire categorically applies this label to all of Shakespeare's tragedies: ". . . il y a de si belles scènes, des morceaux si grands et si terribles répandus dans ses farces monstrueuses qu'on appelle tragédies, que ces pièces ont toujours été jouées avec un grand succès."

congenial to the French temperament, less likely to find a place in the structure of French dramatic tradition. The very label "tragedy" affixed to the play from the earliest mention of it, evoked a work in alexandrine verse, subject to rigid rules adapted from antiquity itself and to a code of conventions rooted in nearly two hundred years of custom and taste. . . . Yet the "monstrous farce" presumably devised for the entertainment of an alien people in a barbaric age, was to become for the poets of the late nineteenth century a symbolic masterpiece transcending nationality and time.[2]

It is true, also, that by the nineteenth century French scholars were quick to point out that it was a Frenchman, the prolific compiler, translator, and historiographer, François de Belleforest (1530–1583), who furnished Shakespeare with one of his most important sources for the play. Belleforest was the first to procure the story from the Latin edition, the *Panorum regum heroumque historiae* of Saxo Grammaticus, printed in Paris in March 1514 on the presses of Jodocus Badius Ascensius by the Canon de Lund (Christiern Pederson).[3] Belleforest's amplified version of the tale appeared in Book V of his *Histoires tragiques* in 1570, but it took nearly two hundred years for the story to make its impact on the French public in Ducis's adaptation of Shakespeare's *Hamlet*. This is not to say that Shakespeare was unknown in France during the seventeenth century. Copies of his works were found in the libraries of Louis XIV and his ill-fated minister, Fouquet (1615–1680). Nicolas Clément, librarian to the "Sun King" wrote: "This English poet has a rather fine imagination; he thinks naturally, he expresses himself skilfully; but these fine qualities are obscured by the obscenities which he mingles in his comedies." [4] Léon

2. Helen Phelps Bailey, *Hamlet in France* (Geneva: Droz, 1964), xiii.
3. See Emile Henriot, "La Première Histoire d'Hamlet," *Livres et Portraits*. Deuxième Série. (Paris: Plon, 1925), pp. 40–45.
4. "Ce poète anglois a l'imagination assés belle, il pense naturelle-

Chancerel, A. José Axelrad, and other critics have remarked similarities between *Hamlet* and the *Folie du Sage* of Tristan l'Hermite and the *Trasibule* of Antoine de Montfleury.[5] Lancaster attributes this "slight resemblance" between the tragicomedy of Montfleury and the tragedy of Shakespeare to a "common source in Belleforest." [6]

With the rising tide of Anglomania that swept the eighteenth century, Shakespeare's reputation began to grow in France. Much of this was a result of Voltaire's well-known criticisms, which were at first mildly affirmative, and then progressively negative to the point of being blatantly unjust. It was Voltaire, nevertheless, who made the first translation of *Hamlet*, a fragment only, the "To be or not to be" soliloquy, a translation hardly designed to whet the literary appreciation of the Gallic reader for the English poet. The *philosophe*'s synopsis of the play from the "Dissertation sur la Tragédie" in *Sémiramis* is a classic example of his stinging wit. "This man with such a bold mind had a timid taste," wrote Brunetière.[7] Herein lies the crux of the matter: After the appearance of Letourneur's translation of Shakespeare, Voltaire felt the Bard was becoming too popular in France. He became deeply concerned that the classical tradition might be seriously corrupted by the intrusion of the barbarian from across the channel. Therefore, the first serious attempt to translate *Hamlet* was that of

ment, il s'exprime avec finesse; mais ces belles qualitez sont obsurcies par les ordures qu'il mêle dans ses Comedies." As quoted in J. J. Jusserand, *Shakespeare in France under the Ancient Régime* (New York: G. P. Putnam's Sons, 1889), p. 137.

5. A. José Axelrad, "Shakespeare's Impact Today in France," *Shakespeare Survey* 16 (Cambridge: at the University Press, 1963): 53.

6. Henry Carrington Lancaster, *A History of French Dramatic Literature in the Seventeenth Century* 5 (New York: Gordian Press, Inc., 1966): 122.

7. "Cet homme d'un esprit si hardi a eu le goût timide." Ferdinand Brunetière, quoted in *Voltaire et la Critique*, ed. Jean Sareil (Englewood Cliffs, N. J.: Prentice Hall, Inc., 1966), p. 14.

La Place in 1746. In order to observe the *bienséances,* the proprieties of his age, La Place combined synopses of entire scenes with passages translated in alexandrine verse and others translated in prose. He summarized the cellarage scene, the nunnery scene, and the latter part of the graveyard scene from the entrance of the funeral procession to the end of the play. He dismissed Hamlet's scathing remarks to his mother as "a few stinging barbs," and he inserted his own ideas on the moralistic values of the drama into Hamlet's advice to the players. No reference was made to Gertrude's shoes; the Queen was not called Gertrude by her husband, but "Madame"; the late king did not die in an orchard, but in an obscure grotto, and Shakespeare's "mere stones" became "marble." [8]

Two hundred years later, in 1946, Jean-Louis Barrault was to remark with justification that the entry of Shakespeare in France began with a crime. In crossing the channel the Bard underwent an operation suffered as a result of vandalism: his verbal form was amputated.[9] *Hamlet,* in particular, suffered much from the literary vandals. Jean-François Ducis adapted the play for the French stage twenty-four years after La Place's translation, and it was the first of Shakespeare's works to be performed there. Although Ducis's adulation of Shakespeare went to the point that he celebrated each year the fete of Saint-Guillaume by crowning a bust of the poet with a laurel wreath [10]—the bust he kept in his study beside a portrait of Garrick in the role of Hamlet—he was seriously handicapped in his undertaking: his enthusiasm for the Bard was equaled only by his

8. Bailey, pp. 8–12.

9. Jean-Louis Barrault, *A Propos de Shakespeare et du Théâtre* (Fontainebleau: La Parade, 1949), pp. 10–11.

10. J. D. Golder, "'Hamlet' in France 200 Years Ago," *Shakespeare Survey* 24 (1971): 79.

ignorance of English. He was, therefore, completely reliant
on the translation of La Place. Ducis attempted to justify
his arduous undertaking in a letter written to Garrick:

> I conceive, Sir, that you must have thought me exceed-
> ingly rash in placing such a tragedy as *Hamlet* on the French
> stage. Not to speak of the barbarous irregularities with which
> it abounds—the spectre in full armour and long speeches, the
> strolling actors, the fencing bout—all these appeared to me
> to be matters utterly inadmissible on the French stage. Never-
> theless, I deeply regretted being obliged, in a certain sense,
> to create a new play: I simply tried to make an interesting
> part of a parricidal Queen and above all to paint in the pure
> and melancholy soul of Hamlet a model of filial tenderness.[11]

In the hands of Ducis the "monstrous farce" became a
scrupulously faithful classical French play. The unities of
time, place, and action were preserved. The time of the
play is contained well within the twenty-four hour period;
the great hall of the palace is the sole setting; and the
action is limited to a court intrigue. A touching scene in
act 1, scene 2, between Hamlet and Ophélie, in which each
one in turn renounces love in the name of filial duty, comes
directly from Corneille's *Le Cid:*

> Mon devoir désormais m'est dicté par le tien:
> Tu cours venger ton père, et moi sauver le mien.[12]

11. Quoted by Paul Benchettrit, "Hamlet at the Comédie Française:
1769–1896," *Shakespeare Survey* 9 (1956): 59. Unfortunately, we don't
have Garrick's reply to this letter, but we do have a letter that he wrote
on January 21, 1773, in appreciation for a copy of Ducis's adaptation of
Romeo and Juliet. ". . . Si votre intention Etoit de venir en Angleterre
pour apprendre notre langue, et de voir plus pres les grandes et Sublimes
beautés de notre Poete immortel Je crois vous devoir les Entrées de nos
Spectacles comme un hommage qui est due aux Soins que vous aviez pris
avec tant de Succes de faire connoitre notre Shakespeare En France,
d'une manière Si avantageuse. . . ." David M. Little and George M.
Kahrl, eds., *The Letters of David Garrick.* II, Letters 335–815. (Cambridge, Mass.: The Belknap Press of Harvard University Press, 1963),
p. 852, no. 741.
    12. Jean-François Ducis, "*Hamlet* Tragédie en Cinq Actes, Imitée de

(My duty henceforth is prescribed by yours:
You go to avenge your father, and I, to save mine.).

It is not surprising, then, that Gertrude should be given a confidante named Elvire. Ducis gave the Queen a role equally important as that of Hamlet. In fact, in Ducis's 1769 version of the play, she has 420 lines to Hamlet's 370.[13] In act 2, scene 1, Gertrude becomes a true sister of Phèdre as she cries out in remorse to Elvire:

Ce qui me plaît, Elvire, en mon trouble funeste,
C'est de sentir au moins combien je me déteste
Je voudrais quelquefois, dans mes justes transports,
A l'univers entier déclarer mes remords.
(While in my fatal turmoil, Elvira, what I take pleasure in is feeling how much I abhor myself, at least. In my sincere outbursts, I should like sometimes to avow my remorse to the whole universe.)

Ducis swept out of the play all the baser characters when he reduced his *dramatis personae* to eight speaking roles: Hamlet, King of Denmark; Gertrude, mother of Hamlet and widow of the late King Hamlet; Claudius, first prince of the blood; Ophélie, the daughter of Claudius; Norceste, who replaces Horatio; Polonius, a Danish nobleman, confidant of Claudius; Elvire, confidante of Gertrude; and Voltimand, captain of the palace guards. Suppressed are the ghost, Laertes, Ronsencrantz, Guildenstern, Osric, the players, Fortinbras, and the gravediggers.

Now, there are two important facts that we should consider: First, this *Hamlet* of Ducis, "Tragedy in Five Acts, Imitated from the English," will be the only *Hamlet*

l'anglais," *Chefs d'Oeuvres tragiques de Ducis* (Paris: Firmin-Didot, 1845), p. 48. All the quotations from Ducis's *Hamlet* are from this edition.
    13. Golder, p. 81n.

staged at the Comédie Française for the next eighty-two years, and indeed, the only *Hamlet* performed by a French troupe until the latter half of the nineteenth century. Second, it is Ducis's *Hamlet* as played by Talma that a number of the French Romantics lauded with effusive praise. Because this play of Ducis shaped so significantly the attitudes of the French for such a long period, I shall give a brief résumé of it using the 1803 edition, which was reworked for Talma.

Act 1: Claudius schemes with Polonius to overthrow Hamlet, whose coronation has not yet taken place. (We see that Ducis has politely, or prudently in 1769, respected the legitimate order of succession.) Claudius is not the uncle of Hamlet and is not yet his step-father. (This, of course, eliminates the incest.) Ducis also gives Claudius excellent reasons for his hatred for the late king. The old king had not appreciated his military exploits and had forbidden his daughter to marry (in the tradition of Racine's Aricie); thus, Claudius's line was to become extinct. Claudius paints a portrait of a weak, overly sensitive, and ineffectual young Hamlet to Polonius. Gertrude, however, when approached by Claudius, has begun to repent of her part in the murder of her husband, and she states that henceforth she lives only to see her son officially crowned King of Denmark.

Act 2: Gertrude relates to Elvire her long love affair with Claudius, the injustices of her late husband, and then confesses that she had carried a poisoned beverage furnished by Claudius to the bedchamber of the king. Her remorse was almost immediate after leaving the poison and she had tried to remove it, but arrived too late. The next scene centers on the arrival of Norceste. It is not until the last scene (5) of act 2 that Hamlet appears on stage, fresh from his encounter with the ghost. He enters with the command:

Fuis, spectre épouvantable,
Porte au fond des tombeaux ton aspect redoutable.

(Flee dreadful apparition. Carry to the depth of the tombs your fearful sight.)

Then Hamlet relates his account of the visits of the ghost, this "ombre chère et terrible" (this beloved and terrible shade) who has ordered him to get a dagger, then obtain the urn in which the ashes of his father rest, but not to water the urn with impotent tears; indeed, he is to run with it and strike down the murderers. Hamlet admits his readiness to punish Claudius, but confesses that he cannot bring himself to kill his mother.

Act 3: In act 3 the mousetrap play is reduced by Ducis to a conversation in which Norceste relates to Gertrude and Claudius the recent assassination of the king of England. This account, of course, is contrived to parallel the murder of Hamlet's father. Gertrude is deeply moved, but Claudius remains inflexible. In scene 6 there is a conversation in which Ophélie admits her love for Hamlet to Gertrude. The Queen is relieved at having discovered the cause of her son's languor and pledges to aid the young couple in setting aside the edict forbidding Ophélie to marry.

Act 4: In scene 1 in the 1803 edition of the play, we find a modified version of the "To be or not to be" soliloquy:

Je ne sais que résoudre—immobile et troublé
C'est rester trop longtemps de mon doute accablé,
C'est trop souffrir la vie, et le poids qui me tue.

(Immovable and disordered, I do not know what to resolve. It is to remain overwhelmed with my doubt too long. It is to suffer life too much and the weight that is killing me.)

In scene 2, Ophélie runs to Hamlet with the good news

that Gertrude pledges them her support. Hamlet can only murmur: "Le bonheur quelquefois est plus loin qu'on ne pense" (Sometimes happiness is farther away than we think). He states that he wishes to die alone ("mourir seul") and refuses any other explanation, first to Ophélie and then to his mother. Claudius, alarmed at his dark mood, decides to begin his insurrection immediately.

Act 5: Ophélie, sensing Hamlet's ill-disguised hatred of her father, comes to beg for his life. The lovers renounce, each in turn, their love for one another in the name of filial duty (*à la* Chimène and Rodrigue in *Le Cid*). Hamlet then confronts Gertrude with the urn and commands her to swear over the ashes of her dead husband that she is innocent of his death. Gertrude faints, thus revealing her guilt, but Hamlet still cannot harm her. He utters these words:

> Votre crime est énorme, exécrable, odieux.
> Mais il n'est pas plus que, la bonté des dieux.

(Your crime is enormous, loathsome, heinous, but it is not greater than the goodness of the gods).

The ghost reappears, invisible to all except Hamlet, including the audience, and pushes the young king to the verge of matricide. Hamlet masters his murderous impulses and urges Gertrude to flee his presence. In the meantime Claudius has assembled his forces and rushes in to seize Hamlet, but is killed by him instead (and quickly carried off stage). Gertrude stabs herself, and Hamlet terminates Ducis's tragedy with:

> Mes malheurs sont comblés; mais ma vertu me reste
> (1803 version).
> Mes malheurs sont comblés; mais ce poignard seul me reste
> (1769 version).[14]

14. *Ibid.*

Mais je suis homme et roi: réservé pour souffrir,
Je saurai vivre encore; je fais plus que mourir.

(My misfortunes are overflowing, but my courage remains
[1803]; this dagger alone remains to me [1769],

> But I am a man and a king: set aside for suffering,
> I shall know how to live again, I [shall] do
> more than die).

The ending described above is a modification of the 1769
version of the play, in which Claudius stabs himself, gives
Hamlet the dagger to take to Gertrude, who obligingly uses
it, and leaves Hamlet to reign with Ophélie.[15] Ducis made a
number of changes in the play between 1769 and 1803.
Talma, however, was still discontent with the 1803 version
ending and finally wrote his own happy conclusion: "Hamlet has been the victim of his own imagination, Claudius is
innocent, Ophelia is going to marry the one she loves and
already calls Gertrude 'mother'; everything ends in universal
happiness." [16]

Ducis's *Hamlet* was a success in spite of biting comments
from critics such as Charles Collé, who termed it an "abomi-
nation" and added ungraciously that the urn device had
been used by Sophocles in *Electra* and by Voltaire in
Oreste.[17] Diderot, even more ungraciously, evoked Boileau
and suggested that Ducis leave off playwriting altogether.[18]

15. *Ibid.*
16. Benchettrit, p. 61.
17. Golder, pp. 84, 85.
18. "O Despréaux, qu'auriez-vous dit si vous eussiez vu *Hamlet?*
. . . Monsieur Ducis, copiez des lettres, faites-en même, travaillez des
dépêches, pourvu qu'il n'y soit question ni d'amour ni de politique; mais
laissez là le théâtre." Diderot terminates his criticism by calling attention
to Voltaire's two translations of the "To be or not to be" soliloquy—"the
one so beautiful when he wanted to exaggerate the merit of Shakespeare
and the other so ridiculous when he wished to denigrate him." Then he
closes with the famous statement that he prefers Shakespeare's monster
to Ducis's scarecrow: "Je finis en vous disant que je m'accommoderai
encore mieux du monstre de Shakespeare, que de l'épouvantail de M.

All that did not diminish the enthusiasm of the public, however. From its first performance on September 30, 1769, until it was retired from the repertory at the Comédie Française in 1851, the play had 203 performances. Between 1831 and 1840, at the height of the Romantic movement, it was played on sixty-five evenings.[19]

Joseph H. McMahon, in an article not unsympathetic to Ducis, stated that ". . . he probably succeeded better than Voltaire in throwing up walls between the Bard and the public." [20] Only a cursory examination of Ducis's *Hamlet* would justify this critical opinion, but one should consider also the comment of J. D. Golder: "It is all too easy to discard this first French adaptation of Shakespeare for the stage as a gross travesty without fully recognizing the fact that Ducis did extend to the Bard a viewing audience in France where formerly he had only a reading public." The play was translated into Italian, Spanish, and Dutch, and it was still being performed in the Netherlands as late as 1878.[21] It inspired two operas, one in Italian, and the other, by Ambroise Thomas, in French, first performed in 1886.[22]

The French Romantic writers had created a myth of Hamlet in their own image by the time the second stage version of the play appeared. This was the Alexander Dumas-Paul Meurice adaptation, presented for the press at St. German-en-Laye in September 1846, and then for the public on December 15, 1847, at the Théâtre Historique in

Ducis." Denis Diderot, "Hamlet Tragédie de M. Ducis 1769," (Inédit) *Oeuvres complètes* 8, Assézat ed. (Paris, 1875–1877): 471–76.

19. Benchettrit, p. 60.

20. Joseph H. McMahon, "Ducis—Unkindest Cutter?" *Yale French Studies* 33 (December 1964): 17.

21. Golder, p. 85.

22. For the elaborate setting for the Thomas opera see the article "Décor, Décoration," in Arthur Pougin, *Dictionnaire Historique et Pittoresque du Théâtre et des Arts qui s'y rattachent* (Paris: Firmin-Didot et Cie, 1885), pp. 268–82.

Paris. Rouvière played the title role. Dumas had had the benefit of complete and faithful translations—by Letourneur, Guizot-Brabante. He had witnessed Kemble and Macready play Hamlet, and he could read Shakespeare in English. All this notwithstanding, the new version is still far removed from Shakespeare. It is sufficient to say that this stage adaptation was also written in classical alexandrine verse, that it begins in the council chamber of the palace, that it incorporates an original love scene between Hamlet and Ophelia, excludes Fortinbras, and ends with the appearance of the ghost who comes to pronounce judgment on all.[23] It tells Laertes to "pray and die," Gertrude to "hope and die," and Claudius to "despair and die." Hamlet asks what he is to do. The ghost replies: "Thou shalt live!"[24] and on this word of condemnation the curtain falls. The play had been destined for the Comédie Française by Dumas, but it would not be performed there until after nearly forty years had passed, all because of a misunderstanding between Dumas and the director of that august society. It had 135 performances at the Théâtre Historique, however, and was a financial success. The critics were lavish in their praise of Rouvière, and one wrote that the actor had "given life to the Hamlet drawn by Delacroix." [25]

This comment brings us to an interesting point in our brief journey with *Hamlet* in France. It was through the paintings and lithographs (sixteen between 1828 to 1859) of Delacroix that the Romantics shaped their image of Hamlet. Delacroix had seen the English players perform in Paris in 1827. He had also seen Kean play Hamlet in London in 1825, and as Helen Phelps Bailey has noted, he "never forgot

23. Bailey, pp. 77–79.
24. Benchettrit, p. 62.
25. *Ibid*

that 'pale and elegant face' which through other models, constantly reappeared in his canvases." [26] Escholier tells us that the face of Delacroix's Hamlet remained unforgettable. It is an "almost feminine" one, and this is easily understood since it was a woman, Madame Pierret, who posed for Hamlet. Throughout the years Delacroix's Hamlet would not vary from this beautifully proportioned body and expressive face borrowed as much from the memory of the actor Kemble as from Madame Pierret.[27] It is also interesting to note that Delacroix was the first in France to choose a woman to represent Hamlet. He anticipated the three actresses who played the role during the nineteenth century: Madame Judith in 1866, Adeline Dudlay in 1898, and Sarah Bernhardt in 1899. Evidently, these actresses felt that Shakespeare's women were a little too dull as compared with the women in the French theater, and in this thought they would have found support from no less a distinguished contemporary critic as Henri Peyre.[28]

René Taupin has stated that the importance of the plastic arts in the formation of the myth of Hamlet cannot be exaggerated, and that it is through Delacroix that Baudelaire understands Hamlet. One might add further that it was through Delacroix and through Talma's interpretation of Ducis's *Hamlet* that the majority of the Romantic writers knew the play, not through Shakespeare's tragedy. The costumes for the Dumas-Meurice adaptation of the play were copied from the paitings of Lehman and the sketches of Delacroix.[29] We note, therefore, that the similarity of Rou-

26. Bailey, p. 63.
27. Raymond Escholier, *La Vie et l'Art Romantiques. Delacroix Peintre, Graveur, Ecrivain,* II, 1832–48 (Paris: H. Floury, 1927): 204–7.
28. See Henri Peyre, "Shakespeare's Women—A French View," *Yale French Studies* 33 (December 1964): 107–19.
29. René Taupin, "Le Mythe de Hamlet à l'époque romantique," *French Review* 27, no. 1 (October, 1953): 16, 17.

vière's to Delacroix's *Hamlet* was by no means coincidental.

On September 28, 1886, the Dumas-Meurice adaptation was presented at the Comédie Française, modified by Meurice after the death of Dumas into a version more faithful to Shakespeare. In 1899, Hamlet was finally permitted to die at the end of the play, and this final version of the Dumas-Meurice adaptation remained in the repertory of the Comédie Française until 1932, when it was replaced by the Swob-Morand translation made famous by Sarah Bernhardt. Mounet-Sully played Hamlet in the Meurice adaptation at the Comédie Française until his death in 1916 and his intense portrayal of the role ranked him with Talma, Rouvière, and Sarah Bernhardt as a major interpreter of Hamlet in France.

Sarah Bernhardt was the first Gallic performer of Shakespeare's *Hamlet*. The Swob text is faithfully translated from the Oxford text and no part of it is deleted or distorted. Therefore, in 1899, not long after English literature was officially recognized as a subject in the French universities,[30] *Hamlet* was given its just performance—not at the Comédie Française, but at the Théâtre Sarah Bernhardt. Clement Scott, infamous for his comments on actresses, was enchanted by the "Divine Sarah." After observing her performance at the Adelphi Theater in New York, he wrote that he never sat out the play of *Hamlet* with less fatigue:

> As a rule the play exhausts one. There was no exhaustion with Sarah Bernhardt—only exhilaration. . . . I begin to think, on the whole, that the French temperament is better for the play of *Hamlet* as acted before an audience than the philosophical German, the passionate Italian, the alert American, or the phlegmatic Englishman.[31]

30. Axelrad, p. 54.
31. Clement William Scott. *Some Notable Hamlets of the Present Time* (New York: reprinted by Benjamin Blom, 1969), pp. 43, 51.

Others, of course, were not in accord with Scott. Haskell Black states that Sarah Bernhardt's performance marked the decadance of the Romantic interpretation of Hamlet—that the pale, consumptive adolescent with black cloak and white plume illustrated by Delacroix "reached its final point in this slight feminine actress." [32]

One of the major difficulties of any French actor performing the role of Hamlet in the first half of the twentieth century was to liberate himself from the Romantic conception of the part and to clear the images of Delacroix from his mind. Axelrad clearly presents the problem:

> The melancholy prince had a special appeal to the romantics, and most people in this country still see him as the contemporaries of Delacroix did one hundred years ago. Our mission of late years has been to try and rid his character of all the romantic mists and hazes, and get, if not a vision of the *real* Hamlet (for each of us has his own Hamlet), at least a plausible image of the character as conceived by the Elizabethans. To destroy the conventional, sickly image of Hamlet in the minds of an audience is indeed a stimulating task. [33]

This was the challenge set before Jean-Louis Barrault, the major interpreter of *Hamlet* in France since the Second World War.

In 1931, after a brief period at the Ecole du Louvre, Barrault, aged twenty-one, came to the Atelier to study under Charles Dullin. There he learned from Dullin "the importance of the body and its expression," the "religious meaning of the masque," the theories of Stanislawski, Gordon Craig, and Copeau. From Etienne Decroux he learned the art of the mime. [34] It was at the Atelier that Barrault

32. Haskell M. Black, "Laforgue and the Theatre," *Jules Laforgue: Essays on a Poet's Life and Works*, ed. Warren Ramsey. (Carbondale & Edwardsville: Southern Illinois University Press, 1969), p. 93.

33. Axelrad, p. 55.

34. Jean-Louis Barrault, *Reflexions on the Theatre* (London: Rockliff, 1950), pp. 19–22.

began what would be one of his lifelong preoccupations—
the search for the elusive figure of Hamlet. It was through
the Swob translation used by Sarah Bernhardt that Barrault
began his quest—through that "magnificent" but "arduous"
text. "My terrors, my eyes starting out of their orbits, my
disordered movements, my wild wheelings around, haunted
some terrace of Elsinore, drawn by Delacroix, even by Victor
Hugo," [35] he wrote. To Barrault the figure of Hamlet was
shrouded by clouds, a figure not unlike the enigmatic
stranger of Baudelaire. Perceiving that he would not capture
this character with a frontal attack on Shakespeare, Barrault
set about perceiving him through the "sensibilité" of the
most "hamletique" [36] of French poets, Jules Laforgue. In
1939 Barrault played Hamlet at the Atelier in a stage adaptation of Laforgue's prose tale taken from the *Moralités
légendaires* by Charles Granval, "who hadn't added a single
word, but had simply done an enormous, skilful, and
reverent job with scissors." [37] Milhaud supplied the incidental music for Granval's production. "This time," Barrault
wrote, "his Hamlet at least came out of the University of
Wittenberg." He added that "Laforgue pointed out . . . a
path which even today seems primeval for approaching the
great Hamlet of Shakespeare: the path of humour. . . .

---

35. Jean-Louis Barrault, "Etre ou ne pas être Hamlet," *Réalités,* no.
198 (July 1962), p. 60.
36. Bailey gives an excellent definition of "Hamletism" as applied to
Laforgue: ". . . the term 'Hamletism' evokes certain traits of personality
associated with a particular approach to existence. It has primarily an
aesthetic connotation—'aesthetic' in the Kierkegaardian sense, signifying
neutrality in contrast to choice. It suggests distractibility and impulsive-
ness as much as hesitation and doubt. There is something in it, too, of
pride—not easily sustained— in one's difference from the general run
of humanity; of darkness and obsession with death; of ambivalence and
frustration; a feeling of ineffectualness, combined with a sense of the
futility of all endeavor. It implies a nostalgia for integrity and a sense of
remoteness from the goal of self-realization. It is akin to fatalism,
nihilism, absurdism." Bailey, p. 153.
37. Barrault, *Reflexions on the Theatre,* p. 77.

Hamlet seemed to me then the artist-hero. Dying he mur-
mured: *Qualis artifex pereo* [What an artist is perishing in
me]. And I found that here, Laforgue hit the mark." Barrault
added that Laforgue had provided him an aerial bridge
that "perhaps" came near to Kafka, a bridge that allowed
him a passage back through time to the atmosphere of the
Renaissance, the climate in which he felt that the true Hamlet belonged.[38]

As may readily be perceived from Laforgue's borrowing
of Nero's dying words for his own dying Hamlet, the poet's
use of humor is ironical. It is also defensive. The poet juxta-
poses trivial phrases of popular speech with semi-philosophi-
cal jargon. One moment Laforgue's Hamlet is crying over his
lost love: "Pauvre Ophélie. Pauv' Lee Lee——."[39] The next
moment he is provoking Laertes to a duel with: "Et ta
soeur," a rejoinder which, as Albert Sonnenfeld has justly
remarked, is an "untranslatable pun, either of whose meanings would have sufficed to justify Laertes stabbing him with
his 'realistic dagger.'"[40] The grave diggers respond to Hamlet's meditation on Yorick's skull with: "And all that will
not keep us from drinking a good round, tomorrow, Sunday."
The tale is ended with Laforgue's observation that "One less
Hamlet doesn't mean the end of the race, don't forget that."

"All that derives from the sad clown, which seemed to
me to be the likeness of Shakespeare, a synthesis of his
work," commented Barrault, adding that "humor is on a level
with true greatness. It is the familiar aspect of it."[41] Now,

38. Jean-Louis Barrault, "A la Recherche de Hamlet," *Cahiers de la
Compagnie Madeleine Renaud–Jean-Louis Barrault,* no. 38 (1962), p. 91.
    39. Jules Laforgue, *Moralités Légendaires* (Paris: Georges Crès et
Cie, 1920), p. 39. All subsequent quotations from Laforgue are from this
edition.
    40. Albert Sonnenfeld, "Hamlet the German and Jules Laforgue,"
Yale French Studies 33 (December 1964): 99.
    41. Barrault, "A la Recherche de Hamlet."

Laforgue, who had based his text on Belleforest, used episodes and names unfamiliar to Barrault—the strangled bird
scene, the use of Fengo for Claudius, et cetera. Therefore,
having previously sought his Hamlet through the Romantics
by way of the Swob text and through the Symbolists via
Laforgue, Barrault decided to make his next step a back-
ward one, beyond Shakespeare to Belleforest. At the
Bibliothèque Nationale he "dug" into one of the texts dating
in the 1570s of the *Histoires Tragiques* and found the contrast between the Hamlet of Laforgue and the one of Belleforest to be striking.

> This approach of my distant Hamlet, of my always elusive
> Hamlet, by the historical Hamlet of Belleforest didn't seem
> useless to me. Hamlet is virile. It seems to me that Shake-
> speare has respected this. In numerous places, when people
> speak of him, whether it be Ophelia, the King, Fortinbras,
> Horatio, or even when he himself mocks the effeminate grey-
> beards, Hamlet is described or acts like a man. At least he
> would be capable of being one. He has within himself the
> material to make one.[42]

In 1940, the year following his experience with Laforgue's
Hamlet at the Atelier, Barrault was engaged by Jacques
Copeau at the Comédie Française. His second performance
there was in the role of Hamlet. This time the text was that
of Pourtalès and the direction was once again that of Charles
Granval. Pourtalès's translation had been made in 1923 and
used by various experimental groups. Barrault termed it a
"bit prosaic," but effective "in the dramatic point of view,"
and in regard to the intelligence of the roles.[43] It was an
easier text than the Swob-Morand translation, which "af-
fected an archaic style, purportedly to render more faith-

42. *Ibid.*, p. 93.
43. *Ibid.*

fully than the modern tongue could do—the quality of Elizabethan English." [44]

The introduction that Pourtalès wrote for his translation gave Barrault what he termed a "window," an opening into the character of his new Hamlet. Pourtalès had called Hamlet "the hero of superior hesitation," and he shared many of Mallarmé's views on the play. In his critical work *De Hamlet à Swann,* Pourtalès had described the work as being primarily "an intellectual drama"—its hero "a perfectionist, a lover of truth, whose hesitations result from sheer lucidity." [45]

In defining his role Barrault took his cues from Pourtalès, in whose *Hamlet* the actor saw the *Shakespearean* hero, the man who is not on this side of action but who is beyond action. In his article "A la Recherche de Hamlet," Barrault distinguishes between the two types of heroes. First, there is the classical hero, the hero of action like Fortinbras who doesn't ask questions for he believes in the ideal for which he is willing to sacrifice himself. Then there is the "typically Shakespearian" hero, the supreme hero, who questions and will not act until he is convinced that his actions will be in accordance with universal rather than with mere human, partisan justice.

Hamlet, "hero of the Renaissance," hero of the "Sickness of Doubt" is, according to Barrault, fully aware of his imbalance and therefore gives his dying vote to Fortinbras, thereby "prophesying the advent of action. . . . The trial of doubt is ended, humanity has passed the peak of the greatest despair, faith is born again . . . life has won." [46]

"The agony, the fragility, the split personality, the black humor, the *esprit libertaire,* all these traits permitted me to feel close to the role," the actor was to comment thirty years

44. Bailey, p. 54.
45. *Ibid.,* p. 158.
46. Barrault, "A *la Recherche de Hamlet,"* pp. 96, 97.

later in his *Souvenirs*, but he felt he had "danced" the part too much—adding that " 'dancing' was [his] worst self complacency." [47]

The play opened on March 16, 1942, and was considered the most important new production at the Comédie Française. It had a total of twenty-nine performances. During the 1942-43 season, it was performed twenty-two times. Margaret Monod remarked in an article written for *Paris-Midi* that never before did one see the theater filled for *Hamlet*. [48]

After the war Barrault formed his own company in 1946 —the Compagnie Madeleine Renaud–Jean-Louis Barrault— at the Théâtre Marigny on the Champs-Elysées. Shakespeare's *Hamlet* was chosen to open the season because Barrault felt that Shakespeare appealed to the age.

> Shakespeare, at our period, appears to us to be more current than Molière; he is more in harmony with us. . . .
> Shakespeare lived in the middle of murders, revolutions and catastrophes as we have. . . . Molière lived in a rich epoch. . . . Above him reigned order, absolute authority— richness, glory, prosperity, order, authority—these are words which are very far from us.
> On the other hand, murders, revolutions, catastrophes, lost faith. . . . doubt: this is what is very near to us. [49]

This time the translation was that of André Gide. Barrault had regretted for some time that Gide had translated only one act of *Hamlet* and he set about trying to persuade him to finish the work. They had met by chance on May 5, 1942, when Gide was in Marseilles getting ready to leave

47. Jean-Louis Barrault, *Souvenirs pour demain* (Paris: Seuil, 1972), p. 149.
48. As quoted in Leo O. Forkey, "The Comédie Française and the German Occupation," *French Review* 24, no. 6 (May 1951): 482.
49. Barrault, *A Propos de Shakespeare et du Théâtre*, pp. 20, 21.

for North Africa. Gide relates the encounter in his journal and describes Barrault as having a "Wonderful face instinct with enthusiasm, passion, genius. . . . Talented enough to remain simple." On July 27 he notes that he is giving most of his time to the translation in order to keep his mind off the anguish of France. Then, on September first, with evident relief he states that he had terminated the translation the previous day after having worked on it from six to eight hours daily for nearly three months with "an adolescent's zeal and an old man's patient equanimity. . . . I should certainly not have persevered if my version had not seemed to me greatly superior to all the earlier ones, and especially much more adapted to the stage and to delivery by actors." Gide admitted to having had within reach for "encouragement" the translations of François-Victor Hugo, Swob, Pourtalès, and Copeau. The last he praised but stated that "all . . . sacrifice rhythm, lyrical power, cadence, and beauty to mere exactitude." In the entry of November 22, Gide continued to muse over Shakespeare's awareness of the full possibilities of each word and noted that the translator "must constantly fear, by being too precise, to limit the flight of the imagination." [50]

A number of contemporary French writers in addition to Gide have stressed the difficulties of translating Shakespeare's *Hamlet*. Christian Pons undoubtedly spoke for all when he wrote that "Shakespeare is the despair of translators and *Hamlet* the despair of the translators of Shakespeare." [51] There are excellent translations of *Hamlet* in German, Pons noted, but the natural resonances of French are poorly suited for the expression of great tragical emotions:

50. André Gide, *The Journals of André Gide*, trans. Justin O'Brien. IV: 1939–1949 (New York: Knopf, 1951): 109, 110, 118, 119, 121, 122.
51. Christian Pons, "Les Traductions de Hamlet par des Ecrivains français," *Etudes Anglaises* 13 (1960): 117, 118.

in the narrow world of our poets in which passions are dominated, or at least enlightened, by *Reason*, the French language,
logical, well articulated, oratorical, is a marvelous instrument
of expression. It is very awkward on the contrary to follow
with Shakespeare the paths of [human] nature into the
shadows of the heart, as into a deep forest where the light
of *Reason* penetrates with difficulty. . . . In brief, if the French
do not have a head for the epic, neither do they have a
Shakespearian soul. . . . French is the least Shakespearian of
all languages . . . nothing illustrates better than a French
Hamlet all that separates the two languages.[52]

André Gide, by no means a novice at the art of translation, had a number of successes behind him when he under-
took the first act of *Hamlet* in the twenties. These included
Rilke (1911), Tagore (1914), Conrad (1918), Walt Whitman
(1918), Shakespeare (*Antony and Cleopatra* in 1920), and
Blake (1922). A translation of Pushkin appeared in 1923.[53]
Therefore, the vexation that he expressed in regard to his
task reflects well the enormity of it. Under the date July 14,
1922, Gide noted in his *Journal* that he had finished the first
act of *Hamlet*, that he felt unhappy with the result, and that
to write well in French one had to go too far from Shakespeare.[54] Twenty years later in the "Lettre-Préface" of the
complete translation which, due to World War II, was published first in New York in 1945, Gide adds in a tone of
exasperation that

> One cannot conceive of a text that is subtler, craftier,
> fuller of ambiguities, pitfalls and traps. All the other plays of
> Shakespeare with perhaps the exception of *Troilus* seem clear
> in comparison. . . . one cannot imagine a more complicated
> manner of expressing thoughts or sentiments which are often

52. *Ibid.*
53. Van Meter Ames, *André Gide* (Norfolk, Conn. New Directions
Books, 1947) pp. 293, 294.
54. André Gide, *Journal* (Paris: Gallimard. Bibliothèque de la Pléiade,
1955), pp. 735–36.

quite simple—the height of artifice which leaves behind the most rambling declamations of Corneille—of artifice—or of art?—for indisputably from all this lyric hotchpotch there arises a heady smoke which goes to the head, the senses, the heart, and which plunges us into a state of poetic trance where reason enters but feebly.[55]

It was the poetic trance that captivated Gide, and what he wanted to do was to bring this, the poetry of Shakespeare, to a French audience. He stated that the writer who translates only the meaning of the text has accomplished "nothing, almost nothing." "Shakespeare is not a thinker," Gide declared, "he is a poet; and his thought matters scarcely to us without the wings which carry it into the empyrean. It is this soaring of the thought which matters to us here, not the thought itself and not the wingless hair splitting." [56] Furthermore, Gide insists that his translation is directed not to the reader but foremost to the actor who must interpret it and then to the spectator who must understand it readily. Therefore, it must not make impossible demands on either. The elocution must be easy and the comprehension spontaneous. Gide warns that it is easy to lose one's footing in preferring lyricism to exactitude in translation, but proposes to lose nothing, neither meaning nor poetry, harmony nor rhythm, élan nor life while maintaining his goals of easy delivery for the actor and effortless comprehension for the spectator.[57] Difficult goals, indeed. Did he succeed? Let us examine his work for the answer.

Gide used the Cambridge text,[53] which he translated into a French that is classic, contemporary, and elegant. Unlike

55. André Gide, "Lettre Preface" in Shakespeare, *Hamlet.* Edition Bilingue, trans. André Gide (New York: Pantheon Books, 1946).
56. *Ibid.*
57. *Ibid.*
58. William Milwitzky, "André Gide: 'Hamlet,'" *Symposium* 1 (May 1957): 147.

Swob, he did not attempt to create the atmosphere of Shakespeare's time by using a language dating from the latter part of the sixteenth century. He did use a few archaisms such as *féal* (ce féal devoir, act 1, scene 2), but they appear in a context that is natural and nondistracting. Like other conventional and purist writers, Gide preferred the *terme noble,* the more refined word to the familiar (e.g., bellicose to warlike), but he did not avoid popular or even crude expressions when he felt that Shakespeare expressly intended for them to be used, as for example

<blockquote>
Shakespeare
  "she is a strumpet"
Gide
  "la Fortune est une catin (act 2, sc. 2)
Shakespeare
  "pious bawds"
Gide
  "ces pieues maquerelles" (act 1, sc. 4)
Shakespeare
  "Would from a paddock, from a bat, a gib"
Gide
  "de ce crapaud, de ce matou, de ce vampire."
                         (act 3, sc. 4)
</blockquote>

To facilitate comprehension, Gide amplified the text from time to time:

<blockquote>
Shakespeare
                   . . . we have here writ
  To Norway, uncle of young Fortinbras,
Gide
  "nous écrivons au roi de Norvège,
  oncle du jeune Fortinbras,"
                         (act 1, sc. 2)
Shakespeare
  "to draw him on to pleasures, and to gather,
  So much as from occasion you may glean,
  Whe'r aught to us unknown afflicts him thus,
</blockquote>

That, open'd, lies within our remedy."
Gide
"Vous l'entrainerez de conserve dans vos plaisirs,
et trouverez occasion de glaner des renseignements
sur le mal secret qui l'affecte, de manière
que nous, instruits par vous, y
puissions porter remède."

(act 2, sc. 2)

Gide even more frequently abridges:

Shakespeare
"Two nights together had these gentlemen,
Marcellus and Bernardo on their watch,"
Gide
"Deux nuits de suite, comme Marcellus et
Bernardo étaient de garde . . ."
Shakespeare
"O God! a beast, that wants discourse of reason,"
Gide
"O Dieu! l'animal sans raison . . . "

(act 1, sc. 2)

Shakespeare
"To-morrow shall I beg leave to see your
kingly eyes;"
Gide
"Demain je demanderai permission de
paraître devant vos yeux;"

(act 4, sc. 7)

Not only does Gide delete words and phrases, he con-
denses whole speeches and passages. An example of this
occurs in act 2, scene 2, in the declamations of the First
Player about the plight of Hecuba. The significance of the
parody is lost for us today, he explains in a footnote, and
substitutes his own version in a style worthy of the seventeenth century. Thus, he justly claims to have preserved the
tone and movement of Shakespeare's parody albeit at the
expense of the exact meaning of his words.[59]

59. Gide, *Hamlet,* pp. 114, 115.

Criticism has been directed at Gide in regard to his choice of vocabulary. Christian Pons asserts that Gide softens the force of Shakespeare. As Pons points out, "Chair trop massive, oh! si tu pouvais fondre! " ("O! that this too, too solid flesh would melt.") is much more elegant than the previous translations of that phrase. However, as Pons maintains, "Shakespeare is not elegant, he is strong." Pons also feels that Gide's version is weak in the passages of lyric force.[60] William Milwitzky shares the opinion of Pons in regard to the passages in which Hamlet denigrates Ophelia, stating that Gide so "toned down the vehemence of the lines as to remind us of the Kittredge regard for the morals of the undergraduate," and he declares Gide's translation of "if I could see the puppets dallying" by "si je pouvais voir vos simagrées" ("if I could see your grimaces") as being inadequate and woefully misleading." [61] One can only agree with the above criticisms while nonetheless pointing out the fact that Gide was quite capable of translating forceful language with language equally as strong. In act 3, scene 4, Gide shows no modesty, no reticence, as he did in the case of Hamlet's remarks to Ophelia, when he translates Hamlet's conversation with Gertrude:

Shakespeare
                         "Nay, but to live
    In the rank sweat of an enseamed bed,
    Stew'd in corruption, honeying and making love
    Over the nasty sty . . ."
Gide
    "Quoi! vivre dans le suint ranci
    d'une couche crasseuse, infuser dans
    la pourriture, et sur un fumier puant,
    faire l'amour."

60. Pons, "Les Traductions de Hamlet," p. 125.
61. Milwitzky, p. 147.

A charge perhaps more serious than that of softening the force of Shakespeare might be that of mistranslating him altogether. Some errors made by Gide are:

Shakespeare
. . ."the sledded polacks on the ice"
Gide
"il écrasa les traineaux polonais sur la glace."
                    (act 1, sc. 1) (Gide translates
                    "the Polish sleds.")
Shakespeare
"Though yet of Hamlet our dear brother's death
The memory be green"
Gide
"Encore bien que la mort de notre cher frère
        laisse une verdoyant souvenir"
                            (act 1, sc. 2)
(*Verdoyant* in French means "green, verdant," not "recent".)
Shakespeare
"Would I had met my dearest foe in heaven"
Gide
"Ah! retrouver au ciel mon ennemi le plus intime"
                            (act 1, sc. 2)
    ("Dearest" here is translated as "closest," rather than being given the Elizabethan meaning "best-hated."
Shakespeare
"Ah, thou poor ghost, while memory hold a seat
In this distracted globe."
Gide
"Me souvenir! Certes, pauvre ombre!
    aussi longtemps que mémoire habitera ce
    monde affolé.
                            (act 1, sc. 5)
    (Gide translates "globe" as "world" rather than "head," as the meaning implies.)
Shakespeare
"Do you think I meant country matters?"
Gide
"Me prêtez-vous des manières de rustre?"
                            (act 3, sc. 2)

(Perhaps a misreading of "manners" for "mat-
ters": Do you credit me with the manners of a
bumpkin?)
Shakespeare
"That liberal shepherds give a grosser name"
Gide
"Auxquelles nos bergers libertins donnent un
vilain nom"

(act 4, sc. 7)
(Gide translates "liberal" [coarse-mouthed] with
the word "libertine.")
Shakespeare
". . . if I drown myself wittingly"
Gide
"Si je me noie moi-même spirituellement"

(act 5, sc. 1)
(In an attempt to preserve the pun, Gide uses
"spirituellement" ["wittily"], which does not, however, have the meaning "knowingly.")

A detailed study of the liberties that Gide takes with the
syntax of Shakespeare would constitute a lengthy volume.
In brief, he often changes both the nature and function of
words and phrases; he changes the tenses of verbs, modifies
prepositions, adverbs, and connectives, divides long sentences, changes the order of sentences, but maintains a fine
sense of balance and equilibrium in his sentence structure. A
rather curious element for a writer who wished to employ a
contemporary style was his frequent use of the *adjectif
epithète*, the attributive adjective: "sa martiale prestance"
(act 1, sc. 1), "votre virginale présence" (act 1, sc. 2), "Mon
obéissante fille" (act 2, sc. 2), "deux particulières raisons"
(act 4, sc. 7), "la radieuse majesté" (act 4, sc. 5).

As French and English prosody are based on two entirely different systems, Gide's express desire to bring the
poetry of Shakespeare to a typical French audience was an
ambitious one. Yet, he succeeded in this domain far beyond

his predecessors. How did he accomplish this? By carefully studying the Shakespearian verbal architecture and imitating it as closely as possible. Where Shakespeare used a concessive clause, Gide does so also if possible. Infinitive is matched with infinitive, participle with participle, and so on. A reading aloud of passages in the two languages shows how well Gide has preserved the rhythm and tone of the original, as for example in act 1, scene 5, when the ghost of Hamlet's father appears to him:

> Horrible! Horrible! Oh très horrible! Si tu
> n'est pas dénaturé, ne tolère pas cela.
> N'abandonne pas à la luxure et à
> l'inceste le lit royal de Danemark.
> Mais tout en poursuivant la vengeance,
> garde ton esprit pur, et retiens ton âme de tramer
> rien contre ta mère. Laisse faire au ciel,
> et à ces épines qu'elle loge en son sein,
> qui la griffent et la déchirent. Maintenant adieu.
> Au pressentiment du matin le ver-luisant
> déjà pâlit sa lueur impuissante;
> adieu, adieu, adieu. Souviens-toi.

In his penetrating study, "L'Art de la Traduction chez Swob et chez Gide," Jean-Claude Noël of the University of Ottawa shows us how Gide is able to obtain a cadence similar to the iambic pentameter of Shakespeare, in such lyrical passages as Gertrude's description of Ophelia's death in act 4, scene 7. By taking liberties with the mute e [ə], Gide was able to obtain both a balanced sentence and an equal rhythm, Noël affirms. He feels that Gide's text reads well, that his sentence is well balanced, well constructed, well articulated, and that this, of course, supports Gide's aim to furnish the actor with a text for easy delivery. Noël states, however, that Gide does this at the price of "completely realtering the sentence, adding here, taking away there, and, moreover, more or less betraying the meaning" that Shake-speare intended.[62] Noël's criticism is just, but one can feel, just the same, that Gide's "betrayals" are perhaps not too serious when one considers that his intention was foremost that of providing a good acting version rather than a literary translation of the play.

On the whole, Gide's translation was acclaimed by the critics both in France and abroad. Henri Fluchère stated that "Gide's *Hamlet* has confirmed his reputation." [63] Wil-liam Milwitzky called it "a magnificent piece of work";[64] Herbert L. Matthews deemed it "intelligent" and stated that "the effect is poetical and the ideas are followed closely enough to catch the spirit of Shakespeare." [65] Justin O'Brien, the translator of Gide, wrote that Gide was able to preserve the poetic qualities of the original and further remarked that Gide's "translation in sensitive, poetic prose is not only the most vivid acting version in French; it is also the French 'Hamlet' that most faithfully reflects the qualities we love in the original." [65]

Even after its completion, however, Gide continued to be preoccupied with his translation. When Barrault's produc-tion opened in 1946, Philip Roddman was asked to interview him for a radio broadcast. To Roddman, Gide expressed annoyance that the American edition of the play had been printed with the English opposite his translation, thus "giving the effect of a blank verse rendition, . . . He main-

---

62. Jean-Claude Noël, "L'Art de la Traduction chez Schwob et chez Gide," *Revue de l'Université d'Ottawa* 39 (1969): 199–206.
63. Henri Fluchère, "Shakespeare in France: 1900–1948," *Shake-speare Survey* 2 (Cambridge: at the University Press, 1949): 123.
64. Milwitzky, p. 149.
65. Herbert L. Matthews, "Jean-Louis Barrault is starred in Gide's version of Hamlet at the Ziegfeld Theatre," *The New York Times*, Dec. 2, 1952, p. 39.
66. Justin O'Brien, "How Gide Translated *Hamlet*," *New York Herald Tribune*, November 30, 1952, Sec. IV, p. 2.

tained that his translation into French prose in no sense intended the effect suggested." [67] He was eager to discuss his interpretation of a number of lines, as for example his translation of "to quit him with this arm?" by "de retourner contre lui ses propres armes?" (to turn against the king his own arms, methods), and stated that he had suspected the Elizabethan slang meaning of "nunnery" but had used the word "couvent!" He reiterated his concern for the poetic, the musical essence of the play and affirmed that he would consider his work to have been useless if he had done no more than render into French the meaning of his speeches "at the cost of the rhythm, the rapture, and the peculiar latent music in which Shakespeare's genius sports." He had wished to lose nothing—"neither logic nor poetry." [68]

During the course of the interview Gide briefly shared his views on the subject of *Hamlet,* stating that "it is not the most perfect work," but adding "that with a like subject perfection is inadmissible." He felt that the secret of Hamlet's character was that he was reflective and that in this he differed from the other Shakespearian heroes who were "impulsive men." Gide attributed this "predisposition to inaction" to Hamlet's long stay at Wittenberg. When Hamlet does act, Gide maintains that he does so in "a quasi-spasmodic manner . . . each of his decisive acts is preceded by a kind of trial act, a flash-in-the-pan. And nothing appears more baffling, more daring, more skillful than this time lag. . . ." [69]

67. Philip Roddman, "Gide's *Hamlet,*" *Partisan Review* (February, 1949), p. 213.

68. *Ibid.,* pp. 214–17.

69. *Ibid.,* pp. 219–20. In this connection, it is interesting to note a comment written by Gide in his Journal on July 12, 1931: "Il n'est pas, dans tout le théâtre de Shakespeare (et je devrais dire plus absolument: dans tout le théâtre), de caractère, non tant germain, mais plus germanisé que celui de Hamlet." *Journal* 1889–1939 (Paris: Editions de la Pléiade, 1955), pp. 1062–63.

With the Gide translation, Jean-Louis Barrault added a new dimension in his search for the ever elusive figure of Hamlet. He states that

> To the mad lucidity of Hamlet two new feelings are added: the chastity of his heart and the purity of his soul. . . .
>
> Certainly Hamlet is chaste . . . the dangers of chastity are dandyism and homosexuality, but why would he sink there? . . . Hamlet always behaves with simplicity and when he fakes madness, he seems to keep his distance in order to avoid contact with the *Others*. He feels repugnance with the odors of men. He is bruised by the shameless conduct of his mother. He revolts at bleeding this uncle when the occasion is offered him to kill him, as it is probable that he would experience a delicate repulsion in opening another wound if he decides to solidify his love for Ophelia. He is haunted by the worm which gnaws at human flesh. . . .
>
> In this respect, I suppose he is completely the portrait of his father. And I imagine also that this was the reason for his misfortune.[70]

Barrault adds that because Hamlet is a chaste man he can bring his sentiment of friendship for Horatio to the confines of what one calls an *amitié particulière,* or special friendship. For Hamlet, as for every chaste man, states Barrault, love and friendship are passions that are equal. "Hamlet loves Ophelia in a condition of purity as he loves Horatio with as much passion." Barrault feels that is the reason why Hamlet destines Ophelia to the convent—to spare her the defilement of the flesh. He also states that Hamlet becomes "smutty" in public as a reaction of his chastity before human coarseness. Barrault reiterates that because Hamlet's soul is pure he does not even bother to examine the rapiers before his fatal duel. For the actor-director, Hamlet is indeed a symbol. "He is the pure man charged with reestablishing

70. Barrault, "A la Recherche de Hamlet," pp. 97, 98.

the universal equilibrium and if not placing on the throne the good, at least the action, that is to say, Life." And Barrault affirms that he tried to confront the prince in feeling "with humor this superior hesitation, this fundamental chastity, this virginity of soul, and consequently, this deep melancholy. . . ." [71]

During his intensive preparation for Hamlet in 1946, Barrault worked in close collaboration and in harmony with Gide. Together they reexamined the English text "word for word." [72] The production, which cost 12,000 francs, [73] opened in October of that year at the Marigny and was an immediate success. In February of 1947 there were fifty performances alone, and long waiting lines. [74] Laurence Olivier came to Paris to see Barrault's production before making his own film of *Hamlet*. (By curious coincidence, Barrault brought his *Hamlet* to Edinburgh in 1948 when the Olivier film was being shown there. [75]) Even after a number of years, the play continued to draw audiences. In 1952, Barrault opened a six-week engagement at the Ziegfeld theater in New York with *Hamlet*. He subsequently performed the play in a number of universities throughout this country, in theaters throughout South America, Japan, and Europe. [76] In 1959 he was appointed director of the Odéon, a state-subsidized theater of France, and reintroduced his production of *Hamlet* there on March 15, 1962, and also several years later, in 1965. [77]

71. *Ibid.*, pp. 98, 99.
72. Barrault, *Souvenirs pour demain*, p. 196.
73. *Ibid.*, p. 184.
74. Nancy Cunard, "Jean-Louis Barrault as Hamlet," *Theatre Today*, Spring Miscellany (1947), p. 11.
75. Barrault, *Souvenirs pour demain*, p. 346.
76 See Barrault, *Souvenirs pour demain*, and André Frank, *Jean-Louis Barrault* (Paris: Seghers, Série Théâtre de tous les temps, no. 15, 1971.).
77. Jean-Louis Barrault, *Odéon Théâtre de France* (Paris: le Temps, 1965).

Barrault, true to form, had carefully coordinated every minute phase of the production. The scenery and the costuming were done by André Masson, the stage settings by Barrault himself, and the music was by Arthur Honneggar.[78]

The atmosphere Barrault sought to create was that of the twilight hour—the "entre chien et loup," when "life itself seems to hesitate, and the mood, that of ambiguity, the period of the passage from life to death." [79] In Paris, the Kleins, Luce and Arthur, commented that "hardly any colors were used—a black Hamlet against neutral-colored curtains . . . and all his other characters seem to bathe in a grayness which allows the attention of the audience to remain entirely on the psychological development." [80] In addition, Nancy Cunard wrote that "of the many scenic interpretations this is probably one of the more austere ones—black and gray and white, and full of restraint.[81] The actors and actresses, with the exception of Ophelia in the mad scene, wore the same costumes throughout the play. Hamlet wore the traditional black, the King and Queen were in monochromatic shades of gray, Gertrude topped by an opulent headdress in that color.[82] In contrast with this atmosphere of neutrality—of gray tonality—is the entry of Fortinbras at the end of the play—"a warrior prince in scarlet and black and white with a tremendous plumed helmet; his soldiers resplendent in chequered doublets and long-hose." [83] The return from ambiguity to action, from death to life, as symbolized by the figure of Fortinbras was thus made to stand out. When the production came to the Ziegfeld Theater in New York on

78. Barrault, *Souvenirs pour demain*, p. 192
79. Barrault, "A la Recherche de Hamlet," p. 95.
80. Luce and Arthur Klein, "Jean-Louis Barrault, An Interview with France's Outstanding Actor-Director," *Theatre Arts* 31 (October 1947): 27.
81. Cunard, p. 9.
82. *Ibid.*
83. *Ibid.*

December 2, 1952, Herbert L. Matthews writing in the *New York Times* called the decor "striking," stating that "basically there are two lofty medievel porches on each side with the change of scenes brought about by moving high curtains and a few simple pieces of furniture. The lighting is imaginative, but sometimes there is not enough of it." [84] Cunard had noted that for most of the time there was a bare stage. [85] For Barrault, what was significant in his stage settings was the object-catalyzer that caused the seminal spark of the work to push forth—as for example a Throne, Power, and Hamlet seated beside them on the ground. [86]

The background music created by Honneggar was rendered by a combination of live musicians and recorded music. Martenot, drum, flute, and clarinet were prominent. Boulez and Jarre played while following the movement of the actors. The trumpets and other brasses were recorded by the best artists of France. In this manner, Barrault felt that he was able to obtain a quality of performance far beyond the ordinary, rightly noting that no great soloist would be willing to be tied up for fifteen minutes of performance during a four-hour period nightly. Through the live instruments, Barrault stated that he was able to continue his studies of organic sonorities—such as the sound of ringing in the ears, heartbeats, and the like. Although Cunard's reaction to the music was positive, Matthews states that the music was "apt and interesting, but . . . frequently drowned out the voices," [87] and Alice Griffin proclaimed that it was more "distracting than dramatic." [88]

The performance was divided into three acts and several

84. Matthews, p. 39.
85. Cunard, p. 9.
86. Barrault, *Souvenirs pour demain,* p. 192.
87. Matthews, p. 39.
88. Alice Venezky Griffin, "Jean-Louis Barrault Acts Hamlet," *Shakespeare Quarterly* 4, no. 2 (April 1953): 164.

scenes and lasted three and a half hours. The second act alone took an hour and a half.[89] This, of course, was an exhausting experience for an actor. Barrault remarked that he lost a kilo each night he performed, that he was struck with Hamlet's disease each evening from five o'clock on, and that he had to adjust to a long-distance race each evening in which he had to pace himself in order to arrive at the end. He felt that Hamlet possessed the "most penetrating consciousness" and he further confessed that the "Melancholy Dane" was both his joy and his torment. The more he frequented him, the actor-director admitted, the more Hamlet frightened him. When he performed *Hamlet* in French for the American public, Barrault stated that he informed his troupe of the risks they were undertaking, and especially that of being a happy company, for if one is happy, one cannot play Hamlet. Happiness excludes anguish, and every major role in the play is steeped in anguish, he affirmed.[90]

One phase of Barrault's production that did disconcert a few critics was the emphasis he placed on mime. The Kleins remarked that "in his approach to the technique of acting he has worked out a synchronization of gesture and speech —especially with an emphasis on mime." [91] Paul Arnold, analyzing the 1947–48 theater season in Paris called Barrault's Hamlet "a curious experiment . . . stimulating in its attempt to express metaphysical ideas through pantomime and postures in themselves remarkably suggestive and beautiful, though obviously foreign to the text." [92] Matthews stated that Barrault's "vivid gift for pantomime carries a

89. Matthews, p. 39.

90. Jean-Louis Barrault, *Nouvelles Réflexions sur le Théâtre* (Paris: Flammarion, 1959), p. 37.

91. Luce and Arthur Klein, p. 26.

92. Paul Arnold, "Actor-Directors in Paris," *Theatre Arts* 31 (February 1948): 28.

sense of yearning, of reaching beyond reason, of gyrating in a supernatural realm which is sometimes extraordinarily effective." [93] This is exactly the effect Barrault intended. He was conscious of what he called "the symphonic movements" of a play, that the dramatic action of a play is shown to advantage more by the tempo of its orchestration than by its psychological accentuations. He felt that the actor should address himself to the heart of his public rather than to the brain, for the impression is everything; the head receives only about 15 percent of the message—the percentage established by Giraudoux, he maintained. [94]

Another element of the production that particularly disturbed Anglo-Saxon viewers was the emphasis placed on the friendship between Hamlet and Horatio. Philip Roddman in his interview with Gide said the reaction of his American friends to the play was "that the Horatio-theme had been given more prominence than it needed, and the evil men less villainy than the action intends." [95] Alice Griffin remarked that "all of the actors used, of course, such Gallic touches as cheek-patting and embracing between men." [96] Barrault relates an amusing anecdote on the subject: "Chastity . . . that is what opened all doors to me in my interpretation of the role. That, moreover, was not without shocking Laurence Olivier, who while attending one of my performances objected that I showed myself to be very familiar in my relationship with Horatio. Hamlet has no ulterior motives —He is fraternal, that's all. . . ." [97]

It is certainly true that Barrault's Hamlet was a rational one. For him, Hamlet's madness was feigned. Indeed, it

93. Matthews, p. 39.
94. Barrault, *Souvenirs pour demain*, p. 193.
95. Roddman, p. 213.
96. Griffin, p. 163.
97. Frank, p. 43.

would have been difficult for Barrault, using Gides's translation, to have interpreted it otherwise. In act 3, scene 2, Gide translates Hamlet's line

> They are coming to the play; I must be idle,

by "Les voici qui viennent. A présent je dois faire l'idiot." (They are coming. Now I must play the fool.)

And even more distinctly in act 3, scene 4:

> Hamlet. Make you to ravel all this matter out
> That I essentially am not in madness,
> But mad in craft.

With

> . . . à reveler que je ne suis pas fou
> réellement, mais par ruse.

(to reveal that I am not truly mad, but by guile.)

Cunard remarks that in Barrault's interpretation "there is no uncertainty, no floating between, no double personality, part-sane, part-demented, no borderlines." She feels, however, that this interpretation does not detract from "the tragic and urgent sense that imbues the play and that he conveys throughout." [98] Barrault, however, was aware of a split personality. He writes on the psyche of Hamlet:

He [Hamlet] receives two blows, like two electro-shocks. The first is that of the apparition of his father; the second that of the episode at sea when he confirms the betrayal of Rosencrantz and Guildenstern and sends them to their death. Before the first shock, the Prince is normal, of melancholic disposition, and has exhausted his tears due to his grief. After

98. Cunard, p. 9.

the second shock, he is a man psychologically depleted in the ambiguous period of the time of the passage from life to death. There is the scene of the cemetery and the significant object: the skull of Yorrick.

Between these two time periods, Hamlet is split: he is *another.* He is never so lucid as at the moment he feigns madness. He is never so threatened not to be able to re-enter his sphere, as when he is alone with himself.[99]

Barrault once compared the virtues of a good play with those of acupuncture, stating that the good play touches us at the very point where there will be the most resonance. A milimeter away and the resonance is lost.[100] "*Hamlet,*" he wrote, "touches man at his most electric point—at the very center of his sensibility." [101] In the actor-director's long quest to reach an understanding of the "barbaric intruder," the "enigmatic stranger" from across the channel, in his collaboration with Gide, in his scrupulous attention to the most minute details of his production, and finally, in his use of mime, Barrault has sought to strike at the most sensitive points of resonance within his French viewing audiences, and here he has succeeded admirably. Gallic and Anglo-Saxon points of resonance differ, however. This Herbert L. Matthews has explained well.

Barrault has clearly studied out and conceived every move and tone. He is too good an actor not to mean what he is doing and it takes more than the language to grasp the subtlety of his conception. To an American he often gives the impression of less emotion than is expected, and yet the part is naturally played at a higher level of expression and feeling than would come from an English or American actor. The range of voice—from a whisper to a shout—the vivid gestures, the extraordinary sensitivity of facial expression are all legiti-

99. Barrault, *Souvenirs pour demain,* p. 193.
100. Barrault, *Nouvelles Réfléxions sur le Théâtre,* p. 36.
101. *Ibid.,* p. 37.

mate on the French stage and, what is more, they ring true, because they are natural within their element. It is this intensely Latin quality that makes Barrault's Hamlet a difficult one for us to appreciate to the full.[102]

One need not be in complete accord with all of Barrault's theories. One need not consider the Gide translation as the definitive acting version of *Hamlet* in France to appreciate the fact that the Gide-Barrault collaboration has made a very significant contribution to the popularization of the play in France. Barrault's innovations have indeed enriched our traditions and have given us much to ponder. Eric Bentley has written, "Barrault must be taken seriously—even as a thinker." [103]

Wouldn't Ducis have been elated at the global success of his countryman with the play he had had to completely transform to make palatable to his eighteenth-century audiences?

102. Matthews, p. 39.
103. Eric Bentley, "The Actor as Thinker," *Theatre Arts* 34 (April 1950): 34.